HORIZONTAL YELLOW

Horizontal

NATURE AND HISTORY

THE UNIVERSITY OF
NEW MEXICO PRESS
ALBUQUERQUE

Dan Flores
april 2003

Yellow

IN THE NEAR SOUTHWEST

Dan Flores

© 1999 by the University of New Mexico Press
All rights reserved.
First edition

Unless otherwise noted, all photographs are by the author, Dan Flores.

Library of Congress Cataloging-in-Publication Data
Flores, Dan L. (Dan Louie), 1948–
Horizontal yellow : nature and history in the Near Southwest /
Dan Flores. — 1st ed.
p.   cm.
Includes bibliographical references (p. 285) and index.
ISBN 0-8263-2010-4 (alk. paper)
ISBN 0-8263-2011-2 (pbk. : alk. paper)
1. Southwest, New—Description and travel.
2. Natural history—Southwest, New.
3. Southwest, New—History.
I. Title.
F787 .F49 1999
979—dc21
99-6382
CIP

Designed by Sue Niewiarowski
Map by Michael Taylor

*For the Flores/Lafitte family of Louisiana,
who for three centuries have known one
thing well: how to stay put*

Contents

Preface

The Horizontal Yellow and the Art of Being Native

*[The vaqueros] said that it was no accident of circumstance
that a man be born in a certain country and not some
other and they said that the weathers and seasons that
form a land form also the inner fortunes of men in their
generations and are passed on to their children and are
not so easily come by otherwise.*
CORMAC MCCARTHY, *All the Pretty Horses*

*The crucial question of the modern world is "How are we
to become native to this land?" It is a question that history
cannot answer, for history is the denativizing process.*
PAUL SHEPARD

There are names for regions—most especially folk names or those of the native peoples—that give places a scent of earth the way directional names never can, and so it is I think with Horizontal Yellow and the part of America that might also be called the Near Southwest. Here at the turn of the twenty-first century most of us know this region as adjoining but separate states—New Mexico, Texas, Oklahoma, with slices of Colorado, Kansas, Louisiana, and Arkansas—divided politically and culturally, each by itself often lumped into regional designations to which the others aren't added. Not often conjured in the same thought.

But for cause I think of them as a piece. In three ways these places make sense as something conjoined, but those three happen to be very fundamental linkages. The first is by water: All these seemingly disparate places constitute a distinctive bioregional watershed, an ecology fashioned by geology and gravity and defined by how the rain and snow draining eastward off the Southern Rockies gets to the ocean. Rivers are how these mountain waters get to the Gulf, of course, all those southward from the Arkansas to the Rio Grande. The second way is history. Until recently and for a long time before, this region was of a piece, stitched together as much by human events and stories as by ecology.

The last is sensory impression. While landscapes that are vertical or green may make up some of its most dramatic spots, the Near Southwest's characteristic topography is one of the grandest, most windswept landscapes of plains, tablelands, and deserts on the planet. Stand upon it now in a spot where the primeval vegetation remains, spread your arms for balance, slowly rotate, and the simple power of the old Navajo name for the western horizon will lift the hairs on the back of your neck. Horizontal Yellow, a land stretched taut like a drumhead as if from the sheer weight of the overarching blue, and for almost the entire year round yellowed (the way anything exposed yellows) by the suck of the sun on an ocean of grass.

So the stories here are first about a place, the great curve of earth stretching down from the Continental Divide—down from places like the chopped Black Range of the Gila Mountains in New Mexico, or the serrated Sangre de Cristo Mountains above that wilderness of dunes in Colorado—along the Southern Plains rivers to their destination in the Gulf of Mexico. For many reasons, but in part because these stories adhere to a setting constituting a sizable block of the contiguous United States, where time and nature have thrown up one of the richest ecological transformations between East and West that exists, the setting of the Horizontal Yellow is a template for its human experiences. The almost endless diversity is part of the country's fascination: piney woods, oak savannahs, blackland prairies and rolling plains and high plains, desert scrub basins, scarp mesas and tablelands, piñon-juniper foothills, and four entirely different *kinds* of mountain ranges all in less than 900 miles of E/W transect.

The seven essays that make up this book are by no stretch an effort at a history of this part of the world. There is history here, some original research, and even a bit of analysis of the kind that appears in books and articles with 30-word titles. But this work is neither a history of the region nor a traditional history of any other kind. I hesitate to join what I've done here with any academic discipline, particularly one as new (and therefore jealous of its reputation) as environmental history. But of course I would be dishonest if I avoided saying that environmental history, with its mandate to focus on the most fundamental historical relationships of all—between humans and nature—is my peculiar preparation for looking at the Horizontal Yellow and its stories. But even environmental history, as welcome as it's been to innovation, is probably unprepared to embrace some of the writing strategies (fiction among them) I use in the pages that follow.

The essays here are more about a part of the world that some 35 million of us (and growing) share than about anything else, but they are also about being in this world, and therefore are to a degree experiential. I was born to the Near Southwest, and during most of the time that the present-day events described here occurred, I have been struggling with my relationship to the place. How long does it take to become native to a landscape, and what are the resulting responsibilities of that condition? I have no new insights to those questions, but if you accept the argument that (say) the Pueblos are not truly indigenous to the Southwest since they, too, migrated from somewhere else and Indians after all have only been hanging around the continent since the Pleistocene, then you'll view my family as a pack of rubbernecking tourists.

My own sense is that I speak from the Horizontal Yellow as a native. I write these words almost 300 years after my European ancestors settled down to live here, and they've been doing so continuously ever since. My dad was born and still lives within 50 miles of where that original Louisiana homesteading took place. Apparently my ancestors were tolerant and friendly folks, for in three centuries our genetic stream has proceeded to incorporate virtually every ethnic group in this part of the world. We've also been right in there simplifying and dismantling the world with the best of them. So all that, it seems to me, gives me a certain contextual claim to an interest in the place and its stories.

It's not that I think I have some privileged ear to the ground and hear what the mountain (or the plain or the desert) is thinking. Far from it. For one thing, with due respect to Aldo Leopold, I don't believe the mountain thinks any thoughts we haven't put in its head. In a literal sense none of us can claim to speak for nature, since none of us knows what it wants, or even if it has desires beyond pure existence. We humans seem to assume that what *we* want—collectively, especially ecologi-cally—is what *nature* wants. As one of the loudest voices nature has produced, we could be right. If so, we've risen to the status of gods, world makers. Which is maybe why our stories have gotten so big.

Environmental history's stories, like places, do strike me as extremely personal, though, relevant in the sense that they seem largely to define and explain something about the world we find ourselves in. So this is a book about history, nature, and place and to some extent my own rela-tionship with them. If the personal is political, then so is the historical! A confession is that my attraction to the mountain and the desert and the plain is one for which the word *passion* seems a bit weak, *biophilic* sounds too overtly scientific, and *religious* makes me wince. But what-ever that feeling is, it does explain why what we Americans have usually called "the wild"—and not just the Western ecology of three centuries ago but buffalo, wild horses, bears, sheep, wolves—shares equal billing with the human players in the stories and essays that follow.

The central core of my own relationship with the Near Southwest in these essays has to do with the wreckage human history has made of the version of the place we found when our ancestors arrived here. Because of the value I place on experiencing Thoreau's entire heaven and an entire earth (or as much of one as possible), I admit to some obsession about this. To a great extent, then, this book is about a search for some-thing—Wild America, if it has to have a name, although I argue here that the *idea* behind a name like that is a gross misapprehension. Nonethe-less, I have looked for what might be called "the wild" in the Near Southwest and found only vestiges, like shadows withdrawing from an aging morning. I have not much known what to do about that or about my strange hunger and am not at all sure that my personal resolution of the dilemma is ethically justifiable, or even workable.

Because this book is so much concerned with place, and because with our stereoscopic eyes and color vision we are eminently visual beings, these essays are accompanied by photographs and occasionally a bit of art. I'm hesitant to say much about the photographs beyond that the basic intent has been to say something visually about the natural world of the Near Southwest, and perhaps to take hold of the time that is my own. So they are best seen as frozen moments (and, I guess, as "narratives" and "texts," too) in the life of a particular part of the earth. I am aware that instinctively (or maybe lazily), my photographs are concerned more with nature than with people or history. And that my way of portraying nature is one that lots of Western photographers (I think of Robert Adams and Richard Misrach) now denigrate as anachronisms in our time of dams and fences and beer can litter. My response is that I am guilty, I guess, of being a less negative son of a bitch than is currently fashionable—and that I am more interested in conveying history and stories with words, and nature with photographs. I think that what I intend to imply with the photographs is that a real and tangible world worth wrapping our societies around still exists out there.

Finally, if this book seems too full of passion for some things and disgust for others, if the Southwestern world as I sketch it here appears wrapped in a kind of barbed wire packaging of paradox and human thoughtlessness, my only defense is that I love the place, yet see it so. There well may be something in our evolutionary arc as a species that has created a Southwest that, while phenomenally rich culturally, seems more impoverished of wildness year by year.

As for me, I love nothing more than celebrating the genius of human history, when it happens. A bit more would be nice.

Yellow House Canyon, Texas
June 1998

Colorado.

SOUTHERN

GHOST RANCH
ECHO AMPITHEATER
Chama R.
TAOS PUEBLO
TAOS

ABIQUIU
CERRO PEDERNAL
SANTA FE

Sangre de Christo MTNS.

Canadian Gorge

N. Fork

Rocky Dell Pictographs

N. Fo.

ALBUQUERQUE

ROCKIES

Pecos River

Palo Dur Canyon

Tule Canyon

CAPROCK CANYON S.P.

Re

Continental Divide

Rio Grande

Journada del Muerto

SACRAMENTO MTNS.

ROSWELL

LLANO ESTACADO

Yellow Hous Canyon

GILA WILDERNESS

WHITE SANDS N.M.

Texas.

ROLLING

BLACK RANGE

New Mexico.

CARLSBAD CANYONS N.P.

GUADALUPE MTNS.

EL PASO

GUADALUPE MTNS. N.P.

CIUDAD JUAREZ

GUADALUPE PEAK

CHIHUAHUAN

DAVIS MTNS.

MT. LIVERMORE

TRANS-PECOS TEXAS

BLACK GAP W.M.A.

LANGTRY

BIG BEND RANCH S.P.

CHISOS MTNS.

Lower Canyons

?

CABEZA de VACA'S *POSSIBLE* ROUTES, 1536- ━━━ ?
JEFFERSON PARTY'S ROUTE, 1806- ╴╴╴
JEFFERSON PARTY'S *FICTIONAL* ROUTE, 1806- •••••
ROBERT HILL ROUTE, 1899- ━ ━ ━

TERLINGUA

BIG BEND N.P.

SIERRA del CARMEN

El Proyecto Reserva de la Santa Elenal Sierra del Carmen (*Proposed*)

DESERT

?

· Mexico ·

Arkansas River

Kansas
Oklahoma

OZARK MTNS.

Canadian River

Canadian River

CROSS TIMBERS

River

River

Red R.

WICHITA MTNS.

WICHITA INDIAN
VILLAGES in 1806

River

Kiamichi River

OUACHITA MTNS.

SPANISH
BLUFF

CADDO MEDICINE
MOUNT

Arkansas
Louisiana

Mississippi River

PRAIRIES

WESTERN CROSS

Brazos River

BLACK

Trinity River

NACOGDOCHES
Jose Flores's
"Rancho
Tortuga"

NATCHITOCHES

NATCHEZ

HILL
COUNTRY
(EDWARDS
PLATEAU)

AUSTIN

Colorado River

SAN ANTONIO

GREAT RAFT COUNTRY
HEAD of RAFT

Red River

GREAT
SWAMP

Bayou Pierre

PIERRE
LAFITTE'S
VACHARIE

MUSTANG
PLAINS

Gulf of
Mexico

FOOT of
RAFT

1 The Great *Despoblado* and Other Fantasies of Wilderness

I fear . . . that the conquest of savagery in the Southwest was due more often to love of adventure than to any wish that cities should arise in the desert. . . . In fact, many of us believed and hoped that the wilderness would remain forever. Life there was to our liking.

BUFFALO HUNTER BILLY DIXON

The greatest happiness possible to a man . . . is to become civilized, to know the pageant of the past, to love the beautiful . . . and then, retaining his animal instincts and appetites, to live in a wilderness.

J. FRANK DOBIE

Is not nature, rightly read, that for which she is commonly taken to be the symbol merely?

HENRY DAVID THOREAU

The burning bush is not an impress anyone soon forgets, and I recall well where I saw mine. The setting—the very pinnacle of a skeletal mountain commanding an immense view of desert, with a porcelain smear of swelling sand dunes below and all around other bony ranges humping their way into the opalescent distance like migrating cater-pillars—was biblical enough, for certain. But this was no holy mountain of the Middle East. And by 1978 religious epiphanies had become rare enough that they tended to go unreported for fear of ridicule on the nightly news.

The mountain wasn't just any mountain, though. It was Guadalupe Peak, the almost 9,000-foot limestone rib cage looming visible for 100 miles on a clear day across the Chihuahuan Desert of West Texas and New Mexico. In some part due to the presence of a Texan in the White House during the previous decade, the mountain had become a na-tional park a few years before. I was up on it out of the lower country far to the east, with the black mud of a handful of years of bluestem prairie life caked in my boots and not a lot of experience yet with the high, seared end of the Horizontal Yellow. But some ancient impulse gave me to understand even then that if you seek the power of a place, climbing some protruding piece of its vertical geometry can lay open rhythms not discernible from the lowlands, the visual equivalent of placing an ear to a seashell. So Jerry Griffin, a West Texas–reared friend, and I had hauled our girlfriends out on an all-night drive from Austin without much of an idea except that since the Guadalupe Mountains was newly a national park, this was a place we ought to see.

The Guadalupes are island mountains of the great Basin-and-Range flats and are thousands of feet lower than Wheeler Peak up by Taos or any number of the source peaks for the Rio Grande or Arkansas River up in Colorado. Guadalupe Peak is the highest point in the state of Texas, though, a point worth mentioning because two decades later one of the only precise details I recall about this climb is reading the climbers' entries in the register on top and noticing that someone I knew had been up the day before and, inspired to a little consciousness alteration, had proudly scribbled that on that date he had the highest high in the state of Texas—no immodest claim within 300 miles of Austin in the 1970s. I also recall that our girlfriends, bleary from helping us dodge deer during the all-night drive, got a sufficient percentage of the rascally steep trail soon enough and decided sensibly that the view from the sleeping bag was the main prize. Fortified by testosterone and caffeine, though, we pushed on—not just to the peak and its astonishing views of the spreading desert but into something else. Something the neat National Park Service signs called *wilderness*.

Earlier that year more than half of the park's 70,000-plus acres had been designated official wilderness in the growing American wilderness system. A son of the South, at the time I had only been in one official wilderness before, a mountain wildlands of the classic kind—the Cloud Peak Wilderness in Wyoming's Big Horn Mountains—up among the moss-campion alpine meadows of glacial cirque lakes and whistling marmots and snowcaps. At the time of that Wyoming experience I hadn't given either the wilderness system or the concept of wilderness itself much thought. But by the time Jerry and I wound our way up Guadalupe Peak, I'd read Roderick Nash's *Wilderness and the American Mind* and much else besides, and the synapses—so to speak—had been properly lubricated for a Big Connect Experience.

Epiphany, baptism, mystic transcendence . . . none of those terms quite fits what I felt in the desert wilderness atop the Guadalupe Mountains in 1978, and (for the literal) no creosote bush actually burst into spontaneous combustion and bathed our faces with the holy light of higher knowledge, either. But from the godlike view atop that arid pinnacle, with the enormous bowl of a seemingly pristine world spread out below, looking as untouched as if it were freshly born and without another human soul in sight except my best friend, I did have a conversion experience. I got religion.

The religion I got in 1978 on top of Guadalupe Peak was the wilderness religion. It's an unexpected religion to come down with in the Horizontal Yellow. Outside a few enclaves of devotees in urban places like Austin and Santa Fe, those of the wilderness faith are a decided spiritual minority in this part of the world. The Baptists and Church-of-Christers and good Catholics far outnumber us. And despite a slew of designated wildernesses up where the Near Southwest's rivers head in the Sangres and San Juans and other ranges of New Mexico and lower Colorado—plus stretches of wild river on the Rio Grande and Chama, some tiny wildernesses in East Texas and atop the mountains of Oklahoma, and of course the oldest wilderness in the whole national system, the Gila, spilling over the Continental Divide in southwestern New Mexico—enormous stretches of the Near Southwest contain no official

Great Sand Dunes National Monument, Colorado, near the sources of the Arkansas River at the northwest corner of the Near Southwest.

meetinghouses for the wilderness faithful. It's a contemporary lack mirrored by history. The regional stories don't much celebrate wilderness characters, either: The Great Culture Hero, the vaquero/cowboy, is a *pastoral* hero, someone who interacts with introduced Old World animals, wages war on natives like wolves, and replaces wild grass with tame imports that make better hay. His legacy is about killing the wilderness, not seeking redemption and meaning there.

Like all new converts, passionate and innocent by turns, in 1978 I set about absorbing all the tenets of a faith my unexamined instincts told me must be true. I wanted to find out all I could about the grand, empty, romantic, *sacred* wilderness that the Horizontal Yellow had been before we humans despoiled and killed it. What was it John Locke had said? In the beginning all the world was America?

It never crossed my mind once as I stood on the crest of Guadalupe Peak in 1978, high on wilderness, that what I would discover was that like most religions, the wilderness one's roots are all too human, and that the wilderness catechism I was learning to recite bore no more relation to the ancient reality of the Near Southwest than the geocentric view of nature bears to the universe.

In 1980, two years after my conversion experience atop Guadalupe Peak, the world-famous microbiologist and Pulitzer Prize–winning philosopher, René Dubos, published a book titled *The Wooing of Earth*, a lyrical and mild corrective, the good scholar believed, to some of the environmentalist excesses of the time. *The Wooing of Earth* took on several of the common premises of environmentalism—ideas like nature always knows best, that civilization and nature represent fundamental dichotomies in the world, that earlier cultures existed in perfect harmony with nature, and (central to the American wilderness idea) that nature is pristine and natural only when humans are absent. What Dubos argued for instead was a human *wooing* of nature, a creation of human places in the landscape through gentle and imaginative symbiosis with the environment. The book held out as an example of what he meant his own homeland, the Île-de-France, which has been occupied by humans almost continuously for several thousand years. According to his taste and that of many other people, Dubos wrote, the Île-de-France was now visually more diversified and emotionally richer than it had been in its original forested state.

Dubos's book may have pleased many Americans, including a reviewer for the *Wall Street Journal*, who at the advent of the Age of Reagan saw the sweetness in a bit of green bashing. But one reader of *The Wooing of Earth* who wasn't so pleased was that articulate lover of Southwestern slickrock, wild rivers, and great emptiness, Ed Abbey. The late Saint Edward of Abbey was a wooer of the great Southwestern wildlands in rather a different sense than Dubos had in mind and had long been a defender of the wilderness. Three years before Dubos's book appeared, his essay "Freedom and Wilderness, Wilderness and Freedom," published in *The Journey Home*, had promoted wilderness as the seat of all human freedom. As we know now that Abbey's journals are in print, Abbey had almost instinctively embraced wilderness before he'd even given the concept much thought. In March 1955, long before he'd even conceptualized *Desert Solitaire* or the wilderness and freedom essay, he wrote these lines in his diary:

6   Like [D. H.] Lawrence, I am taken by the primeval charm and fascination of the simple mysteries: fire, fucking, building in mud, rain, sunlight, the smell of greasewood and live oak after a cloudburst, the luxury of a sleeping hound. I require space, openness, economy, natural resistance, red meat, women, fire, water—the essentials of liberty.

Recognizing Dubos, as he did others (like Gary Snyder) as actually more ally than enemy, Abbey employed uncharacteristic restraint when he wrote what was in essence a review of *The Wooing of Earth* in his mid-1980s essay collection, *Down the River*. In "Thus I Reply to Rene Dubos," Abbey merely pointed out quietly that Professor Dubos brought a European sensibility to his book that an American could not share. Europeans, Abbey implied, were content with and even nostalgic about artificial, manicured landscapes where every inch of ground right to the roadsides was patiently altered and manipulated by the human hand, because for centuries they had known nothing else. But Americans had a different experience, a history intricately interwoven with wildlands, a past played out on a stage of trackless forests, empty plains that were dotted to the horizon with aught but cloud shadows and herds straight from the imagery of Genesis and that gave Americans—among all the world's peoples—one last glimpse of the Garden of the Paleolithic. And a chance to re-create ourselves there.

Edward Abbey was always a quick study and is here when he invokes what we would call context—America and Europe's different historical pasts—as the key to his disagreement with Dubos. But I am suspicious of Abbey's full awareness of how the history of Europe and the Americas has *created* the idea of wilderness. In truth, why is it that I—and Abbey— feel so strongly about wilderness and the wild that the experience of them has something of the religious about it? What was it about their first view of the wild bluestem prairies—a landscape extending from today's Central Texas north across Oklahoma into Kansas, once undulating in the wind like some vast, orange sea and inset with scattered copses of oaks—that struck so many early observers so powerfully, as if it were only there that nature was to be found truly perfect (as one wrote), an enchanting landscape that inspired the soul with sensations not to be felt in any other region of the globe? Why did the drama of peak, desert, and panorama in the Guadalupe Mountains stun the unceasing dialogue in my head to silence in 1978? In sum, why has wilderness seized me, and you, the way it has?

Start with this set of premises, all of which according to current reflection on human nature seem to be true (more or less). That humans are a primate animal. That our genesis as forest foragers gave us stereo-scopic color vision to measure forest distances and to pick out ripe fruit against the dim background of green. That perhaps pushed out of the ancestral forests by competition with other apes, our ancestors emerged into the bright, expansive world of the grasslands and literally straight-ened up and blinked into consciousness there. That the openness and the essential forms of the *place* where this experience unfolded—hori-zontal yellow earth and domed sky in a classic balance of oppositions, cone-shaped green mountains standing above the intersect plane, even the forms that trees take on a fire-swept savannah—became genetically internalized as consciousness budded 3 million years ago. That this place imprinting in the deep genes has been dancing a slow waltz with radiating human culture ever since, flickering into existence an array of aesthetics amounting, essentially, to variations on a set of themes. That words define the world for us humans. That because our evolution is biocultural, there's been an endless conversation between genetic hu-man nature and culture, and the world around us has shifted and shim-mied like a swaying cobra the more we've looked at it and talked about it.

If you've followed all this and have silently nodded more than a couple of times, then you're already on the downhill of this deductive trail: We avuncular chimps are earthlings, a spawn of nature, and we must have come up with a slew of obsessive, imaginative, and colorfully entertaining notions about every aspect of the ancient setting of our deep experience. But Abbey was right: We Americans have had a *particularly* intense love affair with the wild, which via great national preservation schemes we've made into a peculiarly American form of sacred places. That's no particular insight, but on the other hand, the savvy observer of 500 years ago would never have predicted that Americans would invent national parks and a wilderness system in order to preserve what we've taken to be the original continental landscape.

I keep invoking history, but for cause, not gratuitously. In Europe a thousand years or so ago, the old, instinctive ideas about nature and the wild as our original, nurturing home began to change dramatically. The direct cause was the spreading triumph of Christianity over the pagan

A tree form and setting that replicate those of our evolutionary origins in Africa: piñon near the Capitan Wilderness, Sacramento Mountains, New Mexico.

nature religions. In discrediting both pagan ideas and their backcountry shrines, Christian theologians made a useful discovery: Whenever wilderness was mentioned in Judeo-Christian religious texts (almost 300 times altogether), it was presented as a derogation. The wild was the opposite of the civilized, a perception biblical scholars derived from the Greeks. Its principal appearance in the Old Testament is as the dangerous world Adam and Eve were cast into after the Fall, a place of temptation and confusion where the tribes of Israel could wander lost for 40 years. In the New Testament the wilderness is the setting for the Satanic temptation of Christ in Matthew 4:8. Mountain air, spreading grasslands, the instinctive euphoria of great panoramas? As Christianity interpreted it, those feral tugs of impulse were just ole Beelzebub, tempting the unwary back to paganism with the sensuous pleasures of the flesh.

So how did it happen, with the world ordered by those kinds of words so recently in our past, that for many of us in modern America going to the wilderness is like a pilgrimage to a shrine, that altitude equals beatitude? That, too, begs relaxing the conviction that the truths of our existence rest on faith. Not an easy thing, looking your bodhisattva in the eye and asking if he's not made of words.

Winter of 1983, half a decade after the wilderness virus had crawled out of Guadalupe Peak, up my leg, and into my head. I am sitting in a tiny greenhouse tacked onto a West Texas tar-paper shack that, to great ridicule from friends, I have just purchased as a present to myself for having successfully completed the hoop dance of tenure at an academic institution. The tar-paper shack is neither here nor there, just a place to store my worldly possessions and to get out of the weather. The real gift is what's visible out the dusty windows: 12 acres of cliff, mesa, and prairie inset into a scalloped canyon still dominated by big ranches. An environmental study done when the MX missile shuttle game was briefly considered for this same part of the Southwest referred to this canyon as a "natural area." Not wilderness, for sure, what with bison and pronghorns and wolves all gone, Herefords bawling stupidly in the evening stillness, and much of the canyon choked by a mesquite bosque that none of the accounts from a century earlier mentioned. But remnants of the grasses are there, the sky is there, and something is whirring in my head, looking out that greenhouse in 1983. That almost audible *whirrr* had a name: restoration.

In 1983 I'd scarcely begun to examine the *idea* of wilderness. But I did know that however illusory the concept of land ownership might be, Lockean property rights had presented me with the opportunity to manage this 12-acre piece of ground however I saw fit. Like so many of us moving to rural areas as the twenty-first century dawns, I had no compelling need to make this 12 acres pay. So what I saw fit to do with it, at least as I cogitated the question in 1983, was to erase the effect of industrialization and restore this piece of the Southwest to wilderness.

The science of conservation biology, in its infancy in the early 1980s, was then advancing the cause of preserving enormous wildernesses, but I'd read enough Thoreau and Muir and Leopold to believe I saw a tradition of restoring the continent one tiny parcel at a time. However much I might have wanted to, I couldn't put bison or pronghorns on 12 acres and expect them to remain wild animals or expect the ecology of my piece of ground to hold together. But floristically and visually, it seemed possible to restore this little piece. The questions, of course, were how, and restore it to what?

I can say now that the latter is a question I didn't examine very closely at the outset. I did flirt briefly with another environmentalist idea, that nature knows best and that *any* alteration I might make would probably be for ill. That sentiment didn't win out. Instead I gathered up all the exploring accounts and early photo files I could find on this canyon and started reading and looking. And meanwhile, across the 180-degree view of the canyon walls behind my house, I began to obliterate every visual trace that the modern age had ever occurred. Every strand of barbed wire, every fence post, every rusting pile of junk tossed off the rim, every bullet-riddled Coors can—they all went, one by one, until my view to the rimrock was as clean as that cobalt sky.

All those photos and descriptions by trappers and army officers who saw West Texas in the nineteenth century made one thing very clear. While the mesquite and snake broomweed that presently dominated my prairie had once been a part of the local ecology, when Euro-Americans had come to this country, such shrubs had been a minor part. Places I recognized that were mesquite-free in 75-year-old photographs were entirely dominated by mesquite thickets now. And the best estimates we have indicate that in many places in Central and West Texas, the juniper canopy has increased 20 times beyond what it was 150 years ago. Overgrazing by those shit-smeared Herefords I had to listen to undoubtedly was part of the cause, perhaps helped along by the great twentieth-century droughts. But the primary problem, many of us concluded, was that cowboy ecology had suppressed the cycle of restorative fires of the past. The only way really to re-create wilderness on my 12 acres was to start to burn it again.

I did my first restorative burn in the spring of 1984 and have done them on this piece of ground ever since. I won't say that the results were anything like a miracle. Prescribed burns on a parcel this small don't get hot enough to kill mesquite roots, so beating back the *Prosopis* jungle still requires some mechanical effort (read, periodic grubbing with a double-bladed ax). But with fire, restoring my wilderness was well under way, augmented by some judicious johnsongrass pulling, and here and there, in likely locations, the planting of the odd cottonwood or Rocky

The search for a semblance of the wild in the modern Southwest.

Mountain juniper. Within four years I had the 180-degree view sweeping away from my back door and up the canyon cliffs completely restored. Not a sign of a fence, or a vertical post, or a No Trespassing sign. Blue-stem and blue grama and needle-and-thread and two dozen other grasses waving in the wind. Mesquite beaten back to the lowlands. A horse roaming at will across it to perpetuate the ancient effect of grazing. Rapidly improving biodiversity. As a wilderness acolyte, I felt like I was stepping into church when I walked out across it at daybreak, with the coyotes yipping in the distance.

Then you know what I did? I set up a tipi right in the middle of the view.

"Okay, I'll give it to you—last fall was a good one. I really like those deep canyons along the Caprock out there in West Texas. Matter of fact, both your last two have been good choices. That was a sweet little backpack into the Kiamichi Mountain country up in Oklahoma, too, last October. But I think it's my turn now, isn't it?"

Jerry on the phone, fall of 1988, now 10 years after our Guadalupe Peak climb. Having both grown to young adulthood in widely distant parts of the Near Southwest—he in West Texas, me in West Louisiana— Jerry and I had been introduced in grad school by our wives (a move I believe they regretted) and pretty much immediately fashioned a connection based on commonalities of place and time. We were within a year of the same age. We'd both grown up hunting and now thought it strange. We both admired books and talked writers endlessly. Two years after we met, a friend went away for a few days and returned to find, as he put it, everybody divorced and Jerry and me sharing a bachelor apartment. My ex and I settled up amicably, but by the time Jerry and his got around to the process, mine had had a change of heart, and Jerry's been convinced ever since that the pound of divorce flesh I owed had come out of him. Over time I'd moved to West Texas and he'd settled in Austin. But all that past, along with a mutually deepening fascination with the sacred wilderness, kept us in contact, mostly via these yearly pilgrimages.

I realize I'm grinning into the phone. "Well, have you got one?"

"Yeah, I do, one I've been wanting to do for a while. What about we canoe the Llano River in Texas this March? We can put in at a bridge crossing up around Mason and . . ."

"Shit. The Llano? The Llano? Goddamn, man, I knew you were into a river trip, but I thought you were gonna suggest the Lower Canyons of the Rio Grande, or maybe the Chama up in New Mexico. The Llano's too settled up, Jerry. We'll see too many people. Friggin' barbed wire everywhere. No place to camp. Dams. All those idiotic hill country zebras and ostriches and oryx peering down at us, for Chrissake. I'm really hot myself to get into the Pecos Wilderness again after getting snowed off Truchas Peak in '83. Course it'll be way too snowy there if we have to go in March, but we could get into the Gila Wilderness then, I suspect. Hell, we could walk the length of Palo Duro Canyon. Goddamn, Jerry, the Llano River?"

Silence, but not much of it. "Trust me on this. You'll love it. Beautiful river. You'll see."

He was right. It was a good trip. We did three days riding those flashing, green-hued Hill Country waters down through the boulder

Jerry Griffin on our ascent of Guadalupe Peak, newly designated as part of the official Wilderness System in the late 1970s.

fields of the Llano Uplift. Even got cocky through a little pour off and let that orange canoe ride us for a spell. I was right, too: There were fences, too many exotic animals, a dam to portage. And most disturbingly to a wilderness partisan, people. People fishing. Sitting in lawn chairs. Shooting beer cans with .22s. It was no kind of purist wilderness experience as far as I was concerned, and maybe to compensate, when my turn came around the next year, I pointed us at Alaska and the Yukon.

But that little Llano River trip set me to thinking. Just why was it that I thought I needed a wilder and purer wild than that? And why no other people? How was it that I was perfectly okay with a tipi in the middle of the view out my back door but couldn't abide a zebra in the Hill Country or floating by an Aggie with a Coors in a lawn chair? This was an unexamined bit of dogma not to be taken on faith.

In the beginning all the world was America. I'd always assumed I knew exactly what Locke meant. Starting in Africa, we humans had colonized around the world, eagerly seeking every new, previously untouched hunting and gathering ground (our aesthetic preference for trees with clean trunks and spreading crowns doesn't extend to those with broken limbs or too irregular foliage—makes us think subconsciously that we've already been beaten to a place). The North American wilderness was thus the last great, unexploited Eden.

Like the English-speaking arrivals on the Atlantic Coast, the Spaniards and Frenchmen who were the first Europeans to witness the Southwestern wilderness saw the region in biblical terms. Wilderness in this tradition was and supposedly always had been unlived in by humans, the haunts of wild beasts but not people. Exploring westward out of Louisiana, the French used terms like *pays inculte* (uncultivated or uncultured lands) and *brousse* (bush, scrub, wilds) to refer to the Horizontal Yellow beyond their settlements. *Pays sauvage* was used, too, and implied that although the country might be inhabited, the Indians were actually just another kind of natural fauna capable of producing no more transformative an effect on the landscape than a herd of deer. As for the Spaniards, they distinguished between Indians like the Pueblos, who farmed and lived in permanent villages, and hunters who roamed the deserts and plains. Terms like *naturaleza salvaje* and *salvaje silvestre* at least implied a human presence in the wilderness that *selva virgen* and *tierra inconnigia* did not. More specific to the Near Southwest, the

Spanish name for the prairies and plains, Llanos del Cibolos, ignored the Apaches and other human inhabitants, stressing the dominating presence of buffalo instead.

But for reducing humans to invisibility, not even that name approached the term Spaniards used routinely to refer to the Big Bend country, the great Chihuahuan Desert, and the Jornada del Muerto between El Paso and Albuquerque. Those the Spaniards called by their most common name for wilderness: *los despoblados grandes*—the great uninhabited lands.

If we are romantic about American wilderness as a kind of last Eden, a paradisiacal continent of natural innocence, then the initial firsthand descriptions of that world ought to stand as holy texts. Before we came and ruined it, this is how it was; when we preserve wilderness today, this is what we should replicate. When we seek it out, this is what we should find.

Accept these premises and one of the holiest of our texts ought to be Álvar Núñez Cabeza de Vaca's *Relación*, describing a shipwrecked Spaniard's traverse of what is now the Near Southwest in the 1530s. The famous *Relación* is not just the first written description of the Horizontal Yellow from observation; it's the first good account, period, of *los despoblados grandes*—the great North American wilderness of our imaginations. So what was it like?

The first outstanding fact about Cabeza de Vaca's story is that as a true American wilderness adventure, nothing else in our literature comes close to it. Later European explorer/adventurers all remained far more in control of their circumstances than Cabeza de Vaca and his companions, who took on an unknown continent stripped of every Old World technological artifice. That alone would seem to make the story almost mythic. Civilized Europeans pitch up on the coast of the last great wilderness continent, and by their wits a handful of survivors strolls, marveling, through paradise. Or, you might think alternatively, they fight their way through bears and wolves and stampeding herds of buffalo and survive to tell the tale. Neither of those versions would be right, because it turns out that what de Vaca and his companions saw was nothing like the great wilderness of our imaginations.

The story up to the time this modest, well-educated Spaniard and fewer than two dozen survivors straggled ashore on the Texas mainland in 1529 is the kind of classic study in European arrogance we've all heard by now. In the wake of the Spanish conquest of Mexico, an aristocrat named Panfilio Narvaez had petitioned for a grant in the New World, and without even considering what any resident natives might think, the Spanish Crown turned over the keys to North America, between Florida and Tampico, Mexico, to him. The colonizing party set out in five vessels in June 1527, 600 strong, soon reduced to 300 after a storm and desertions in Santo Domingo. When finally shipwrecked for the last time on the Texas coast in November 1528, only 80 men remained, and disease brought the number of survivors to 15 by the spring of 1529—among them Cabeza de Vaca, a strangely portentous name (Head of a Cow) for future Southwestern popular culture.

Up to this point the evidence in the *Relación* is a bit contradictory with respect to the qualities of the North American wilderness. No European who actually experienced America during this first-encounter period could long operate under the illusion that America was uninhabited by people. Certainly the Gulf coastline was inhabited, and by many different groups whose reception was often less than chamber-of-commerce friendly. On the Florida mainland one group had made many signs and menaces and appeared to say the Spaniards must go away from the country. These Indians tried what must have been, judging from its frequency of use, a stratagem on the order of, "Hey! Aren't your shoes untied?" They tried to deflect the Spaniards elsewhere, mentioning a province called Apalachen where there was much gold. No misfire this time. Off the Spaniards went, en route traversing a Gulf Coast forest very difficult to travel and wonderful to look upon, where the trees were astonishingly high. Apalachen turned out to be a disappointment, not least because of the Indians' tendency casually to shoot arrows at them as the Spaniards walked about the town.

As for the interior, Cabeza de Vaca was given to understand by the coastal tribes that it was very thinly peopled and that there were great lakes, dense forests, immense deserts and solitudes. A great interior *despoblado*, the vast wilderness the Europeans expected? Or another stratagem? The Spaniards were destined to find out, because within weeks shipwrecks and panic collapsed the expedition into an every-man-for-himself situation, and at some point during this dark time the tiny rafts they'd built passed the Mississippi's mouth and finally crashed on the island Malhado (Misfortune). Galveston Island, likely.

Almost everything that happened to Cabeza de Vaca over the next seven years turns the idea of a classic wilderness, in this part of America at least, into a fantasyland that shares about the same relationship with authenticity as Six Flags Over Texas. The world that takes form in the *Relación* was no Spaniard's idea of paradise or Eden. And if you assume that his adventures were mostly, or even partly, with ravenous wild beasts in great, empty wastelands, you'd be a good acolyte of the Wilderness Church but 100 percent wrong about Cabeza de Vaca. As for nature as primary foil, it is true that the Texas Indians insisted that the country stretching away westward (toward other Spaniards in northern Mexico) was immense, and also very cold and thin of people. This was yet another Indian reference to a *despoblado grande* in the interior, and the idea of it did give the Spaniards pause.

A pretty long pause, and one that conveys the idea that the main actor in the fate of these dwindling Europeans, stranded in the wilderness, was not nature but the very numerous and very diverse native peoples who in fact surrounded them on all sides and interacted with their every move. Anthropologists who study first encounters like this think that such complex exchanges are particularly good expressions of Franz Boas's cultural relativity: In an initial encounter each group has no recourse but to interpret the other through its own distinctive cultural lenses, to fit other people into categories already in their heads. For the Europeans, in other words, the natives were most easily understood in the context of medieval Europe's idea of the Wild Man of the Forest.

So this initial ethnography of the natives of the Horizontal Yellow lumps many different groups of humans into a category that, in European eyes, was basically acultural. The Indians knew the seasons well and how to use them, the *Relación* says, and they were practiced at knowing the positions of the stars, but they were all ignorant of time, either by the sun or the moon, nor did they reckon by the month or year. They married but separated for the slightest cause. Men without children seemed to have an endless succession of wives, while those with children stayed with one wife. "Some among them are accustomed to sin against nature," de Vaca wrote, observing that there were men who took men as their wives and that these were more muscular than other men and taller. The women were drudges, working 18 hours a day; they were also the diplomats to other nations and sometimes the cause of wars. All believed that dream events were more real than waking ones, and at least one Spaniard was killed because of a dream. They were warlike and skilled at tactics and waylaid their enemies constantly. Their method of fighting was to leap about, and in battle one could never show fear or they would bore in on it. All of them were great thieves, great liars, great drunkards—exemplary early Texans. They ran deer down on foot and were a merry people, and the happiest season was when they ate prickly pears. "I believe these people see and hear better, and have keener senses than any other in the world," de Vaca says. Strip away the details and in essence this is a description of the European Wild Man.

What finally saved the last four of them—three Spaniards and Esteban the Moor—was not their technology or wits but the way the Indians interpreted *them*, how these strange and hairy white/black men were worked into the native worldview. The natives of the Horizontal Yellow tended to view unconventional people—epileptics, those with handicaps or deformities—as individuals possessing special powers. Medicine people, healers, and shamans, in other words. Apparently wild, otherworldly strangers fit the bill perfectly. And since the Europeans very obviously had unleashed diseases among the natives, there was plenty of call for healing.

The Spaniards who thrived through five years of loose captivity were the ones who had already become physicians "without examination or inquiring for diplomas," as Cabeza de Vaca put it. At first Cabeza de Vaca laughed at his fellow Spaniards' efforts at becoming shamans, telling the Indians that it was folly, that "We knew not how to heal." But the Spaniards had crucifixes, and they acquired rattles and other accoutrements, and a design began to unfold. Becoming shamans turned out to be not only a lucrative move in a material sense but gave them freedom of movement inland through the wilderness; it made a return to civilization possible.

The Spaniards were now preparing for the first transcontinental crossing of North America by Europeans. Setting out westerly, they were called upon to cure among the first group of Indians they encountered inland, and the possibilities for existing off the fat of the land in right shamanly fashion became clear when somewhere (apparently) along the edge of the Texas Hill Country, Cabeza de Vaca brought a man back from the dead. That's what the *Relación* says. Back home this would get him in trouble for the equivalent of performing miracles without a license. I think I'll reserve judgment on that part of the story, personally, but whatever he did, the Indians were ecstatic with the result. At that point *all* the Spaniards became physicians.

Perhaps predictably, but unfortunately, his time spent as a shaman became something of a blur for Cabeza de Vaca. They encountered many peoples—Cuthalchuches, Malicones, Coayos, Susolas, Atayos, Arbados; indeed, so very many and of so many different languages that their names became impossible to remember. The Spaniards were five when they struck inland in 1534, but Oviedo deserted them, leaving Dorantes, Castillo, Esteban, and Cabeza de Vaca. I cannot tell you where they went, and every route proposed so far (including one south of the Rio Grande) is a fat target for criticism. A cold guess with the *Relación* and Erwin Raisz's physiography map in hand and no preconceptions once led me to favor a crossing of the Hill Country between the Colorado and Llano Rivers, then westward along the Balcones Escarpment to the Pecos, southwest to the Rio Grande above the Rio Concho, and finally across Chihuahua and Sonora to the Río Sonora. The buffalo gourds, the metal (meteoric iron among the Hill Country Indians?), the proximity to the great bison economy—all those references influenced me. Frankly, now I don't know where they went.

Wherever it was, though, they missed the *despoblado grande*. The vast yellow plains and the deserts with their blue mountain islands were the base reverse of uninhabited (nor was it, except infrequently, very cold). Surrounded by great and ever growing throngs numbering in the thousands, the four Euro-shamans pressed into the interior, and as they traveled, the people they encountered became better fed, more kind, and more populous. Indeed, like Hernando de Soto a few years later, Cabeza de Vaca and his companions seem to have spent virtually every night of this wilderness journey in a town. If the *Relación* conjures a big image of this time, it's of a holy pilgrimage through dense settlements, but a pilgrimage as much biological as spiritual. It proceeded across the Horizontal Yellow as a smoky plume of diseases that afflicted the inhabitants of the towns in its path and continually grew its size with the hordes of those sickened and clamoring for healing, all while the camp followers extorted and plundered everyone they met, telling them the Europeans were children of the sun.

How were they able to heal? That one stumped Cabeza de Vaca, too. His most cynical explanation is also the most logical, that the Indians "are all very fond of romance and are great liars," particularly so where they had any interest. Shamanism usually incorporates ethnobotanical knowledge, although the *Relación* doesn't say that the Spaniards were using plants. But few modern healers dismiss the roles of hope and belief. The power of suggestion and lady luck seem to have been with them in 1534 and '35, but those weren't infallible, as Esteban would find out dancing and rattling his way to the Zuni pueblo of Hawikuh with Marcos de Niza four years later.

One last interesting detail with respect to our idea of a North American wilderness appears in Cabeza de Vaca's *Relación*. All the country they passed through continued very populous—until they began at last to draw near the Christians in present Sonora. Then, in response to European disease, the lands became vacant, and where they were not, Spanish slave hunters were seen in the distance, riding the Indians down with horses.

Only near civilization did the land begin to seem like wilderness.

Early nineties. The situation was getting disturbing. The more reading and thinking I did, the more dubious the notion of a great North American wilderness seemed to be. Looked at clear-eyed, ignoring faith, wilderness was beginning to have about the same relationship to the ancient reality of the Near Southwest that Bullwinkle shares with a flesh-and-blood moose.

However genetically deep our subliminal responses to the wild, it was turning out the more I read that much of the dogma of the American wilderness idea was only two or three centuries old, at best. The maturing sciences of geology and botany and eventually Darwin's great insight about natural selection had been critical in wresting wilderness from the grasp of churchly approbation, explaining all that chaos of nature and topography as part of evolutionary process. So had experiential immersion with wilderness, like mountain climbing, for example, which had the effect of chasing the rumored pagan hobgoblins beneath the scree forever.

It was the poets, painters, and mystics of the Romantic Age, though, who'd really reclaimed the wilderness—people like Thoreau and the German-American landscape painter Albert Bierstadt (one of my favorites even before that conversion experience in 1978), who for us Americans had effected a final transformation of wilderness gloom into

Wilderness detail from the Horizontal Yellow.

wilderness glory. Culturally, many Americans seem to have put the spectacles of romanticism on then and there, and we've only wiped them a time or two, never removed them, since. Bierstadt, Thomas Moran, even the photographers who often were alongside them in their portrayal of the nineteenth-century West, were shamans of the first rank. As visual translators they were obsessed by the mystery of the once-forbidden. Their art turned a formerly shunned, fallen part of the world into *scenery* and the old genetic and reflexive human awe at vastness and topographical complexity into a positive emotion they referred to (borrowing from Edmund Burke and John Ruskin) as the Sublime.

And since romantic ideology had by no means escaped religion's influence, remote country that once had been Satan's lair now became . . . *wilderness,* no longer fallen. Instead, its ancient and mysterious power was newly seen as good and transcendent. In short, the romantics had performed the hat trick of entirely inverting the previous idea. The wilderness was now *holy,* the freshest and best remaining example of

God's creative handiwork, and it was civilized humanity that was suspect. Meditate on that nineteenth-century romantic art sometime and do an emotion check. In the play of holy light in paintings by Bierstadt and others, the wilderness landscape quite literally becomes the face of God. As usual, Thoreau got it before almost anyone else when he shrieked, from atop Maine's Mount Ktaadn in 1846, "Contact! Contact!" The romantics in effect were alchemists who had resurrected the pagan worldview. They'd made the wild synonymous with the divine, and we've fashioned our world in the American West around the idea ever since.

Who cares? Discovering all this, I realized that I probably ought to, and that I certainly wasn't going to be alone.

Ralph Waldo Emerson once wrote, in his essay "The Method of Nature," that nature exists in the mind in solution; now it has been precipitated. Postmodernism, with its focus on how language defines reality, has to love an Emersonism like that. By thinking for so many centuries of America as a kind of Edenic and empty continent, a place where a timeless, pristine balance of nature held sway and humans either were absent or—when they were acknowledged—were considered a kind of native fauna moving lightly across the landscape, we had defined wilderness in a way that barely glanced off reality.

What I was starting to grasp from Cabeza de Vaca's *Relación* and a slew of other early descriptions was the extent of the irony, what a stupendous effort of imagination had been required to convert North America into a virtually uninhabited landscape lying outside human agency. Was wilderness in our classic definition actually a species of historical hoax, a great lie? A few years ago I was willing to indulge that idea. Now I think the image of *los despoblados grandes*—the wild continent of our imaginations—in fact is more like the great foundation myth of our history. And there were causes for its emergence that went beyond the alchemy of the romantics.

The reason the myth of the wilderness could emerge and carry so many of us away in the rapture of it says something about religious sentiments themselves. The Spanish and French colonists in the Near Southwest who pioneered places like Santa Fe, San Antonio, New Orleans, and Natchitoches, and certainly the English settlers on the shores of the Atlantic, saw America through the prism of Christianity, whose

holy text made no mention whatsoever of Indians. If they weren't the lost 23
tribes of Israel, which meant their presence in the Americas extended
back only two millennia, then who were they? Misapprehension of the
continent begins here.

What archeology and history have come to understand only relatively
recently is confirmation of what Cabeza de Vaca describes in the Near
Southwest in the early 1500s. At that time, at least 350 generations of men
and women had been living in and dramatically transforming North
America over a time span of at least 11,000 years. (Seven hundred generations and a time twice that deep is now looking more likely.) What
Europeans saw when they confronted the Americas was anything but a
selva virgen. From Alaska to Tierra del Fuego there were probably close
to 100 million people at contact, one-sixth of the world's population.
When Cabeza de Vaca made landfall on the Texas coast in 1529, the
most sparsely inhabited parts *were* north of the Rio Grande, as the Indians told him. Yet the native population north of Mexico was then
probably 10 million and had been approaching that level for 500 years.
Multiply that out. Considering merely the last 15 generations before
contact, it means that what the wilderness tradition had taught me (and
you) to imagine as a virgin continent had been home to 150 million
people over the previous five centuries.

In the Near Southwest, later Spanish and French chroniclers (and
recent archeologists) have confirmed Cabeza de Vaca and Coronado:
There may have been as many as 50,000 people in South Texas when the
Spaniards were shipwrecked there, perhaps 10,000 in the towns called
La Junta near Big Bend and another 30,000 up the Rio Grande to El
Paso. The 70 or so Pueblo towns along the Upper Rio Grande reached
upward of 80,000 when Coronado visited them five years after Cabeza
de Vaca's return, and archeology indicates that the Wichita towns Coro-
nado saw in southern Kansas then numbered as high as 100,000 souls.
Add another 20,000 or so Apaches of various groups, roaming the Near
Southwest from Taos and the Chihuahuan Desert eastward into the
Texas Hill Country. Factor in the Caddoans of present Louisiana, East
Texas, and Arkansas, with at least 30,000 people then. It means that
roughly a third of a million people were inhabiting the wilderness of the
Near Southwest in its pristine condition.

One of the thinkers who's pondered the significance of that, geographer William Denevan, argued in a classic essay he called "The Pristine

Myth" in 1992 that the ecological changes so many generations of people could produce over such a long period were so significant that early European observers just couldn't have missed them. Indians, as we've come to understand, had produced a profound effect on a continent the Euro-Americans kept insisting was a virgin wilderness. They had cut trees, drained swamps, engineered water diversion systems, and built highway systems like the one radiating out from the Chaco Canyon cultural center in New Mexico, in what Denevan calls a mania for linear lines across the landscape. Indian civilizations like the Mississippian Culture had erected enormous earthen mounds along rivers like the lower Red and tributaries of the Arkansas that for centuries were larger earthmoving projects than anything the Europeans attempted in America. I'd spent many hours walking over the great ceremonial mounds of ancient America in the very Louisiana and Arkansas woods where I grew up and never thought of that. Denevan believes Euro-Americans were around for three centuries before our efforts produced as much ecological alteration as existed on the continent in 1500.

In our self-hatred and guilt over what we've undeniably done to shrink biodiversity across the continent, we've continued to indulge the fantasy of native peoples as a species of fauna, now evolved into the ecological Indian who scarcely disturbed a blade of continental grass. That's conspired to obscure the role Indians really played in creating the perceived grand wilderness. It's not just industrial or capitalist cultures that alter the natural world, after all. Some of the earliest native cultures in the Americas, the purist big game hunters named for the towns out on the Horizontal Yellow (Clovis, Folsom, Plainview) where their artifacts were first found, unquestionably participated in the extinctions of the great mammoth, camel, and horse herds of Pleistocene America, the most significant ecological transformation (almost 75 percent of large animal species became extinct) in North America since human occupation, and an extinction scenario with enormous implications for floral and faunal evolution in the so-called wilderness. Indians had domesticated dozens of plant varieties and at least two animals (wolves and wild turkeys). Pueblo and Caddoan farmers in the Southwest had introduced a host of exotic plants from Mexico, and their manipulations had produced disjunct ranges for several native Near Southwest plants, the Chickasaw plum and the bois d'arc tree, particularly.

And as the geographer Carl Sauer speculated long ago, Indians relied on fire as their most effective technology of ecological alteration and changed every habitat from Louisiana's swamplands to the high prairies and right up to the peaks of the Rockies with it. Cabeza de Vaca describes fire matter-of-factly. He says the Indians of the Texas interior fired the countryside regularly and for every kind of manipulation: to encircle deer, to drive lizards and other edible creatures into the open, to manipulate bison movements, and to dry the country from mosquitoes. Sauer's speculations three-quarters of a century ago have been confirmed and exceeded many times over.

The end result when Europeans first journeyed into the Near Southwest was not wilderness at all. Coronado and Oñate in New Mexico perceived that the Pueblo world was a constructed world, and St. Denis and Bienville in Louisiana recognized the same thing about the Caddoan setting. What the Europeans saw as a wilderness world beyond these agricultural societies, though, as *despoblados grandes*, was in truth another, if more subtle, human construction, an environment that centuries of Indian inhabitation and use had made into an ecological subclimax of vast, waving grasslands. Yellow grasslands extending from the Blackland Prairie across the plains well into the foothills of the Rockies. Desert grasslands dominating the basins and bajadas of the Chihuahuan Desert. And in an impression that must have triggered some primal ripple through the genes—*Africa!*—enormous, awesome herds of bison, elk, deer, and pronghorns across those grasslands. Desert and Rocky Mountain bighorns on almost all the mountain ranges. And wolves, cougars, grizzlies, and black bears as accompaniment to that hunters' world—animals that all seemed as tame as the creatures of Eden to the Europeans, not because they'd never seen humans before, but because they'd interacted with humans for so long.

There may be one more explanation for our wilderness assumptions in the hurricane of Old World diseases that swept the Americas after the Europeans arrived. The epidemics and pandemics that evolution had reduced to childhood diseases in Europe swept through formerly unexposed Indian populations as virgin soil infections in the Americas, obliterating 60 to 90 percent of the Indian population in a single generation, surfacing (with less effect) again and again across the centuries. The stories in the Near Southwest are just too grim to recount, the regional version of an unintended holocaust. But as a by-product they seem to have had the effect of making the countryside appear for a time far emptier and less influenced by humans than it had been. There is also mounting evidence that as diseases wiped out Indians, animal populations underwent an explosion. There were no buffalo in the woodlands near the mouths of the Near Southwest's rivers when Spaniards like de Soto and Moscoso explored that country in the 1500s. But French settlers found buffalo there 75 years later, after the Caddos and other tribes had been devastated by disease. The herds reached a zenith about 1700, but as the human population built back, buffalo disappeared. The last buffalo seen in Louisiana was killed in 1803. That ecological rebound effect must have made much of America, for a few generations, seem more like an Eden of animals than it had been in many dozens of centuries.

By the nineteenth century, in any event, the wilderness idea had been so internalized that it's been almost impossible to get out of our heads since. I have a for-instance that's considerably sobered my own wilderness faith. In the 1820s and '30s one of the prominent naturalists in the Near Southwest was Gideon Lincecum, botanist, collector, and correspondent with Darwin among other things. As he naturalized across the Southwest, Lincecum convinced himself that the world through which he rode was a wilderness of wild maiden forests with no indications of its ever having been occupied by any people. So taken was he with this grand conception that one fine day in Texas's San Marcos valley, he rhapsodized that the country then about him was the beautiful face of paradise, existing in a perfectly natural condition without a sign or scar to disturb the supreme quiet of the birds and beasts.

I understand. I've been there. But for all Lincecum's bliss, there's just one small snag to that scene. Ignore the Indian influence if you want. But the naturalist was then overlooking a valley that half a century earlier had been occupied by a Spanish mission.

The geographer Martyn Bowden puts it neatly: "The grand invented tradition of American nature as a whole is the pristine wilderness, a succession of imagined environments which have been conceived as far more difficult for settlers to conquer than they ever were in reality." Maybe if the geographers were the shamans and mythmakers of our culture, we'd have had less trouble understanding the continent.

In truth it's artists who are our primary mythologizers, though. And historians, the storytellers of how we got from there to here. So accept the inevitability that it was a historian who recognized the wilderness

Ruin of an early High Plains Anglo homestead established in 1877—in a Near Southwest "wilderness" once inhabited by 350,000 people.

tradition as an American canon and set it to mythic verse. It was Turner (as in Frederick Jackson) who encapsuled and articulated the evolving wilderness myths of the seventeenth through the nineteenth centuries in the short scripture he called "The Significance of the Frontier in American History," penned in 1893. Turner captured it all in under 40 pages. Influenced by Darwinian thought, he rejected the idea that American traits and institutions had diffused from Europe to America and instead saw Americans as the unique products of interaction with a new habitat, the North American wilderness. Much as a new habitat will tend to produce speciation, Turner argued that a set of traits—democracy, individualism, a work ethic, and so forth—had been selected for by the American wilderness, and that these traits made Americans entirely unique. (Left unspoken but implied was the Romantic Age notion that this interaction with the divine had probably made Americans more noble, more moral, than other peoples.) The process might have produced a few unsavory traits, like grasping materialism, hostility toward urbanites and intellectuals, a gross plundering of nature—all those beloved classics we today tend to ascribe to redneckery. But in fact they're part and parcel of the pioneer tradition we inherited, and the pioneers who had conquered and tamed the great American wilderness were literally superhuman, overachievers capable of anything. In a word, John Waynes. Or so our histories have long argued.

Turner's explanation for America introduced one tricky little problem. If it was the supposed wilderness that had made Americans unique, what in the twentieth century and beyond was to be done to sustain that uniqueness if the wilderness was all conquered, with all those Indian and animal representatives of the wild driven to their lairs? In the shrinking of the wild continent, whose loss as reported by the census of 1890 had set Turner to work on the frontier thesis in the first place, Turner could imagine only two possible solutions: either continued American expansion or a social welfare state to perform the function of societal pressure valve the way the frontier supposedly had.

But there was a third answer, the final link in this explication of the gospel of wilderness. In 1919 a young Forest Service architect named Arthur C. Carhart began correspondence with another youngster in the Forest Service, Aldo Leopold, whose experiences had been in the Southwest, over the possibility of preserving certain parcels of the national forest lands in the West from grazing, logging, mining, and summer home building. In other words, leaving them in the condition they'd been in when the first Euro-American adventurers had looked up, wiped the tobacco juice off their chins, and presumably shouted in ecstasy, "Sweet Jesus, it's the Garden of Eden!"

Looking back, as we all do, with passing curiosity on my own incarnations, I see myself now as the most typical—even predictable—of wilderness parishioners over much of my adult life. As a group, the wilderness congregation tends to a form of agnosticism. It's not so much that the gods are either nonexistent or on vacation. More like the only tangible and touchable form of the divine is nature. And that (thank a litany of dead white males in Western literature and religion for this) nature sacredness is banished once the blighting touch of fallen modern humanity lays ahold of it. Because we're only now starting to understand it, the Indian touch on the landscape seems not to count. These were my own thoughts for more than a decade, but not just my own. Like all initiates reciting their catechisms, I learned these ideas (as the postmodernists say) as a constructed reality. I also know whence many of these ideas entered my own head.

In the Southwest the good Baptists tend to share similar views of the world because they (or their ministers) all read Billy Graham and Jerry Falwell, or else they absorb their dour view of a world run to ground by liberals via Pat Robertson's *700 Club* and Oral Roberts with a bit of nonsectarian evidence from Rush Limbaugh. Similar clues to the depth of one's wilderness faith reside in how much of the holy canon from the American wilderness writers you've absorbed. John, Son of the Wilderness Muir, an amalgam of Old Testament prophet and Calvinist Puritan, is essential, of course. And Thoreau, who gave us sensuous (if not sexy) woodlots and sacred local wildlands. And Edward Abbey, of course, who popularized the Southwestern deserts as the ultimate wilderness, argued for wilderness as a form of penultimate human freedom and turned us on to the idea that the wilderness was the place to get in touch with the sexy animal within.

Who I've left out and cannot is Aldo Leopold. In terms of a national policy of preserving wilderness, he is the most important of them all, and in the Southwest particularly, he ranks along with Abbey as a cultural force. Leopold merits some special consideration, too, because he is such a transparent bridge working off the myth of the *despoblado grande* and spanning the generations down to us. In a series of essays with titles like "The Wilderness and Its Place in Forest Recreational Policy" (1921), "Wilderness as a Form of Land Use" (1925), "The Virgin Southwest" (1935), and "Wilderness" (1935), Leopold translated the historical myth of the existence of a vast North American wilderness and its transforming effects on Americans into the foundations of national policy. This passage is from "Wilderness as a Form of Land Use":

Many of the attributes most distinctive of America and Americans are [the result of] the impress of the wilderness and the life that accompanied it. . . . If we have such a thing as an American culture (and I think we have), its distinguishing marks are a certain vigorous individualism combined with ability to organize, a certain intellectual curiosity bent to practical ends, a lack of subservience to stiff social forms, and an intolerance of drones, all of which are distinctive characteristics of successful pioneers. These, if anything, are the indigenous part of our Americanism, the qualities that set it apart as a new rather than an imitative contribution to civilization. . . . Is it not a bit beside the point for us to be so solicitous about preserving [American] institutions without giving so much as a thought to preserving the environment which produced them and which may now be one of our effective means of keeping them alive?

Leopold spent two stints in the Southwest, one of them early in his career, during the heady years of the Great War when Taos and Santa Fe were attracting thinkers from around the world. He eventually became superintendent of the Carson National Forest (and even a public relations hack for the Albuquerque Chamber of Commerce from 1918 to 1921), and then later, in the early 1930s, supervised Forest Service erosion work in the Southwest. By all accounts, including his own poetry, the Southwest virus never let go of him. The existence of the Gila Wilderness in New Mexico as the oldest wilderness preserve in the American system is proof of his impact on place. But as a wilderness acolyte trying to see the fire rather than the shadows on the cave wall, for me it's Leopold's *ideas* about wilderness that are most intriguing.

In 1933 Leopold set about reworking (for a talk at the Laboratory of Anthropology in Santa Fe) an essay he presented under the telling title "The Virgin Southwest and What the White Man Has Done to It." Although he incorporated the thoughts and research from this piece into other essays, what became more simply "The Virgin Southwest" was not finally published until 1991. Wilderness was an issue Leopold had been thinking about for 15 years by 1933. He was *the* seminal thinker on the subject in the period when wilderness values were beginning to enter policy. In "The Virgin Southwest" he is primarily interested in the differences between the virgin condition of the Southwest as described in explorers' accounts and the degraded Southwest he saw around him in the early twentieth century. As to the cause of that degradation, one need look no further, he thought, than the devegetation of the range through overgrazing by domestic livestock.

Perhaps I shouldn't critique Leopold too much for relying, in a public talk, on the journal of James Ohio Pattie as the centerpiece of his description of the so-called virgin Southwest of the nineteenth century. But I have to point out what an unfortunate choice Pattie was to show us what the Southwestern wilderness was like. Historians are now convinced that Pattie's personal narrative was not an actual firsthand account at all but a work based mostly on interviews and imagination. Pattie's eye for game, grass, and timber, as Leopold put it, certainly reflected some widespread nineteenth-century sentiments about the West, but for the most part that eye did not actually view the world it claimed to describe. Remarkably, though, Pattie's hovering eye did see the world Leopold wanted it to see.

Leopold's evocation of Pattie leads him to conclusions like this about the Rio Grande Valley in the second quarter of the nineteenth century:

> In Pattie's day the Rio Grande drained a stable watershed, devoid of abnormal erosion. Even the sand dunes adjoining the river carried a heavy growth of grass. By reason of this grass, prairie fires swept across the valley and kept it devoid of large trees. . . . There was grass everywhere, little erosion, a normal river, and bottomlands of sweet well-drained soil.

Note the critical adjectives: normal river, heavy growth, sweet soil. This virgin Southwest, according to Leopold, did not erode until livestock was introduced. To Leopold the lesson was clear: The Southwest had been a pristine paradise, with all the characteristics of an untouched garden, until the white Forty-niners started traveling the Santa Fe Trail and introduced their domestic cattle to the Southwest. He got so rapturous about this vision that he even quoted Pattie's patently absurd statement that the Colorado River somehow managed to drain the vast red beds of Utah while still flowing entirely clear.

I find five things notable about "The Virgin Southwest." One is that James Ohio Pattie's personal narrative, however much it was faked, did portray a Southwest that fit conventional wisdom that America was an

Eden when first seen by Europeans. By further extrapolating from an account of faked experiences, Leopold continued that convention, added to it, in essence using Pattie to create the Southwest he wanted. In that vision, which became ours through his ideas, Leopold treated the Hispanos in New Mexico essentially as Spanish explorers had treated the Indians: He acted as if they had not really been present in New Mexico all those years. Like them, he scarcely mentioned the very ancient Indian occupation at all. And finally, he blamed the perceived changes in the landscape exclusively on the white pioneers.

"The Virgin Southwest" was a talk Leopold gave to the public. The Forest Service had already been moved by his arguments and in 1929 had issued the L-20 regulations establishing an official policy of wilderness preservation in the national forests. By the late 1930s Bob Marshall's U regulations had restricted roads, settlement, and economic development on more than 14 million acres of national forests and the evolution of policy leading to the official Wilderness Act of 1964 was in motion. It ought to be no surprise to hear that during testimony on the bill, which went on from 1955 until its passage, the role of the pioneers in subduing the virgin continent and the wilderness's function in shaping American uniqueness were probably the most winning arguments in convincing legislators to pass the original bill, designed to preserve 54 areas totaling 9 million acres (up to 90 million today) as vignettes of a pristine American Eden.

And add one final characterization, straight out of myth: According to law, in America official wildernesses are places that humans only visit, where man and his works do not remain. Eden but no Adam, and as for Eve, she doesn't even come in for a mention. *Los despoblados grandes* may not have existed in real, historic North America, but we could always legislate them into existence.

One end-of-October morning in the late 1980s, on the fourth day of a walk down the length of one of the Horizontal Yellow's most secret places, a friend and I entered one of the wildest places in all my experience, rivaled only by the Lower Canyons of the Rio Grande in Texas. Walking up Tule Canyon in the Texas Panhandle that morning was like being granted the keys to a magical kingdom. Birds I'd never seen in West Texas flitted along the rimrock, 700 feet above us. Coyotes sat a stone's throw away, barking at us in amazement. The great canyon was

The author in Tule Canyon.

far from empty—in fact, it teemed with life—but except for footholds in the sandstone and the ubiquitous beer can washed down the drainage, it seemed utterly devoid of human influence. Wilderness?

If an absence of Old World humans and anything associated with us is truly the definition we want to give wilderness, if a place like Tule Canyon is sacred primarily because it's too rough for cows and thus the cowboys aren't interested, then far more de facto wilderness exists in highly privatized parts of the Southwest, like Texas, than anywhere else. Tule Canyon was nothing like the Wheeler Peak Wilderness outside Taos, where I was used to seeing 50 or 60 people by the time I'd hiked to Williams Lake at the base of the mountain. Lacking trails, designated campsites, or Forest or Park Service managers, a place like Tule will strike you as more truly wild than official wildernesses like the Gila or the Pecos or the high Guadalupe Mountains. *If* it's the absence of the despoiling human—or at least *other* humans—that truly defines wilderness.

I no longer endorse that view. Very likely the search for a mythical land without people is a vestigial Paleolithic impulse of the kind that originally sent human hunter-gatherers searching out the planet. I recognize how old it is. Yet my own journey in search of the wild has caused me to be suspicious. I don't believe we humans are fallen any more than I think wild nature ever was. And I certainly don't buy that culture (or religion) has extracted us and separated us from the world of nature. So I think there's a paradox at the heart of our American definition of wilderness: We've sanctified an imaginary continent and attempted to make our interaction with it defining for us as a people. Perhaps that's why the United States is still the only country to create an official wilderness system; not a single nation anywhere else has emulated our program.

Because wilderness as we have defined it is certainly a myth, an ethnocentric idea based on the false premise of a virgin and uninhabited continent, there are those who argue that we ought to throw it out entirely. Various proponents of constructed realities (like historian William Cronon) and defenders of traditional wilderness ideas (like biologist Michael Soule and philosopher George Sessions) have argued a great deal about whether the wilderness idea should be abandoned. Cronon seems to believe that because wilderness (and, indeed, nature itself) is a construction, we might as well dispense with it and get on with substituting simulated Disney World or video experiences for what we seek when we go to wilderness. And there's the view of biologist Daniel Botkin, who has pointed out that the endless changes that take place in nature literally make it impossible for wilderness areas to capture and fix snapshots of the frontier, that we ought to start thinking more accurately of wilderness as protected reservoirs of natural processes and biological diversity. Which after all is how the Wheeler Peak Wilderness differs from a wild place like Tule Canyon that could be dammed or made a dude ranch any fine morning.

I suspect my own journey to the roots of the sacred wild isn't over yet, but it has brought me a ways. I try not to long anymore for some *despoblado grande,* and as intrinsically annoying as it is to encounter others of my kind just when I think God has assumed the form of a cliff face in the Chisos or in the lines of some meltingly organic badlands configuration across the prairie, I'm trying for a view that sees humans as integral to the wild. After all, we are wild animals.

This doesn't mean my sacred wilderness isn't historical, though. I'm still rapturous over places where ancient, native America yet resides, places that still possess the full range of species making up the ancient community that evolved here through deep (rather than shallow) time. The Horizontal Yellow I've inherited is a disturbed world, badly diminished in numbers and variety of deep time species, still in the shock wave of exotic introductions from other places. But the deep time animals and plants—wolves, bears, bison, cottonwoods, needle-and-thread grass—still mean far more to me than the shallow time ones. So I still labor to restore the little piece of prairie on my canyon homestead with those eighty-odd forbs and grasses whose *longue durée* histories give them more poignant meaning on this piece of ground. I'm yet a partisan of the wild natives.

And I still go off in an unceasing search for . . . what? On those afternoons of looking across the great sweeps, with the blue Rockies in the yonder distance or even the thought of them there, or the bright winter mornings when I drop into the Horizontal Yellow's plunging desert canyons and the ancient air rattles my heart around inside my rib cage from sheer ecstasy, what is it I long for? *Wilderness* no longer seems the correct name for it. *Despoblado* is certainly not.

What I *really* yearn to touch and honor—to give proper credit—is *Indian* America.

2 The River That Flowed from Nowhere

*I have proposed in conversation, & it seems generally
to be assented to, that Congress shall appropriate 10.
or 12,000 D. for exploring the principal waters of the
Missisipi & Missouri. In that case I should send a party
up the Red River to its head. . . . This will be attempted
distinctly from your mission.*

THOMAS JEFFERSON TO MERIWETHER LEWIS, 1803

*The Valley of the Red river is one of the richest and most
beautiful imaginable. . . . It cannot be exceeded either in
fertility or beauty, by any part of America, or perhaps of
the world.*

NATURALIST PETER CUSTIS, 1806

*Opposite: Thomas Jefferson never imagined this place—the origin of the Red
River's canyonlands.*

April 1995, the sunrise side of the Blue Ridge Mountains, with dogwoods and redbuds firing the first bolts of color through the drab winter woods of Virginia, and I am standing on Thomas Jefferson's veranda atop the small mountain where he built his experimental home of Monticello. Standing here, and facing west. For the past half hour I've toured the domestic world of this long dead American president whose life I've admired across the years. I've looked with a kind of numb shock at the bed he rolled out of as soon as the morning light was strong enough to see the hands on a nearby clock and at the writing table where in this same month in 1804 he composed a seven-page letter that set in motion the long American love affair with the part of the continent we now call the Southwest.

Now I stand in the cool spring on his west veranda and imagine that under similar conditions 187 years ago he rose from his desk and walked to this exact spot and did what I am doing now. He would have looked out across Albemarle County to the pale undulation that is the Blue Ridge, used his memories to construct the hidden Shenandoah Valley and ridge upon ridge beyond, finally leaving to his imagination and the words he'd read to penetrate farther and farther westward until even imagination failed against distance and rumor and the opalescent unknown.

Inside, I had been stunned to find hanging on the west wall (appropriately) of the receiving room one of his maps of the continent as Western cartography had known it two centuries ago. Sure enough, there was the Red River of the Southwest, its confluence with the Mississippi fixed by mathematical coordinates, the old French city of Natchitoches portrayed, and upstream from it the lands of the Caddo Indians. Beyond that the line of the Red River, the western stream Jefferson regarded as, next to the Missouri, the most interesting water of the Mississippi, angled off into . . . nothing. A runeless big empty.

Before he died in 1826, Jefferson's contemporaries did piece together parts of the puzzle of the region Americans were beginning to call the Southwest. An army officer, Zebulon Pike, traveled along the Arkansas River in 1806, raised three cheers for the Mexican Mountains (the Southern Rockies), pronounced the peak now named for him unclimbable, then got lost searching for the sources of the Red River and got himself arrested by troops from Santa Fe. Six years before Jefferson's death another American expedition, led by Stephen Long and including the sort of scientific naturalists and artists (Edwin James and Thomas

Say in the former category, Titian Peale and Samuel Seymour in the
latter) that Jefferson wanted so badly to send into the interior, traveled
along the Platte to the Rockies, then searched down the Front Range for
the Red River. They found it—they thought—and in a blistering summer
drought in 1820 descended the rusty stream only to find themselves back
on the Arkansas. The bewildering geography of the Southern Plains had
somehow put them on the Canadian River. And the Red? The river that
led into the viscera of the Horizontal Yellow, that supposedly penetrated
the most sharply changing geography of the West to provide the most
direct link between the swamps of Louisiana and the mountains of New
Mexico, the Rosetta stone to that runeless blank? Jefferson died with that
terra on his Western maps still incognita.

He *must* have stood here on this veranda many times looking westward and wondering what it was really like out here.

It's hard not to look at the Red River now, from the perspective, say, of
one of the bridges crossing it in Louisiana or a bit farther up, where it
defines the border between Texas and Oklahoma, and not think of it
merely as a chute for the delivery of red mud, salt, and sand to the Gulf
of Mexico. Up close is another matter altogether. Once two friends and I
spent a week descending the Red through this stretch. The sense of it
that still resonates in my memory is of a ponderous, Amazonian sort of
river, its waters the color of *latte* coffee, slow whirlpools belching up
entire trees that broke the crawling tension that carried us along with the
emergent power of surfacing leviathans. That Red River felt to me then
like a living thing, some ancient entity whose secrets and history were
worthy of a quest.

I have a great regret about the Red River, and standing on his veranda
in 1995, I realized that it's the same one Jefferson had. In the year
1806, two springtimes after the American president had dispatched Meriwether Lewis and William Clark to examine the Missouri and Columbia Rivers through the Northern Plains, Rockies, and Pacific Northwest,
Jefferson saw his second major scientific probe into the unknown West
turn its flatboats into the mouth of the Red River and head upstream.
There was, in other words, to have been a second Lewis and Clark
expedition, another epic Jeffersonian exploration whose mission was to
follow the Red toward the setting sun and unreel for Jefferson, for science, and for Americans the innermost secrets of the Horizontal Yellow.

When it is grandly successful, as it was with Jefferson's world-famous probe across the northern Louisiana Purchase, exploration can quench all sorts of yearnings having to do not just with national mission but with the simple desire to *know*.

Once Lewis and Clark were under way in the spring of 1804, then, Jefferson devoted the time and energy he had for exploration to assembling and launching what he and all the principals came to regard as the Southwestern counterpart to the Lewis and Clark expedition. Nearly two years of detailed planning and preparation finally poised the president's grand excursion for a scientific strike into the heart of the Southwest in April 1806. With Lewis and Clark then crossing the Bitterroot Mountains en route for Saint Louis and home, one triumph seemed ready to proceed on the heels of the other.

Why, specifically you might ask, the Red? Aside from the geographic symmetry of aiming his second Western expedition at the most southerly tributaries of the Mississippi, the reasons as Jefferson saw them were diverse and compelling. For one, there was the matter of the boundaries of the Louisiana Purchase. When Jefferson asserted that the Rio Grande ought to be the western boundary of the Louisiana Territory, Spanish diplomat Pedro Cevallos had responded that the American claim was absurd reasoning that did not merit refutation. But the president's claim did have the important consequence of turning the Red River into a reasonable boundary compromise.

Geographically, where, in fact, would the Red River lead American explorers? The truth, despite the long-standing presence of Euro-American settlements in New Mexico and Louisiana, was that only the Indians and a handful of traders knew the answer to that question. Unable to imagine the actual nature of Southwestern topography, Jefferson and everyone else in the American government assumed that major rivers head in mountain ranges and that given its lower course and size, the Red River must have its origins somewhere in the southern ranges of the Stony Mountains, at the foot of which lay Santa Fe. Indeed, these assumptions seemed corroborated by the most recent maps available, particularly Alexander von Humboldt's *Carte générale du royaume de la nouvelle Espagne*. Based on manuscripts in Mexico City, this map merged the Pecos River—which heads in the Sangre de Cristo range east of Santa Fe—with the river the French called *rivière Rouge* (Red River) in Louisiana. So Jefferson saw in the Red River an arteryway to New

Mexico, one that would open trade with that isolated province (and perhaps pry it loose from New Spain?) the way the Missouri-Columbia route was to open trade with Asia.

Actually, revisionist knowledge about Red River reality gleaned from traders did make it back to Washington via General James Wilkinson. In 1804 Wilkinson laid before the presidential eye a twenty-two-page letter detailing trader knowledge about the Southwest, mentioning volcanoes and other marvels of natural history and providing a description of the upper Red River country that combined reality with confusion. This is the passage that must have cemented Jefferson's convictions:

> About 20 leagues above [the Wichita Indian villages] the Red River forks, the right descending from the northward and the left from the westward. . . . It appears that the right branch . . . takes its source west of a Ridge of mountains, in the East side of which the Arkansas and Ouichita or Black River head.
>
> The left branch which is reputed to be the longest is said to have its source in the East side of a height, the top of which presents an open plain, so extensive as to require the Indians four days in crossing it. . . . West of this high plain my informants report certain waters which run to the Southward/ probably those of the Rio Bravo/ and beyond these they report a ridge of high mountains extending North and South.

What was being conveyed here was someone's firsthand knowledge about the upper Red but embroidered with secondhand syllogisms. It accurately portrayed the heretofore unsuspected Llano Estacado, the great Southwestern escarpment and plateau on which the Red River heads, well beyond which lay the southward-running Pecos River and the Sangre de Cristo front of New Mexico. While this ought to have raised doubts that the Red would lead American explorers to the Rockies, Wilkinson's muddled account of the North Fork probably alleviated those doubts. True enough, like the Arkansas, the North Fork of the Red does flow through a ridge of mountains, but in the Red's case they're the Wichita Mountains of Oklahoma, 200 miles short of the Rockies.

With hindsight, Jefferson's fascination with the Red seems to have been ill-starred from the first; the river was not going to lead his explorers where he thought it would. And there was one other, really big problem.

Unlike the Missouri, the Red would bring Americans threateningly near and accessible to the settlements and presidios of New Spain, and that country had already deciphered the handwriting on the wall of the future. But Jefferson's fascination with Southwestern natural history and the potential of trade between the Americans and New Mexico goaded him onward.

It was the natural history of the country—what we would now call the progression of its ecology, which captures the transition between East and West so well—that really intrigued him. The Red was said to be navigable for a thousand miles above the town of Natchitoches, penetrating westward into a country of immense and rich prairies. Alligators, buffalo, tigers, wolves, and innumerable herds of wild mustangs were said to abound. The Scottish expatriate scientist who helped Jefferson organize the Southwestern expedition, William Dunbar of Natchez, wrote to the president of the Red's long course, its medicinal plants, its sources in mountains of pure or partial salt. Dunbar also dangled wonderful stories of wonderful productions before Jefferson, among them wispy accounts of unicorns and giant water serpents. And from Dr. John Sibley, his Indian agent at Natchitoches, Jefferson learned that the keepers of the gates to New Mexico, the Panis (Wichitas) and Hietans (Comanches) of the upper river, were openly interested in the Americans.

In April 1804, then, Jefferson sat down in his study a few feet from where I stand in 1995 and composed a seven-page letter of instructions for Southwestern exploration based closely on his now famous 1803 letter to Meriwether Lewis. The Southwestern version differed on routes, of course, but its scientific emphasis—a canvassing of every scrap of geography, natural history, and Indian information possible—remained at the core. It also included a line that had its origins with the Lewis and Clark letter but that would prove far more significant in the Southwest: "If at any time a superior force authorized or not authorized by a nation should be arrayed against your further passage and inflexibly determined to arrest it, you must decline its further pursuit and return."

It took two more years to make the grand excursion happen. The delay primarily lay with the difficulty of finding leaders, since no second Meriwether Lewis, groomed by the president for just such a task, was waiting in the wings. The man Jefferson finally settled on was neither a military man nor, in fact, an American native. His name was Thomas Freeman, a young engineer and surveyor who had emigrated from Ire-

land in 1784 and who was promoted for the job by Robert Patterson, 43
the mathematician at the University of Pennsylvania who tutored Meriwether Lewis in the use of scientific instruments. On November 16,
1805, Freeman dined privately with the president at the White House
and had the honor of seeing Jefferson inscribe, *To Thomas Freeman,
Esquire*, across that letter of exploring instructions. As Freeman wrote to
a Tennessee friend shortly after that dinner, he well understood the
hazards of travel in the neighborhood of Saint Afee (Santa Fe) because
of the Spanish troops there: "[A] Great many difficulties, and some
personal danger will attend the expedition, but, I will—'Stick or go
through.' The more danger the more honor." Then he added the kicker:
"How would you like to be my Cashier in that country?"

Criticized for his failure to add a naturalist to Lewis and Clark, Jefferson wanted someone with real scientific training for the department of
natural history in the voyage up the Red River. After considering many
of the famous names in American natural history (Constantine Rafin-
esque, Alexander Wilson, and the legendary William Bartram among
them), he settled on 25-year-old Peter Custis, a medical student from a
well-connected Virginia family—an Albemarle County family related to
George Washington, in fact—who was in medical school and studying
with Benjamin Smith Barton at the University of Pennsylvania. Jefferson
personally selected Captain Richard Sparks, familiar to him via Meriwether Lewis as one of the best woodsmen, bush fighters, and hunters in
the army, to head the military escort. Other characters in this story
include Lieutenant Enoch Humphreys, so eager to go that he volun-
teered to do so without pay, and one Lucas Talapoon, probably a Louisiana métis, who a few years earlier had wowed the American scientific
community with his expertise in Indian sign language. As with Lewis
and Clark, there was an African American in the party, too, although his
name is a mystery.

Jefferson got Congress to appropriate $5,000 for the expedition (twice
the original appropriation for Lewis and Clark), and from it the leaders
assembled the best scientific instruments available in America—among
them a high-quality chronometer for establishing longitudes, a portable
barometer to take elevations, an achromatic telescope of either 60X or
75X to fix latitudes by observing the eclipses of Jupiter's moons, a camera
obscura (forerunner of the camera), and Custis's field guides, plant
presses, and taxidermy instruments. Also a flotilla of special flatboats and

pirogues and enough goods to trade for horses from the Indians once the river was no longer navigable.

You have to be Zen about lost opportunity, but the scent of palpable regret still lingers around this event even two centuries later. When Jefferson's party entered the mouth of the Red River on May 1, 1806, they anticipated a year-long probe penetrating some 1,300 river miles into the interior. But no one could have missed the warning signs on the Spanish border. As Custis put it, ominously, in the second of his four lengthy reports to the administration, "This expedition seems to have thrown their whole Country into commotion." In fact, when word of Jefferson's party reached Spanish officials, they were so alarmed at the potential outcome of allowing American explorers along their borders that they dispatched not one but two bodies of troops to intercept Freeman and Custis. One, commanded by a ramrod-straight adjutant inspector of troops, Francisco Viana, was sent from Nacogdoches to confront the Americans on the lower river. The other, known in Southwestern history as the most important military exercise ever carried on from the province of New Mexico till that time, was the insurance policy. Its commander was Lieutenant Fecundo Melgares, a future governor of Spanish New Mexico, and it left Santa Fe bound for the plains in early June.

In his *Wonderful Life*, Stephen Jay Gould lays out an argument for the time line of history that explains its progression from point to point far better than any resort to cycles, waves, or the circular time of hunter-gatherers. Gould suggests that history is hardly a linear march of events, either, but rather a layer cake of contingency events and decisions that pile atop one another to create direction. If human history (or the history of life) were a tape that could be rewound to the beginning, it would never play the same story twice, since at numerous critical contingency points, any small change could alter the flow of events, building up a new time line based on another set of contingencies. What such a view of history means is that within the big parameters of physical laws, virtually everything that actually happens is unique, to be savored. It also means that many other worlds are possible.

In the time line of the history that actually happened, the summer of 1806 merely waited out the rendezvous of the opposing historical forces. On July 30, three months after starting their journey, near the present eastern border of Oklahoma and only 615 miles up the Red, Jefferson's party found itself facing a Spanish army four times its size. The Spanish commander, Viana, politely but firmly insisted that the Americans turn back. Freeman consulted his orders—and I am certain drew in a long, ragged breath at what could have been—and complied.

What befell this exploration has a personal dimension, I admit. It just so happens that the Spanish army that stood between Thomas Jefferson and the mysteries of the Horizontal Yellow included as one of its officers a direct ancestor of mine, José Flores of Nacogdoches. Yet standing here on Jefferson's veranda, looking west two centuries later, my own feelings are only minimally conflicted. Anyone who knows this history and is also fascinated with the nature encounters that have so shaped the way we perceive the West simply has to be disappointed with the arrested promise of this expedition. Peter Custis, particularly, represented the best that Jeffersonian America could launch at the West. His four reports even now amount to an extraordinary encyclopedia of early Red River ecology. In only three months he cataloged a total of 267 species, 22 of which he recognized as new to Western science, among them the bois d'arc tree, the beautiful Mississippi kite, and the black-tailed jackrabbit. A portion of his botanical collection, which (I discovered several years ago) still exists among the Lewis and Clark specimens at the Academy of Natural Sciences in Philadelphia, concentrated particularly on ethnobotanical plants used as medicines by the Indians. Befitting a young man about to receive a medical degree. And a student of the classics, as his experiences with the Caddos kept reminding him of the stories in Homer!

In contrast to Lewis and Clark, history tells us almost nothing about Peter Custis. He did finish his degree in 1807, and he did become a physician—in New Bern, North Carolina—where across the arc of a long life he married the daughters of fellow physicians and named one of his children after Linnaeus. Other than a single characterization of him as somewhat blunt and caustic in his manner but (counterintuitively) also highly popular, I have no insight into his personality except from the four letters he wrote about the Red River. The rather formal stylistic qualities of those aside, Custis's letters provide the best (and only real) scent of flesh remaining from this ill-starred expedition.

Take a careful look at them now and you get a time-travel glimpse of a Red River "wilderness" extensively shaped by the Indians, with their fires and their clearings and their habit of transplanting useful species from one place to another. And shaped by the previous European presence: Custis found 15-odd Old World plants already growing in the Southwestern wilds in 1806. Together he and Freeman left us tantalizing descriptions of the lower course of this major river of the Near Southwest, with lines like, "The Valley of the Red river is one of the richest and most beautiful imaginable" (Custis), and, "In some places the growth of timber is observed to be of one particular kind, whilst in others, there is an admixture of almost all the species here enumerated, and all of large dimensions" (Freeman). Their accounts of climbing to the top of the Caddo Medicine Mount with their Indian guides, of the Great Raft—an enormous five-centuries-old logjam plugging the river and ascending its channel like some gigantic serpent—and of the semitropical Great Swamp that the Raft spawned are hard to read without a grimace at what might have been.

Standing in his space, then, I convince myself that Jefferson and I would agree on this: That one of the most seductive mysteries of Southwestern nature and history is what those never penned fifth and sixth Peter Custis reports would have told the president.

So what the hell? The crucial contingency in this story is clear enough. Let's rewind and let that tape play back one more time. What follows is fiction, but this is how it *ought* to have happened. And how a good core of the Horizontal Yellow must have appeared two centuries ago.

Peter Custis's Reports on the Upper Red River, 1806–7

Pani Villages on the Red river, 97 deg., 37 min., 30 sec W of Greenwich, September 10, 1806.

Dear Secretary Dearborn,

Obedient to the President's instructions, you will have, from Mr. Freeman's hand, another description of our ascent of the river to this point, including a fuller account of the diplomatic arrangement entered into by our party & Capt. Viana, who commanded the Spanish force sent out from Natchidoches to arrest our exploration of the river.—Here I note only Mr. Freeman's & Captain Sparks' agreement with the Spanish representatives, that in our further progress *we confine ourselves, per the President's own orders, to an examination of the Red river only, & locate our encampments & examine only the country on the right bank, or north side of the main river,* until such time as a formal agreement delineating an accurate boundary between the

possessions of the King of Spain & those of the U. States be made.
The latter part of this agreement, I should add, has been somewhat
injurious to my efforts to compile as thorough a natural history &
study of the Indian inhabitants as could be made.

Fortunately given this arrangement, thus far in our journey the
country lying to the south of the river has not presented a face materially different from that to the north.—Indeed, the only interesting
topographical variations we have seen in the extensive meadows that
characterize the region 1,000 miles above the river's mouth, have
appeared on the north side. And while one division of this village,
where we have been encamped since the first instant of the present
month, does lie south of the channel, the two larger divisions, including the lodge of Awahakei, the main chief of these peoples, are fixed
on the north bank.—

Our tents, space for which was cleared by the women of these
tribes (I say tribes, for contrary to assumption, there are four different,
'tho related, peoples in this village), now sit comfortably on a rise of
ground well north of the riverbed, in part to escape the sandstorms
that the frequent winds of this region stir from the channel.

Agreeably to the orders of the President and Mr. Dunbar, as with
my previous four missives I have attached a list of species observed,
viz., 41 additional botanical observations & 28 new specimens properly dried & packed in a leather cartouche sealed with bear grease for
delivery by messenger into Mr. Dunbar's hands. This accompanies a
description of 11 additional trees not found below the place where we
treated with the Spaniards. We have surely entered a new & very
different country from that of the river below, & many of the animals I
described from hearsay in my last communication are now familiar
companions on our journey.—My measurements, descriptions, &
proposed scientific names for several species, both floral & faunal,
probably new to science are also enclosed, although I will take occasion here to mention a few of the more remarkable.

From the point where we met the Spanish army to this, a distance
of 380 river miles measured by line & approximately half that distance in a straight tangent according to Lieut. Humphreys' calcula-
tions, required a full month's travel on the river. While in no wise a
challenge approaching that presented by the mazes of the Great
Swamp earlier in summer, this part of the Red river affords its own

obstacles to navigation, chiefly in the form of low water at this season of the year.—On two separate occasions our party were obliged to encamp for several days awaiting thunderstorms, which occur but infrequently in this country in summer, but fortunately discharge astonishing quantities of precipitation when they do, in order to raise the level of the river sufficiently to float our barges. Thus did we precede to this spot, stopping, waiting, with much-appreciated opportunities to hunt & botanize, then hurrying upriver with the freshets. Doctor Sibley was undoubtedly correct when he presented the Pani Villages as the upper limit of navigation on this river.

As to the nature of the country, if the river between the head of the Great Raft & the bluffs where we encountered the Spaniards appeared to me as the Paradise of the World, awaiting only our countrymen to claim its fertility, the country to here has presented equally an image of a Garden, but of a different kind. It is not like anything I have seen before, & indeed, unlike the descriptions we had received of it, causing me to wonder if it can be properly described, by firsthand observers, to people who have never seen its analogue.

The transformation of the country begins almost immediately beyond the point where we met the Spanish force, which we named Spanish Bluffs. The cause of the transformation of this region from tall woods to vast, open meadows is not yet obvious to me, but direct observation seems to refute the notion, expressed in the recent literature, that the *prairies* of the interior of Louisiana are the dried beds of ancient lakes. Nor can the soil be faulted for its fertility, for it is so rich, black, & even greasy in the hand that we followed the hunter's custom of calling this region the Black Prairies. The first evidence for the alteration appeared two days upriver from our encounter with the Spaniards, when, with our Caddo guides Cut Finger & Grand Ozages, Mr. Freeman & I left the boats under command of Capt. Sparks & ascended out of the Cotton Tree bottoms of the river to look over the uplands extending away on the right bank. What immediately demanded attention was that the tree growth of the hills, although composed of many of the same species as those downriver, were here sensibly dwarfed in size. Species of *Quercus*, of which there are several, which were 60 feet in height in the vicinity of the Raft were here no more than 35 feet. Nor was this a local phenomenon of soil, for the same dwarfing extended to many other common species,

& was observed across all the face of the country we traversed.— Equally worthy of remark, the small copses of upland meadows we had seen here & there downriver, almost exclusively occupied by an orange-hued bunchgrass growing to knee-height, here were much extended, so that woods & meadow occupied almost the same balance of ground. No doubt linked to these same phenomena, the horizon had now become visible, in many places, at a distance of a mile or more.

I thought this inexplicable transformation might correspond to the slowly rising elevation of the country (for our course to the Pani Villages remained almost due west & none of our latitude readings with the telescope have so far fixed us at above 34 degrees N.), a view reinforced when, during a delay occasioned by low water, the Indians, Mr. Talapoon & I had the opportunity to ascend the Kiomitchie, a tributary of the Red river famous among the hunters for its beaver.— Three days travel by pirogue brought us into a piney mountainous country, & eventually to a fine, long mountain valley that in aspect and elevation so closely resembles the Blue Ridge that my eyes filled with tears for *home*. The mountains here, however, run E/W rather than N/S, & under close examination the similarity is only partial. With much difficulty on account of heat & the swarming ticks we ascended the sandstone & slate ridge on the S margin of the cove, where the barometer showed an elevation of more than 2,400 ft. above the Sea. The view to the N was of immense meadows inset by picturesque peaks, thro' which flowed a branch of the Arkansa. Down the cove to the W were the several striking, piney knobs that deflect the Kiomitchie towards the Red river, while S of the narrow hogback that was our perch was the facing ridge, equally lofty & decorated atop its summit with a medicine tree. The three head forks of the Kiomitchie were distinctly seen below us at the upper end of the cove.

The Caddos use the same name for this river & the mountains, which means Horned Screamer and refers to the cries of the woodpeckers, the great ivory-bills being particularly numerous. In these mountains I observed that the vegetation often differed markedly from one side of the ridge to the other. I here collected several species of plants I believe to be new to science, among them a shrub bearing a resemblance, 'tho different, to the *Phyllanthus* of Linn. Seeing the heights of these mountains so thinly clothed with scrubby oaks &

specimens of *Pinus* twisted into fantastical shapes gave me the notion that, as in the Blue Ridge, perhaps it was elevation which was producing the change we were witnessing in the country.—

That change grew even more startling when freshets upriver once again set our main party in motion above the mouth of the Kiomitchie & into a region the hunters called Horse Prairie, for soon we found that we had entered a world composed of prairie almost entire, the only trees away from the river being those found in the declivities of the hills. The country also grew choppier, the crests of the swells from one to three miles apart. The meadows of the Red's alluvial bottoms, lush with June grasses & wild rye & needle & thread, along with many new species in the awn & grama families, were matched by the spangled prairies of the black-soiled uplands, where the prairie bluebell I collected near the village of the Coashattas was common, along with thousands of *Rudbeckias* & a pure-white *Coriandrum* I believe is new.—The Bow-Wood Tree is plenty on the margins of these prairies. Here also I first saw, at great distance, a small group of quadruped animals I thought to be goats escaped from a Spanish settlement. But when they turned from me they escaped across the prairie at a speed only a winged, Pegasus goat could reach. This may perhaps be the astonishing one-horned creatures described by LaHarpe & Mr. Hendry. We have since seen such animals several more times, 'tho always at great distance. This is a mystery I hope soon to resolve.

In these same prairies, at about W. longitude 96 degrees, we also met with the first of a peculiar species of ground-burrowing Squirrels, in size little different from the new Fox Squirrel I reported below Natchidoches, but with a very short tail tipped in black & with a yellowish coat. I give a more precise description of it elsewhere, along with a proposal for a scientific name, from a specimen Mr. Freeman collected with an admirable rifle shot.—The small Owl is also from one of these Squirrel Towns, for the two species live in colonies & appear to co-exist. I have wondered many times since what Mr. Bartram would think of such an arrangement!

The appearance of these vast & fertile prairies, almost constantly dappled with the shadows of clouds floating above them, & grazing peacefully upon their surfaces the first small droves of Buffalos & bands of Wild Horses we had seen, produced a strange & unexpected

reaction from almost the entire party. We were filled with a kind of
euphoria & had we possessed horses I have no doubt we would have
dashed madly across its surface in pursuit of distant herds. The President may envision something of the appearance from the view he
commands to the SE from his mountain home in Albemarle County,
except that no imminence of any height whatsoever is required for
such views in the country approaching the Pani Villages. Such views
surround one on every side.

A great salvo of thunderstorms played across the horizon west of us
as we followed the river through these extensive prairies, which effected a steady rise & muddying in the river's waters but eased our
ascent.—By 10 August the black prairies began to fall behind us &
we entered a sandier country, thickly overgrown as far as the eye
could penetrate both N & S, perhaps 20 miles in each direction, with
dwarfed Oaks of several species, and in some cases so dense with
Smilax & other underbrush that the woods were impossible to penetrate. This the hunters called the First Cross Timbers, for the Red
river is bisected by two such unruly tangles. If soil not be their cause,
then I am at a loss. Prairie openings continued to appear, however, &
on several occasions Mr. Talapoon returned with the choice cuts of a
Buffalo he had killed, certainly the most sumptuous meat I have ever
tasted.—

On the morning of August 16 I accompanied him to a point that
brought us within rifleshot of a young Elk, a male of the species
with antlers yet in velvet, which we brought down by firing together.
Dr. Barton is certainly correct in his argument that the Elk of North
America is very different from the animal that goes by that name in
Europe. This animal also seemed different in particulars from the
description given in Linnaeus. Its skin and antlers accompany my
natural history collection in case it be something new.

By August 19 we had emerged from the sandy Oak country into a
prairie more extensive & vast than any country I have yet seen, the
soil calcareous rather than loamy black as below, with white limestone full of shells exposed in the streambeds. Indeed, rather than
prairie, this country might more properly be called, following General Wilkinson's map, *the Great Plains*, or Grand Prairie, for at first
it appeared to stretch as far as the eye could penetrate. Open &
elevated away from the river, it is more exceedingly pleasant & insect-

free than any country in my experience, and was full of plants new to me even with flowering season over for most species. Among them is the Gourd species collected. I found it growing in all the buffalo wallows that indent this plain, & so profusely that at the low angles of the sun their craters cast a pox of shadows across the smooth grasslands. We found Buffaloes & Wild Horses in such plenty in these Great Plains that the mind cannot grasp their abundance & I must ruefully acknowledge that my doubts at these descriptions two months ago were an excessive caution.—Alligators, so numerous downriver, are no longer found on the Red river beyond this point.

Four days before reaching the Pani Villages the Great Plains gave way to another broken country & once again Oaks and common Cedars overspread the land, but growing in more parklike fashion here, as if the country were regularly swept by fires, as indeed the hunters & Indian guides assured us it was. It was here that I collected the spiney shrub the hunters called Muskeet, which grows in the declivities only, never on the uplands, as it appears to be sensitive to the great prairie conflagrations, which burn it up.—According to Talapoon, who has traveled extensively in the direction of the Spanish settlements, it becomes more common and grows to a larger size farther south.

Due to Mr. Freeman's urgency to reach the Pani Villages so we might continue our journey westward before winter, I did not have sufficient opportunity to study the habits of the Buffalo & the Wild Horses. But knowing the President's keen interest in the latter, particularly, I will seek occasion to do so as soon as possible. I do note that Bears & Lions remain common, that the Virginia deer, not being hunted much by the Indians in Buffalo country, are as common & tame as barnyard stock round about the Pani Villages. In addition to the Mexican Wolves I mentioned in my last report, which on more intimate acquaintance are truly grizzled gray, not white, & both numerous & very tame, there is another Wolf midway in size between the Fox & the Mexican Wolf & more sharply made than the latter. I am sending along a skin & skull. I have called it *Canis ludovicianus.* One final observation about the country: Bee trees and the Honeybee, which the Indians call white man's fly, do not now occur past about 97 degrees W. But our Caddo guides say they find them farther upriver every year.

On account of emissaries sent in advance of us by Dehahuit, the Great Caddo chief, to apprise the Panis of our mission, our arrival here was expected & greeted warmly by the Pani chief Awakahei, whose name means Great Bear. After some haggling he has agreed to trade with us for sufficient horses for twenty-four of us to continue our journey upriver, for which we embark tomorrow, accompanied by Talapoon & three Panis. Corporals Reid & Osborne, with two enlisted men, will remain at the Pani Villages to guard one of the flatboat & three pirogues our party will use to descend the river when we return from its exploration. The rest of the party, 22 in number & commanded by Lieut. Humphreys, will set out downriver tomorrow, in the other flatboat & pirogues.

Obedient to the President's instructions, in our short stay I have attempted to compile a Pani vocabulary, several words of which appear similar to those of the Caddos. A young Pani woman, She-day-ah, remarkable for her address & intelligence & a great favorite at these villages, was my principal informant in this & other endeavors. Her name is that of one of the most common shrubs in this great wilderness, & means Wild Sage.

The Panis, some of whom call themselves E-skan-ees, others Tao-vays, others O-wah-heys, & still others Wish-e-taws, are a beguiling and handsome people numbering about 400, now greatly reduced by the smallpox, they say. They came to this fine spot on the river within the memories of some of those still living, & say they formerly lived on rivers to the N, including the Arkansa, & knew white men there, many generations ago. Several Spaniards, raised from childhood as Indians, reside among them. At a distance their houses resemble those of the Caddos, but are constructed on a different plan & include space inside for their best horses, on account of frequent attacks on their villages by the Osages. Like the Caddos, their women grow maize, squashes & beans of various sorts, also melons, which they raise in sufficient quantities to store & to trade with the Hietans for products of the chase. The Panis themselves generally only hunt Buffalo extensively in winter, when they desert their villages.

They are a generous people in every respect. One example will suffice. The women of the villages were much taken with my black man, exhorting him (& indeed not him alone) to sport with them in their Green Corn dance & their gaming, which goes on nearly

The real She-day-ah, painted by George Catlin, 1834. (Courtesy National Anthropological Archives, Smithsonian Institution.)

every night. He did so with such enthusiasm that he caused Mr. Freeman a certain anxiety, yet none of their husbands uttered a word of reproach.

As I wrote the above sitting outside my tent, with a fine view across the yellow grasslands, which form overlapping horizontal planes into the distance, She-day-ah came to me with refreshments & disturbing news. The Pani warrior Tatesuck, a fair Spaniard captured as a child in Monterrey & raised to adulthood as a Pani, has confirmed other reports to Mr. Freeman that the Spanish force dispatched from Santa Fe, under command of a man named Melgares, is still upon the prairies.—He also confirms that the river we are exploring forks, but says that while the right fork will take us to the Rocky Mountains it will not take us near Santa Fe; that the left fork is longer but reaches into a place known generally in these wilds as El-Yan O-sta-kah-doh. He says this last is a very dangerous place to the unwary or unlucky, a place entirely destitute of water. A place, he says, that can confound & confuse.

Yr Obedient Servant,
Peter Custis

January 15, 1807, Natchitoches, Doctor Sibley's home

Dear Secretary Dearborn,

While I address this letter to you, Sir, as directed by my letter of appointment, & intend no disrespect, I am aware that its contents are intended ultimately for the Presidential Eye. So if you will tolerate my presumption, I will direct my remarks most specifically to the concerns of Mr. Jefferson.—

Mr. President, I inquire of your health, as always, as well as that of my old friend, Mr. Lewis. Doctor Sibley tells me that his voyage on the Missouri & Columbia has been an entire success & that he is the toast of Washington. My family will be relieved at his safe passage & glad to hear that his melancholia has been vanquished, but, I fear, are yet alarmed for my own safety.—So soon following post dispatch delivery of this & Mr. Freeman's accounts, our last & final reports of our expedition, into your hands, I beseech you, Sir, to assure my family of my safety. Doctor Sibley has told me of the false account of our fate which appeared in the New Orleans papers. I fear it may have found its way to Charlottesville. Assure them, as well, that I will return to my studies with Dr. Barton in Philadelphia this winter, but that certain other matters (which I will take up with them on my return) require more immediate attention. Beyond that I should not speak, but request of you, Sir, to ask my family to have the guest quarters near my room placed in a state of preparation. Mr. Dunbar will no doubt wish to entertain us in Natchez & examine my specimens, but assure my family that this delay in the interest of science should not detain me long.

You will learn from Mr. Freeman's report the chronology of our exploration to the source of the river. As before, his account is more detailed in some matters, as in describing his success in delivering your message to the Indians respecting our wish for peace & trade & the transfer of their allegiance to us. His report also includes our celestial reckonings, so I will take few notices of them here. Mr. Freeman has given me to understand, in very confidential terms, your certain disappointment that the Red river did not access Santa Fe & the possibilities thereof, & has much more to say than I to your specific regrets at this unexpected turn. I will only add that this negative result is ameliorated by a positive: we now know which river to take to reach that city.

My account of our journey from the Pani Villages to the head sources of the Red river, in Louisiana, with a brief notice of our return to Natchitoches, follows.

We left the Pani Villages on September 11, 1806, at day-break, the party selected to penetrate to the remotest sources of the river consisting of 23 citizens of the U. States, my black man, & three Indian guides. Our cavvy (a word the hunters use, to refer to a party's drove of horses) consisted of 37 riding horses & 18 mules which were employed to pack our scientific instruments, collections, & presents & flags for the tribes upriver.—Mr. Freeman will have more to say to you about the unfortunate accident to the achromatic telescope, which occurred on our first day upriver. The latitude of our journey varied but little to the heads of the river, but unfortunately its loss prevented us from determining the exact positions of the major head streams.

We left the scattered Oak woods the first day & soon entered a country that for vastness & desolation I took (at the time) to be the equal of any on earth. During all of our stay at the Pani Villages there had been no rain, & except for several astonishingly fierce storms, which I will in due course attempt to describe here, many days at a stretch passed with no rain at all & the sky an immense, inverted blue bowl over our heads.—The sun was harsh, the light exceedingly bright to the eye, & in this stretch of the river the yellowed grasses began to mimic the dwarfing we had earlier observed in the tree growth. I attempted my first images with the camera obscura of this region. They will show the Presidential Eye a land rolling away like gentle ocean waves in every direction from our tiny party. Consistently the effect of such travel was to surmount the wave-crest before us with the expectation of having achieved an overlook, only to find another, higher crest directly ahead.

Species new to science in this region, the measurements & descriptions & proposed names for which appear in my appended lists, include a kind of Wild Chicken different from the Grouse of the E. states, & the Prairie Goat, which I believe on close examination to be an Antilope or Gazelle similar to those of Africa. It is an exceedingly actively-made animal, remarkably light of frame & with bulging eyes that seem made for seeing across the great distances of the country it inhabits.—It was just above the Pani Villages, also, that I came upon the peculiar shelled animal that appears in my collection. Even the Indians said they had never seen this creature before & interpreted its appearance as a kind of omen. In form it resembles the Anteater of S. America, except attired in gray armor. We found it crushed by a passing travois alongside an Indian trail. The Indian who found it related that the creature had shown itself only a moment when a Pani woman with horse & travois appeared from nowhere & ran it over.

Herds of Elk & droves of Wild Horses inhabit this wild, desolate country, & in many places we saw regularly used Indian trails. On our outward trek, however, we saw but few Buffalo here, although old sign of them abounded. Their scarcity the Indians said had to do with their rutting season being extended by the dryness, which kept them mostly north of our line.

We traveled for four days along the right bank of the river when we began to see the blue profile of mountains some distance to the north. On the morning of the sixth day above the Pani Villages we met with the great forking of the Upper Red river. In truth, there are three forks altogether, a considerable streambed with but little water entering from the SW first, followed 10 mi. upriver by a division in the main stream, the smaller fork flowing a wholesome, clear water down from the mountains, which were still in view, whilst the widest of the three beds presented a coiling swipe of sand disappearing into the plain directly westward. While counseling with the Indians on our course of action, we thought to name these rivers the Dearborn, the Dunbar, & the Jefferson, to honor our expedition's sponsors. Chronometer readings & such observations as we could make without the achromatic telescope proved this place to lie at 99 deg., 15 min. W of Greenwich.

Mr. Freeman's account will explain at greater length the reasons behind our decision to explore only two of these, the main, or Jefferson, fork to its source first, while attempting an examination of the interesting mountain, or Dunbar, fork on our return journey. Agreeable to the document we signed with Capt. Viana, we did not explore the Dearborn Fork nor any of the country S of the main stream.

Mr. Freeman had employed Tatesuck as our chief guide into this unknown region, for Mr. Talapoon had only vague & second-hand knowledge of it, & on the 20th day of September, 1806, we pointed our horses up the Jefferson Fork & proceded on.—I will not here duplicate Mr. Freeman's chronology & daily mileages for this part of our journey, but from a natural history standpoint I should say that it was in this region that I added the lightning-shattered calcareous rocks to my mineral collection. This followed one of the great storms we met with in this country, on a day that began entirely clear but by noon had produced directly before us a columnar cloud climbing ever higher above our heads which by 4 p.m. had spread into the very shape of a smithie's anvil & grew dark & angry. The storm commenced with several bolts of lightning, two of them striking the prairie in plain view less than a mile from us, which threw geysers of mud & rock & grass 40 ft. into the air. This was followed by rain, falling in such blinding sheets & with such fury of wind that we were fair amazed. Yet this wet & wind were nothing to the pummeling we received from stones of hail the size of hens-eggs which soon began to fall about us like artillery. We covered ourselves & instruments with blankets & indeed anything within reach, but the frightening storm entirely stampeded our cavvy, which required most of the day following to gather. Within an hour of starting the storm had passed & the sun came out, showing a country glistening white with hailstones. The storms of this country appear fully the equal of its vast scale.

We traveled for almost a week thro' this sandy desert, inhabited principally by the Burrowing Squirrel & its Owl companion & vegetated in places by fully-matured Oaks now reaching only to the height of the knee! Also, increasingly, by kinds of Cactus & by a new species of the Soap-Plant, different in particulars from the one collected downriver. Wild Turkeys continued exceedingly numerous, as they had been throughout our journey, & we here first encountered the new species of Crested Quail that appears in my collection. Also, the large, Crested Cuckoo, which the Indians call snake bird for its skill in killing rattlesnakes. It seems a country where the birds save their wings & walk about.

On the 22nd of September, the Autumnal Equinox, a line of mountains rose portentously in our path to the west, appearing at first like a low stratum of blue clouds before us. I say *line* because from the distance, which we thought very near but that required two long days to cross (a frequent miscalculation in all this upriver region, we soon discovered, owing to the extreme transparency of the atmosphere), these mountains appeared to constitute an almost uniformly horizontal summit with but few peaks visible & those of an odd, block shape.— To our discomfort, as we neared this line of mountains the water in the river, though clear, assumed a taste so salty & so liable to expand in the mouth that it was with difficulty that we drank of it & I was kept busy treating the men for the cramping. These, indeed, may be the Salt Mountains about which the President has been so curious.

We had now entered a country much gashed & torn, where the soil was as red as blood, like the redbeds of Georgia, & crystalized spiderwebs of salt, most often laid in horizontal strata, were exposed in an array of striking patterns in the tributaries away from the river. Wild Horses were here extremely abundant & repeatedly we were forced to rout the stallions which sought to toll away our remounts.—Here, too, a new kind of Deer made its appearance, different from the Common Deer in several particulars, among them its tail and ears but most readily its gait, hence our name for it: Hopping Deer.—All the while the mountains loomed before us, assuming forms & shapes such as I have never seen in the art of Rosa or Turner or anyone else.

Some agreed that these bizarre & astonishing forms, carved from rock layers of the mountains, remarkably resembled the turrets, towers & porticoes of castles on the Rhine, whilst others with Oriental tastes thought they must have been built by the same hands that constructed the towers of Constantinople.

On the 30th of September, with the river commencing to flow from a NW direction & the strange mountains gathering around us, we came to a considerable stream of water coming in from the west, directly exiting the mountains, its waters salty but less so than the main river. Tatesuck advised us that this was the last point for several days where the river's waters could be drunk, that we must ascend this west fork, called Too-lee, with our packmules to where the water became sweet & fill every skin bag we possessed for the journey beyond. Mr. Freeman thus split the party, leaving 18 at a camp at this place while 9 of us followed the Too-lee into its mountain fastness. Wholesome & sweet water was obtained within five miles of travel up this little stream & our skinbags were soon filled to brimming. But so weird and oddly enchanting was the country that it drew us onward, & with one of the Indians & Mr. Talapoon, Mr. Freeman & I decided to explore further this narrow & interesting defile.

This was our first experience with a kind of scenery which became frequent ('tho never common to our eyes) during the next months of our travel, a scenery, if I may, never before known within the confines of the U. States. The majority of the views we here submit to the Presidential Eye, recorded with our camera obscura box, are of this region & of the rock mountains along the River Dunbar. Yet, I must add the sensible fact that none of the profiles we recorded can give an adequate impression of this country, which would require all the imagination & skill of Europe's best painters of landscape to capture. It is now four months since I have returned from this region, yet the fantastical shapes of it & the hues of its coloring linger in my mind like the faint impressions of a dream. Had I not seen it all with my own eyes I would not believe such a place as the region about the head sources of the Red river exists.—

The chasm of the Too-lee, which is called by those familiar with the country a *cañon*, continued for at least another 20 miles beyond the point where we left the packmules. The reading with our instruments was taken far up it, in a grassy basin surrounded by astonishing free-standing columns of red sandstone rock, but short of its ultimate

source. Here was the first place in more than 15 miles that the cañon
could be crossed by horse & through it a large & well-traveled Indian
road was found. Remarkable as this place was, however, it paled in
comparison to a point passed the day before. This place, which we
called the Defile, for stirring the mind to thoughts of awe exceeded
any view we had during the entire journey. In this Defile the opposing red-brown sandstone walls, filled with pebbles & shells, closed to
less than 60 ft. apart, one from the other, & rose sheer & vertical to
giddy heights above us. Strange, lyrical birdsong & the gushing of a
voluminous spring filled the cañon about us with sound. Owing to
some superstition, Tatesuck was struck by a sudden desire to escape
this spot, & finding some footholds carved into the north face he
attempted an ascent which I accompanied with the barometer. A two
hour's climb brought us to the crest of one of the surrounding peaks,
yet imagine my astonishment when we found ourselves not atop a
mountain, as I had supposed, but instead at the margin of a plain so
flat, so extensive & so glaring in the sun that its effect, coupled with
the stupendous rent in the earth from which we had escaped, produced in me several moments of utter disorientation.—El-yan O-sta-
kah-doh, Tatesuck said to me, simply. The barometer showed a difference of 800 ft. from the floor of the Defile to this spot.

On returning from this journey, on October 7, we found our main
camp well supplied with meat from the fortuitous appearance of
herds of Buffalo, which except for a few stragglers had been almost
absent since we had left the Pani Villages. Thus provisioned, on the
8th we once again turned our horses up the main, or Jefferson, fork &
began to follow its wide, sandy bed in a N/NW direction. Here again I
wish to refer the Presidential Eye, for corroboration of my impressions, to Mr. Freeman's account, for of all of us I believe he was most
astonished at the country, finding it so utterly unlike the misty Ireland
of his youth that he wondered aloud more than once whether we
could yet be on the same planet as that fabled isle. As the river wound
deeper into the surrounding mountains the strangeness grew daily,
the colors becoming brighter, ranging from brick reds & oranges to
yellows, chocolates, & myriads of other hues, often laid one atop the
other in striped mounds that appeared & disappeared & appeared yet
again as the eye cast about.

During the time when Mr. Freeman & I had ascended the Too-lee
our waiting party had found much sign of Indians, & on several

Tule Canyon, high-drama canyon on the eastern escarpment of the Llano Estacado.

occasions had observed smokes at a distance. Having traveled the entire distance from the Panis without meeting with any Indians, although signs of their camps were abundant, we therefore daily expected to have an encounter.—These expectations were further augmented by the truly astonishing numbers of Buffalo that now began to appear before us, much muddying the stream, filling the nights with their bellowing, their ranks sometimes barely parting enough to allow us to pass. Throughout the day they poured in brown streams down from the mountains on every side, thousands in view at a glance. We noticed that where earlier the herds had been of all sexes & ages, with bulls, cows, & yearlings mingling amidst great shoving & butting & bellowing matches between the bulls, now the herds tended to be segregated by sex. We had the impression that in entering these deep cañons our little party had stumbled onto some secret *sanctum sanctorum* of the buffalo tribe.

On October 12, having traversed in a rare morning fog one of the most fantastical & colorful parts of this narrowing cañon we were ascending, a place so bizarre to the experience of civilized man that the language to describe it fails, the course of the stream turned abruptly to the west. Now we began a journey through yet a different setting. Springs gushing from the walls now grew abundant, the water became sweet, & the winding cañon became clothed in a forest of Cedars, some low & rounded like hedges and carrying berries that were blue on some bushes, red on some, others growing as tall & pointed & massive of trunk as the Cedars above the Coashatta Village, 1,200 miles downriver. Our way now was much blocked by boulders falling from the rocky rims rising above on either side, so on the 14th, discovering what appeared to be a wagon trail leading into the valley, we ascended the north wall to the summit line above & once again found ourselves confronted with the great plain. Apart from Mr. Freeman & myself & a few others, most of the party had yet to witness this phenomenon, & great were the exclamations of surprise when the summits of the mountains thro' which we had traveled yielded up a featureless plain stretching into infinity, where the only vertical objects were the dried stalks of the Soap-Plants stabbing like daggers into its sterile surface.

Except for its exposure to the sun & the occasional drain running into the cañon below, the great plain presented no obstacle whatsoever to travel. We were thus moving more rapidly than heretofore when one of the Panis appeared with word that a very considerable camp of Hietans was fixed in the valley some miles before us. By midafternoon we were in sight of their tents, gleaming whitely in the sun & scattered about the cañon floor just above a place where the stream created a series of very picturesque waterfalls. Mr. Freeman sent Tatesuck & Talapoon forward to announce us, & well before sunset

The Horizontal Yellow, eastern New Mexico.

we once again descended into the cañon, where we entered a camp of 120 tents, almost 1,000 persons, many hundreds of very noisy dogs, & round about which grazed several thousand horses & mules. Hoping for precision, I later made an effort to count them, giving up at more than 3,000 because of the constant coming & going of herds to pastures scattered at some distance from the main camp.

This camp had more than one chief, for it was made up of several divisions. But we were escorted to the tent of its generally acknowledged leader, a man who appeared near 50 years of age, extremely fit, with a bright eye & (as we were to learn) a quick mind. Wary at first, for they had been in the country upon the Arkansa & had heard nothing of our coming, he soon inclined (as some others were not) towards greeting us in friendly fashion, & inside a spacious hide tent, copiously fitted, he bade us smoke with him. Thro' our interpreter, Talapoon, who spoke to him in both signs & Spanish, Mr. Freeman explained the nature of our journey.

When he began to speak he said he was called Cordero, that his people were the Kot-soh-tee-kas, or Buffalo Hunters, that they traded

in both Santa Fe & San Anton where the Spaniards called them by
the name Cumanchee. His people, he said, were as numerous as the
stars & owned all the country from San Anton to Santa Fe & north to
the Missouri. He told us quite frankly & with a prim satisfaction that it
was good that the Great Mystery had placed a forest towards the
sunrise to hem the Cumanchees in, for if there were prairies &
buffalo & horses in that direction he would fear for the people of the
U. States, as the Cumanchees would surely overrun us!

He said they were at peace with the Spaniards, who traveled &
traded among them freely, & who they suffered to raise horses for
them! He called the river we were on Ke-che-ah-que-ho-no, meaning
Burrowing Squirrel River, & said the traders from Santa Fe called this
cañon the Pa-loh-doo-roh. On specific inquiry to Mr. Freeman's questions, Cordero said that this river would not take us near to Santa Fe,
but that at a day's fast ride to the N was another river that came from
the snowy sierra, on the far side of which lay the Spanish towns of
New Mexico. Told of our explicit instructions to explore only the
head sources of this river, he remarked that it & the river to Santa Fe
were not a part of the same water, but that if we wished he would
show us all the waters of this Rio Rojo & any others we wished to see.
Cordero accepted Mr. Freeman's offer of a U. States flag & showed it
utmost respect. He said they welcomed our traders among them but
that Natchitoches was too far to come to trade. He did not like the
idea of a trade factory in their country.

Thus embarked a period of near to a month when a significant
portion of these Indians traveled with us, a circumstance not entirely
pleasing to us because of the inclination of their young men to make
off with our horses & goods. With apology Cordero returned or replaced what he could, yet the annoyance sometimes strained our
daily intercourse.

The Hietans or Cumanchees are a large people, heavier than
many Indians, with broad faces & slow movements until they alight
their horses, at which horse & rider achieve a remarkable unity of
movement & activity. Watching their feats of horsemanship in their
home country & more especially the flair with which they pursue &
drive their arrows entirely thro' the Buffalo whilst riding at full gallop,
I was put in mind of the cavalry of the Tartars on the steppes of
Mongolia. Like the Mongols, they are herders of horses. Yet they

rarely eat of them; their horses are but a means to hunt the Buffalo. They live exclusively in Buffaloskin tents, the covers & poles of which they are endlessly replenishing, but which endure the constant winds which sweep this open country & are disassembled so rapidly by the women that a camp can be broken, to search of fresh pasture for their herds, in moments. The men have as many horses as they can accumulate & as many wives as they can care for, the younger of which accompany them on their hunts & raids. They are at war with the Osages & the Apachees, but were at this very time in the process of making peace, thro' intermarriage, with their neighbors, the Kioways. Beyond any expectation, Indians from other tribes & a great many Spaniards, captured as children, are found among them, living as Cumanchees & apparently wishing for no other life.

I befriended one of their physicians, a man of particular influence among them, who instructed me in their materia medica. Particularly interesting are three of their cures, the first a plant which they say inhibits a woman's ability to conceive of child. Another is a kind of small Cactus, which they have only recently learned the use of & which grows far to the south, which a few among them ingest as a general tonic & to speak with the Great Spirit. They also have a method of curing toothache or the common aching head, viz., by the chewing of the stems of the ordinary Willow.

On the morning of October 19, having remained here as long as we thought prudent, we commenced our journey up the river, now dwindling rapidly in size, accompanied by Cordero & more than 100 of their warriors & young women. We now found ourselves traveling thro' a shallow, cañon-like valley set 200 ft. below the surface of the immense plain. As we moved W various branches split off from the main fork, but Cordero directed us to one with the best water, altho' scarcely a trickle, which he called La Tierra Blanca, which contained a highway ascending it fully the equal of the road across the Cumberland.

On the 22nd, at a spring below one of the last of the rocky bluffs that defined this valley, Cordero bade us fill our bags full & gave us to understand that we were now only a short distance from the sources of the Red river. The streamwater, found only in some holes at wide intervals during the previous day, now gave out entirely, as did the white rock strata along the drain, & the bed became merely a low depression winding thro' the plain, which was thick with Buffalo &

herds of Gazelle Goats as far the eye could penetrate, their forms very often appearing outrageously distorted in the wriggle of heat waves emanating from the ground. One pair of our hunters had earlier endured merciless hilarity from the general company when they had reported the difficulties of shooting Buffalos walking on 20-foot stilts, but now had their satisfaction atop the shimmering surface of the El-Yan.

Thus it was that at midday on the 23rd of October, 1806, the depression we had been following having faded into the general surface of the great plain, one of the men gave the shout that he saw some break ahead, & within an hour we had all gathered on the brink of a tremendous precipice falling 1,000 ft. below us, its cliffs stretching as far as we could see SW/NE. Before us to the W lay outliers broken off from the enormous tableland over which we had come, a country of flat-topped mountains extending away into the opalescent distance. It was the grandest sight I ever beheld in these U. States. Our readings indicated a position of W. longitude 103 deg., 30 min.

Mr. Freeman asked of the Indians if there were a route to Santa Fe thro' this tortuous country, and how far? They answered yes, that only a short distance N was a cart road regularly traveled by the Spanish traders, but that the sun rose & fell 12 times on them between here & and the Spanish towns.

During the rest of this day Mr. Freeman took no counsel but consulted his orders by lamp well after dark. A huge, golden moon rose out of the plain to the east this night, illuminating the prairie in a silvery blue cast when one walked away from the fires, & lighting the gashes & throwing immense shadows across the wild tablelands W of us. The Wolves sang & the Buffaloes bellowed. Homesick as we all were &, I confess, with thoughts of other, recent, moonlit nights in my head, I shall never forget that night.

Before I retired Mr. Freeman came to my tent & told me with very evident regret & not a little heat that given the specificity of his orders & and his agreement with the Spaniards, our outward journey was now at an end, & to prepare for the return journey two mornings hence, for our original plan to seek winter quarters among the settlements of New Mexico was now untenable. That because the Spanish force from Santa Fe might still be searching for us, he & Capt. Sparks agreed we should attempt to return by a more direct route to the Pani Villages & descend the river with our barge when the water &

A look off at the Horizontal Yellow from the Llano Estacado on the New Mexico side.

weather permitted. That the Hietans with us were in any case urging escape from the surface of El-Yan before the great cold winds from the north swept the exposed plain. But that he & Capt. Sparks, with Talapoon & Tatesuck & our escort, Cordero, had thought to ride along the precipice on the morrow & welcomed my company.

We rose before the moon set & rode from camp in a SW direction as the glow began in the east. Notwithstanding that our course lay away from the sunrise, over the next hour we repeatedly reined in our horses to observe a phenomenon of these immense deserts, the sun's rays fingering the eastern sky in a most regular pattern resembling the spokes of a wheel. At one point Capt. Sparks, who as the President knows is a Virginia hunter himself & who had befriended Talapoon in the course of our trip, rode up to tell me that the hunters referred to this singular occurrence by the name Prairie Aurora. Given Mr. Dunbar's interesting studies of the rainbow, I preserved a sketch of it to show him. Although the rays of the aurora lack a prismatic effect, I suppose that refracted sunlight must account for it. The Indians had no interest in this explanation, but made much of the phenomenon, & when it had finally faded & at the moment the bright orb crested the flat horizon, I observed Cordero to face the sun with outspread arms & perform a small ceremony of immersing himself, horse & weapons in smoke.

We used up this day riding the great western precipice of El-Yan, I collecting plants & mineral samples in the declivities of the steep & dry sandstone mountains below the brink, Mr. Freeman & Capt. Sparks in taking readings at the head of a more southerly headwater drain of the Red river than we ascended. It was here that I saw the new species of dwarf *Pinus*, collected the delicate little pea-shrub I believe a new genus & found a new variety of the *Cassia chamaecrista*, different from that downriver. Also, the silvery shrub of the Aster family, growing with and in appearance very like the feathery *Artemesia* of this country, but with flower bracts blooming a most vivid yellow. I believe it a new genus. Here, too, were crotons & cacti & many other species of an alien world.

At midday we crossed a narrow neck of ground to the surface of what appeared the most westerly of the peninsulas of this tableland. Here seemed to be a divide, the gashes and rills going both N, to the river that leads towards the settlements of New Mexico, and S, towards a distant & unseen river the Indians say flows to the Rio Bravo considerably below El Paso del Norte. The barometer showed this spot to lie at an elevation of a mile & 400 ft. above the point where the Red river enters the Mississippi. The view from this redoubt, with the rimrock stretching away from us to the S and NE as far as the eye could penetrate, was a most strange mixture of pleasure & awe.

On October 25 we reluctantly turned our faces eastward once again & began to follow a trace to the NE that Cordero's people led us along, with the broken lands below the plain & to the N sometimes visible & close, while at other times we crept across the stupendous, flat surface of El-Yan as if the world were aught but plain & sky. No one was allowed to straggle or even hunt during these crossings, for fear of losing them in a country of no landmarks. The plain is dotted at intervals with shallow ponds, round like plates, usually of cracked mud trampled by the surrounding herds. But when watery the ponds are much frequented by animals & by such an array of Ducks, Geese, Waders, & a species of gray Crane, smaller than the Hooper, that first, viewed from afar, we thought the air above the ponds to be suspended vortexes of Bee swarms, when we finally heard the cries of the Geese & the Cranes.—I & others of the men found this enormous plain, swept by constant strong winds, monotonous in its scenery, entirely lacking an echo, to be oddly stirring in spite of its sterility & alienness. This is undoubtedly one of the largest plains in the world, & it has the kind of stern, self-assured grandeur of a great ocean, a confidence (if earth may have such!) perhaps springing from the certainty that man will ever be a traveler, never a tamer, of its desert wastes.

We made the crossing from the sources of the Jefferson Fork to the head gullies of the North, or Dunbar, Fork in five days of riding, always angling towards particular springs & camps, known to the Indians, hidden away in the broken lands on the northern periphery of our route. At the second of these there occurred an interesting encounter. By mid-afternoon of this day Cordero's young men led us to a most fascinating spot, an alcove, carved by sweet water gushing out of a spring in a rock amphitheatre, covered top to bottom in various painted & carved Indian symbols. These were many & varied, some painted in red ochre, some (including what appeared to our eyes as a Spanish bull) in black charcoal. Situated in the midst of these frescoes, however, & extending almost the length of the alcove, was a large & remarkable Serpent, painted in red ochre & capped by a single horn on its forehead!

Whilst in investigation of these interesting symbols a party appeared in sight on the same trace we had just traversed & within an hour descended to our encampment. They proved to be 15 traders, some Spanish, the greater part Indians, from the New Mexico towns & the Indian pueblo (they said) of Saint Domingo. They were much astonished to see us. With two rickety & noisome carts, possessing wooden slab wheels & but a single axle apiece, yet filled with breads, vegetables, blankets & wares, they were bound for a res-cah-tay, or trade fair, at a place along the eastern precipice of El-Yan they called Kit-ah-kway. They told us the spot where we were encamped was one of their regular rests along the route.—

Here was presented an interesting opportunity & so I engaged them, through Talapoon's translation, as to the meanings of the symbols on the wall behind us, particularly with respect to whether the Great Serpent depicted represented some creature not known to science. Their response was that the Serpent did indeed represent a creature, which they called Gah-nah-doh, the Great Horned Serpent That Protected The Waters, & that because of its appearance on this wall, weary travelers could always find water here. To further inquiry they said that Gah-nah-doh appeared in the flesh only in dreams or ceremonies, but that the Rattlesnakes were his familiars & more common emissaries.

This group accompanied us for two days more before turning SE to their rendezvous with certain Hietan bands, during which time I treated several of them for various ills. One of these was a Spaniard from a town called Ab-ee-kyou, on the waters of the Rio Bravo, a man of about 40 years who surprised me not only by being literate but, indeed, literary. We made ourselves known to one another using Latin terms & phrases, & he gave me to understand that he had been born in Galacia, where he studied some law, & had emigrated to New Mexico in search of adventure & wealth, that the former had found him but that he had eluded the latter entirely. His name was Tru-hee-oh & he expressed a most interesting view of the surrounding country & its potential. It was his opinion that between our two peoples, the Spanish approach to these vast plains & mountains would be the more workable, for they would leave the country a grazing commons—or ee-hee-dohs, as he pronounced the term—& the only harm would be to the wild herds. But we Anglos, with our zeal for possessing the world, would try to turn these lands into a place of individual grasping, & having no tolerance either for the wild beasts nor the Indians would banish both. Thus we would destroy the country. To my protests he wondered good-naturedly if I had read Cervantes, & gave me to understand that our two nations' jousting for this region was in fact an affair of the windmills, that Nature had ever owned these expanses & ever would.

Among the other interesting particulars of our short acquaintance, he showed us his method of hunting el-see-boh-la (the Buffalo) from horseback with a lance. Mounting their fastest horse, he proceeded to run at one of the herds that constantly surrounded us in this region, & within a space of minutes after mounting had plunged a steel-tipped lance deep into the vitals of two fully grown Buffalo running flat out across the prairie! It was as daring a display of courage & skill as I have ever witnessed. He told us he had learned the technique watching bullfights in the city of Pamplona as a child.

On the afternoon of October 29 we began to come within view of the head gullies of the northern branches of the Red river, on the eastern border of the tableland. Less precipitous & deep than the cañ-ons of the Jefferson Fork, the rills draining the plain here nonetheless possessed springs of good water & small copses of the Cotton Tree, & their sides were rich in the bright hues of the country. At the begin-ning point of the gully, which Cordero assured us was the river that flowed through the mountains we had seen on our outward journey, the barometer indicated an elevation of only 3,200 ft. above sea level, leading us to the conclusion, surprising to all, that the apparently horizontal plain over which we had come actually pitched downward almost 2,500 ft. from its western perimeter! Celestial readings taken here indicated a longitude of 101 deg., 7 min. W of Greenwich.

During the night of October 31, having rested & provisioned our-selves for beginning our exploration of the mountain, or Dunbar, fork on the morning next, we were struck by the first of the great north winds of which the Indians had spoken with such awe & urgency. Nowhere in the Eastern states, save during the hurricanes along the Carolina shore, have I ever experienced the equal of this wind. The thermometer, which had stood at 67 degrees F. the evening before, had dropped to 6 deg. F. by morning! All day the wind blew re-lentlessly & consistently from the NW, pushing before it a fine yellow dust that coated us as if with volcanic ash. Had this wind caught us atop the open plain I would have feared for our lives. But we hid away from its furies in the gullies of the stream, like Burrowing Squirrels in their holes, until it sensibly slackened some 30 hours after it com-menced, & clouds of stars appeared in the intense cold of the night. For most of our travel across the El-Yan we had seen & heard Geese & the species of gray Crane frequently in the skies overhead, but this night was filled with the cacophony of strange flutings & weird cries from unfathomable numbers passing over us, heading south.

Frost lay across the rolling lands east of the El-Yan as we de-scended the river on the morning next. But the day soon warmed & for the remainder of our journey down the Dunbar Fork & through the Rocky Mountains the weather remained clear, delightful & invig-orating. Four days journey down this little river & still passing thro' immense numbers of Buffalo, all drifting southward, we left the last outliers of the strange, flat-topped table mountains. The next morn-ing, Capt. Sparks, Tatesuck & Talapoon, riding ahead of the party,

Where have all the pretty horses gone? The bluestem prairies of the Wichita Mountains in southwestern Oklahoma, where wild horse herds once speckled the landscape.

spied the blue uplift of conical mountains on the eastern horizon, & by that afternoon we made camp in a place where the river cut directly thro' the most westerly range of them.

It should now be understood that these ranges of peaks (for there are several of them scattered, one from the other, across the plain), 'tho deserving the hunter's appellation, Rocky Mountains, are not a spur of the Western Sierra, or Mexican Mountains. They stand separate from the main sierra by a distance of perhaps 250 miles. Nor are they lofty. We ascended to the topmost points of several of them, including the highest peak in the main cluster, & measured an elevation, by barometer, of 2,400 ft., about 1,000 ft. above the surrounding plain. The peaks of these mountains thus lie below the lowest surface we measured on the El-Yan! They are composed uniformly of barren, gray granite, & indeed present the appearance of immense piles of granite blocks, a rock not found elsewhere in our investigations of the country. Their vegetable clothing is Oaks & Cedars only, 'tho the main range preserves atop it several spacious meadows, glowing very orange in the sun, of the Bunchgrass mentioned in my last communication.

We found Elk & Buffalo plenty about these mountains, but no animal caught our attention in this region so much as the droves of Wild Horses, which here appeared in great numbers wherever one cast an eye across the country. Knowing the President's fascination with the subject, I took special pains to observe them. In its wild state the horse naturally segregates into droves, or mahn-yah-das, as the old horse-catcher Talapoon calls them, each ruled by a stallion whose chief occupation seems to be the difficult work of keeping his harem of mares together & adding to it, by theft & seduction, whenever possible. The stallions, especially, are vigilant & wary, & will not suffer close approach.

Unattended by grooms, the Wild Horse presents a striking sight, its mane long & flowing, its tail sweeping the ground, its eye glowing & alert. Many appeared exceedingly well made, 'tho small, & they present all the colors of hounds in a Virginia kennel, the tan with black mane & tail predominating, 'tho the brown & white spotted horse appears frequently. Sometimes entire droves are composed of one color only.—The Indians & Spaniards have devised successful means of capturing them & say the younger ones are easily tamed. Given the cost of horses in the U. States, these immense droves are already being sought out by our hunters, who in this commerce stealthily avoid the Spanish patrols which jealously guard this prairie resource. On our descent of the river in December we thrice met with hunters ascending to engage in the horse trade, & it was one of these to which Mr. Talapoon attached himself rather than return to Natchitoches with us.

The country about these mountains appeared the best & most fertile we had met with in our exploration of the upper river. Indeed, Tatesuck, the Pani warrior, took particular interest in the site of our first camp in these mountains, where the Dunbar Fork so tumbled thro' fertile bottoms almost enclosed by the rocky summits that we gave it the name, Devil's Cañon.—We had now re-entered the range of the Black Walnut, which grew tall & stately along the streams below the mountains, & with great delight began to encounter the Bobwhite, Bluejay, & other familiar birds of the Eastern states. Here, too, a group of Pani hunters hailed us, with eagerly-welcomed news from the Pani Villages.

On November 14, following a night when the north wind lay four inches of snow across the country, we ended our descent of the mountain fork of the Red river to its confluence with the main stream, arriving at our campsite of September 18–20 on the afternoon of the 16th. The weather becoming disagreeable, we did not tarry but camped that night at the mouth of the Dearborn Fork. Here Cordero & his people, anxious to join their companions wintering in the deep canons of the El-Yan, begged to take their leave of us. Notwithstanding certain minor frictions which had developed from so long a travel together, Mr. Freeman honored them with a feast & dance which lasted, for some, until the morning planet glowed a molten silver in the rose sky, as if to beckon us homeward. My friend Esa-wah-we, the Cumanchee physician, presented me in the morning a bundle of herbs & cures. And he directed my attention to a cluster of conical mountains some distance to the S, of which he spoke with apparent reverence, repeating the term, pu-ha, pu-ha, meaning medicine or magic.

Anxious now to return down the river, we proceeded rapidly along the N bank, bound for the Pani Villages & encountering nothing noteworthy except for one unusual circumstance.—During the morning's travel after we parted with Cordero & his people, a short distance up the tributary the hunters call Faux Ouachita, we came on the spectacle of a large herd of Buffalo dead from some unknown cause. Wolves, Vultures, & Eagles, among them a small Eagle of a type with which I was unfamiliar & possessing a black cap atop a white head, were making grisly work of the bodies. But I was able to observe that several of the poor creatures suffered from a common malady of carbuncles on their sides & legs & a black discharge from nose & anus, common symptoms of the dreaded anthrax. The number of dead animals in this drainage we estimated exceeded one-thousand.

Throughout the whole of the time that we descended the river from the forks to the Pani Villages, the plains 'round about us were seen to be on fire, both nearby & (judging from the smokes we saw) at great distance also. These fires the Indians had set, to direct the movements of the Buffalo, freshen the grass for their horses, & to burn up the Snakes & annoying insects. This practice seems to confirm Mr. Dunbar's assertion that these immense & grassy plains exist because of fire, a view in which Mr. Freeman concurs & contributes the observation that the dwarfing of the vegetation we have observed is related to the same cause.

I am not so certain. The rising elevation of the country up the river, which is seen to correspond sensibly with the diminution of the grass & the Oaks & other common species, should not be dismissed. But I am anxious to discuss with Mr. Dunbar & Dr. Barton my theory that neither fire nor elevation is the ultimate answer, that both the spreading grasslands & the dwarfing of vegetation are related instead to a sensible & gradual decrease in atmospheric precipitation as one journeys farther into the interior of Louisiana. The effect may be amplified, perhaps, by the cloudless nature of the skies in this part of the world & the tremendous force of the sun on the soil. For it was observed that even when saturated by the sporadic downpours, the ground was very soon after always baked dry of its moisture by the incessant beat of the sun's rays. While we noticed a few fertile & well-watered tracts above the Pani Villages, the general impression much of the country upriver imparts is thus of a sandy desert. In contrast to downriver, the country about the sources of the Red river can never beckon the farmer. It is a region fit only for pasturage.

We were greeted warmly at the Pani Villages on the 20th, finding them anxious that we would fail to arrive before they had set out on their winter hunt southward on the waters of the Rio Brassos & Rio Colorado, in Texas. Indeed, two of their divisions had already departed. Our craft & stores, left with them, were in good shape, except for some barrels of flour, which Corporal Reid had distributed among the Indians for some favor.

We remained here, awaiting a rise in the river, until the 2nd instant of December, during which time I was able to dry & re-package my specimens from the sources of the river, a total of 41 vegetables (13 of which are used as cures by the Indians), 15 grass, shrub & tree specimens, 17 birds, & 11 quadrupeds, including the skins & horns of another Buck Gazelle & an Elk & those of the Hopping Deer. Also, live specimens of several curious Lizards beset with projecting horns & knobs & an active, vividly-colored collared Iguana from the Pa-loh-doo-roh. The greater part of this collection I believe to be new species & in several cases new genera. Also, 18 ink sketches of the country upriver done with the camera obscura, to which notes have been added designating coloration in hopes that paintings may be worked up from them, although I dare not speculate on the receptivity of our nation to what such art of our Western borders implies. Three boxes

of minerals representing all the geological strata we met with accompany the collection as well. Those who may be inclined to doubt our
reports as to the astonishing hues of much of W Louisiana may herein
satisfy themselves.

I must also inform you, Sir, that I took the liberty during this interval to ask She-day-ah, my Pani informant, to accompany our party
downriver, to which she readily acceded. She wonders much about
the world I have described to her, and altho' she fears it also, she has a
desire keen as a blade to know things. It is my hope to have the
pleasure of introducing her to your company, & towards this end she
brings a present we hope you will do the favor of accepting. In a place
like Lexington he would not be so outstanding for conformation, but
in pattern of coloration & sense he is a prairie apotheosis.

On the 2nd we pushed off into the river & began our descent to the
village of the Coashattas, where Mr. Freeman planned to leave the
barge until the high water of the spring enabled a more favorable
penetration of the Great Swamp. The voyage downriver was made
without incident. On several occasions we made camp with parties of
hunters ascending the river in quest of meat, honey, & horses. On the
18th, encountering a group of Caddos hunting Buffalos in the black
prairie above where we met the Spanish army, several of us joined
their sport for one last taste of the prairie life. The Caddos, 22 in
number, organized us into a surround & bade us not to suffer a single
animal to escape, lest the beasts warn others of the stratagem! In the
space of time required to re-charge a piece three times, we killed the
entire bunch, a total of 41 animals, & that night gorged on Buffalo
until we fell into a stupor around the fires.

We passed the great southward swing in the river the day before
Christmas, 1806, & made the Coashatta Village five days after. There
being insufficient horse to transport all our party overland to Natchitoches, Mr. Freeman left the major portion of our party, under command of Capt. Sparks, to march the road eastward around the Raft &
Great Swamp, while he & I, with Echean, the Coashatta chief, &
She-day-ah, rode in advance. We reached Doctor Sibley's house here
on the 5th day of the New Year.—

With respect to the country up the Red river, it is unnecessary to
say more. Neither it nor the course of the river have turned out, upon
examination, to bear a close resemblance to what the President may

have expected. Indeed, certain of us (altho' Mr. Freeman refuses to concede the idea) have begun to wonder whether the Spaniards permitted our explorations precisely because they knew this. The country is so entirely unlike any other in the U. States, the scenery of vast horizontal spaces & stupendous defiles of bizarre rock formations & astonishing color so strange, nay, even alien, to the eye, that one wonders even now what our people would ever make of it. Many of us wonder if it might most practically be left to the Indian, the hunter, the Buffalo, the Wolf, & the Wild Mustang, forever.—

I am, Sirs, Yr Most Obedient Servant,
Peter Custis

Pulling my jacket tight against the chill of April in Virginia, 187 years to the month after the West's most famous dreamer first unleashed that blowtorch mind on the Southwest, I finally accept the nature of my relationship with Thomas Jefferson. Standing downstream in the flow of time from the point he occupied, I have an advantage. I know how it all turned out. Or, at least, I know more of this story than he was ever destined to.

The simplest part, which requires only being born downstream in the time flow in this part of the world, is that those Spaniards of Jefferson's day—like my ancestor—were absolutely right to throw themselves body and soul in the path of this exploration. Jefferson's party, however innocuous and purely scientific, was the first swell of a wave that would threaten to rinse them off the map of the Southwest. You can't help but applaud such an act of self-preservation, even if it amounts only to delay.

In terms of sheer knowledge about the world, though, in our (and Jefferson's) time line of history, this outcome meant that unlike virtually every other major river in the American West, the Red River continued to shimmer and dance like some High Plains mirage beyond reach of scientific knowing, and it did that for another 75 years after Jefferson tried to unlock its mysteries. After both Pike and Long failed to clarify the whole mystifying puzzle prior to Jefferson's death in 1826 (although Long's botanist, Edwin James, at least provided the former president some of the Southwestern natural history particulars he craved), in 1852 Captain Randolph Marcy at last located the maze of deep canyons sluiced by the Red's exit from the Llano Estacado. The world went on to

Tule Canyon in West Texas, unimagined landscape of the Red River Thomas Jefferson was destined never to know.

hail him as the elusive river's conqueror. Yet Marcy's romantic descriptions and drawings of the head sources have turned out to be of Tule Canyon, the sheer side gorge 125 miles short of the river's actual headwaters.

So. It was not until 1876, the same decade that Sir Richard Burton finally tracked the Nile to Lake Victoria, that Lieutenant Ernest Ruffner at last spent two months exploring and mapping the windswept draws and desert canyonlands that give rise to the river draining that runeless blank on the map in President Thomas Jefferson's receiving room. At last the river he had targeted so many years before as next to the Missouri, the most interesting water of the Mississippi, was graspable. But it was a river Jefferson and his explorers never got to understand. For them it remained the river that seemed to flow from nowhere.

I take one more look around me, and with a shrug for the wonders that we all are destined never to know in our lifetimes, walk down the pathway of Thomas Jefferson's mountain to my car.

3 Where All the Pretty Horses Have Gone

The prairie near the horizon seemed to be moving, with long undulations, like the waves of the ocean. . . . The whole prairie toward the horizon [was] alive with mustangs.
JOHN BARTLETT, 1852

They hunted the wild horses in the upland forests in the pine and madrono and in the arroyos where they'd gone to hide and they drove them pounding over the high mesas and penned them in the stone ravine fitted ten years earlier with fence and gate and there the horses milled and squealed and clambered at the rock slopes and turned upon one another biting and kicking while John Grady walked among them in the sweat and dust and bedlam with his rope as if they were no more than some evil dream of horse.
CORMAC MCCARTHY, *All the Pretty Horses*

It is the horses who make men wild. With a horse under me, I myself am no better than a Comanche.
GABINO RENDON, LAS VEGAS, NM, CIBOLERO

[Opposite: An animal that made men wild. Plains Indian petroglyph, Cowhead Mesa, Texas Panhandle.]

Where are the wild horses?

Odd question though it may seem across the Horizontal Yellow at the turn of the twenty-first century, it deserves an answer. Superficially the response might be that the wild horses exist in the same place that the grizzly, the wolf, the bison, and most of the other charismatic mega-fauna of the Old West exist—on the pages of books or in our minds as we stand looking out across the strangely empty Southwestern landscapes of the end of the twentieth century. Like the one I'm presently in, the Chardon Gardens Wilderness in the Wichita Mountains National Wildlife Refuge. Casting my eye about the oddly satisfying tumult that is the granite rock garden of this Southern Plains mountain range, I'm appreciative of the herd of bison I communed with an hour before, lying about like statuary as the wind-whipped bluestem rose and fell around them. And I'm happy to know that the bugling of bull elk still reverberates through these mountains on frosty late October mornings, even if they aren't the native (and extinct) Merriam's elk of these mountains. As for the Texas longhorns loose across these ridges, I'm less than indifferent. What the hell are *they* doing here when the far more characteristic animal of the wild plains of two centuries ago is nowhere to be seen?

Only someone who's read the earliest history of the Horizontal Yellow would have any inkling of this (maybe a good argument against knowing anything about the past), but three centuries ago this world was ground zero for the return, after 80 centuries of absence, of a true American native, evolved with the stipa and grama and buchloë grasses that even now are bending to the breezes against my legs here in Oklahoma's Wichita Mountains. Gone from here for 8,000 years but preserved in slightly new form beyond the Bering land bridge in Asia, the horse came home when Spaniards suspended them in slings aboard swaying ships and hauled them back across the Atlantic 500 years ago. Forget the fairy tale that the horses of the American West trace their ancestry to some equine Adam and Eve escaped during Spanish exploration of the Southwest. Indians who'd never thought to mount an elk or buffalo skewered those bizarre, hornless strays for the sake of science and cuisine. But accept, because it is true, the more beguiling story that when horses managed to stay loose, escaping their herders during the Pueblo Revolt of 1680 or abandoned lame in the woods by packtrains supplying the East Texas missions in the 1690s, they went feral across the Horizontal

Yellow by the millions in an ecological instant. Why? And why, given
that efflorescence, are they all gone from here now?

Or *almost* entirely gone. I have actually seen wild horses in the Near Southwest—in Oklahoma, in fact, traveling a ridge in the Ouachita Mountains in the eastern part of the state. They appeared before my companion and me on a gray November day and seemed for a long moment some unrequited dream of wild horse materialized from the fog of our longing. Visible briefly through dense oak woods high on a mountain hogback. Just a slurry of horse motion through the texture of tree trunks, a brief clattering of hooves on rock, and then the fading, thumping, and rustling of a big animal escaping across a flooring of autumn leaves. But the glimpse was like an icicle breaking in my mind. Whole— a black, no, a dark dapple-gray, pony-size horse, eyes rolling in alarm, its mane and tail dirty white and amazingly, impossibly long, the mane matted and below its withers and the tail sweeping dried oak leaves. Then gone. Snip.

At the end of the twentieth century that glimpse stands as wild horse summary statement for this part of the world. But 150 years ago? This is what artist George Catlin, traveling through the very Wichita Mountains country I'm now hiking, saw in the summer of 1834:

> The tract of country over which we passed, between the False Washita and this place, is stocked, not only with buffaloes, but with numerous bands of wild horses, many of which we saw every day. . . .
>
> The wild horse of these regions is a small, but very powerful animal; with an exceedingly prominent eye, sharp nose, high nostril, small feet and delicate leg; and undoubtedly, have [sic] sprung from a stock introduced by the Spaniards, at the time of the invasion of Mexico; which having strayed off upon the prairies, have run wild. . . . There is no other animal on the prairies so wild and so sagacious as the horse. . . . So remarkably keen is their eye, that they will generally run 'at the sight,' when they are a mile distant . . . and when in motion, will seldom stop short of three or four miles. . . . Some were milk white, some jet black—others were sorrel, and bay, and cream colour—many were an iron grey; and others were pied, containing a variety of colours on the same animal. Their manes

were very profuse, and hanging in the wildest confusion over their necks and faces—and their long tails swept the ground. Whilst on our march we met with many droves of these beautiful animals.

Take any space on earth. Ecological change across time is inevitable. But why does such change so consistently impoverish us? As I look about the part of the world where I live, I do not like to think that the nature I see and interact with has by my time not just been blunted but sheared out of existence, so that not even doppelgangers of the older, richer, more interesting world yet remain.

Where have all the pretty horses gone?

You don't doubt, in southwestern Oklahoma, that you're in Indian country. Driving out after my day of hiking the little wilderness area in the Wichitas, I'm surrounded by the descendants of all those people Catlin painted catching horses here 150 years ago. The modern Wichitas, Comanches, and Kiowas may have swapped the ubiquitous paint pony for the ubiquitous F-150 pickup, but with all these Indian faces, Comanche Nation High Stakes Bingo bumper stickers, backyard ceremonial grounds, yard art of carved black bears clawing carved trees (a reenactment of a mythic Kiowa story), and the Quanah Parker Historic Trailway under construction, you know you've crossed out of Texas or Kansas, and you're sure not in New Mexico, either.

I stop for gas at the Trading Post Indian Store in Cache, on the south side of the mountains, and while the tank is filling wander inside and at once step into the best collection of dime store, Western eclectic, pop culture knickknackery I've ever seen assembled under one roof. Here are your bolo ties with the rattlesnake head clasps, lazy-stitch beaded rosettes at a buck and a quarter apiece, Indian superhero comic books, velvet paintings of Jesus hung halo to earlobe with likenesses of Mickey's pal Goofy, and old photos of Quanah and a pencil drawing of Quanah's Star House, built (so they say in Texas) for Quanah by cattlemen south of the river to keep the goddamned Comanches out of the state. Painted electric-illuminated tipi lamps seem to be a Trading Post specialty; the Galleria Mall in Dallas can't touch this selection of styles. And of course there's a wooden Indian, more than one, I see; in fact, a wooden couple that'll stop you in your tracks and chill your guts at the long life of stereotypes.

George Catlin preserved for us an image of a Horizontal Yellow covered by herds of wild horses as the wild plains reverted to their Pleistocene form two centuries ago. (Courtesy National Museum of American Art, Smithsonian Institution.)

After Cache I head west on 62, Quanah's new Trailway, into Kiowa County to 54, where I turn north around the west end of the main Wichita range, with many scattered mountains to the west (the Glens, the Twins, the Navajos, and the Quartz range according to my topo map), most of them topping out at no more than 500 feet above the rolling plains but looking blue and lofty across the distance. This is the first real basin-and-range country as you move westward across the Southwest, unexpected in the vast expanse of the plains.

A few miles down 54 I pull over beside an Oklahoma/Kiowa Historical Society marker designating Cutthroat Gap, a pass visible a couple miles east where in the summer of 1833 the Osages famously fell on an unprotected Kiowa camp under the charge of Islandman, killing 150 and seizing the sacred Tai-Me medicine bundle. Little Bear recorded it in his calendar as The Summer That They Cut Off Their Heads, since those killed were decollated, their heads left in cooking pots. I look up from reading this and gaze across a couple of miles' distance at the mountain pass where the grisly deed occurred. It strikes me as an uncommonly serene setting for such an event.

Glancing down, I notice I'm not the only traveler to find some dissonance between the story and the scenery: There in the dirt is a fresh, bright pink *condom* of the novelty sort available in the familiar metal dispensers in every becrudded men's bathroom in every truck stop in America. The incongruity of the continuum makes me laugh into the sky. These Oklahomans are gonna be all right. Their ancestors, like mine, may have helped erase all the wild mustangs from the countryside, but they're survivors.

The answer to my horse question is not as simple a one, in its sum, as you might think. But the parts that are simple serve to open another one of those unpleasant windows onto the human condition that stories about nature always seems to be opening. Of course those who think on such things argue endlessly about the causes of our impoverishment. Have we simplified and ripped away at the natural world around us in the Near Southwest because of materialist reasons merely, because where 350,000 people lived 500 years ago we now cram nearly 35 *million?* That simple? Or is there something amiss in the Western worldview, something inherently damaging to nature in our philosophies, which tend toward a utilitarian view of the world around us? Or in our religions, which in the case of Christianity and Judaism regard us humans as special players, the only residents of the place with a physical likeness to God, therefore the only ones with souls? Is it that science and modern technology have run amok, destroying every sense of the sacred in nature and tripping off ecological chain reactions that we don't understand? And what does economics have to do with our situation, especially given capitalism's exalted pedestal in this part of the world? Did the coming of the global market to the Near Southwest unleash humanity's selfish gene in a way that ate up the richness of the Horizontal Yellow before our generation arrived on the scene?

Keep those questions in your head and consider this story from one of Colonel Richard Dodge's books about the West in the nineteenth century. It was October 1872 and Dodge, a fellow officer in the American army, and three English gentlemen were idling away a few days on the North Fork of the Cimarron, a plains river given its name because of the bands of wild sheep and horses that frequented it. And what did one do whilst idling away time out on the Horizontal Yellow a century ago? Why, what else but turn your guns on everything in sight, so that in a few days of sport you might amuse yourself by shooting dead (according to Dodge's obsessively kept scorecard) 127 buffalo, 13 deer and antelope, 154 turkeys, 420 waterfowl, 187 quail, 129 plovers and snipe, assorted herons, cranes, hawks, owls, badgers, raccoons, and even 143 *songbirds* (including a bluebird). Total take: 1,262 animals, in just 20 days.

What preparation from culture is required to fashion that kind of view of nature, where animals exist not merely as resources but, more carelessly, as live targets worthy only of assassination? No lurking bloodthirstiness embedded in human nature explains it. Adolescent curiosity about the natural world, the frontier equivalent of rural boys with BB guns and .22s? Dodge, his companions, and the bulk of the farmers, ranchers, cowboys, and settlers who tore apart the old ecology of the Near Southwest a century ago were grown men and women.

I could not argue, on the basis of diaries and journals from the last century, that what happened to most of the wild horses of the Near Southwest was that they were shot down, although a great deal of that did happen. The fuller truth is that the wild horses were virtually erased from this part of the world primarily because they became objects of pursuit in what loosely could be called a Southwestern variation of the fur trade. It was an economy aimed at live capture, all right, and eventual sale of the horses as light draft and riding animals. But it was a cruel enterprise nonetheless, aimed directly at reduction of the wild and the remarkable. J. Frank Dobie regardless, it's a story—or a set of them—that not even historians know much about.

Ruminating on all this as I point my Jeep westward toward home, I still wonder at the *mind-set* of it all, that mode of thinking that leads so thoughtlessly to extinguishing from the world the very elements that lend it beauty, grace, romance, richness of experience. And not just as it played out a century ago or in other minds. I wonder about it in all of us today, certainly in myself, that teenager who tried so hard to capture nature with traps and guns. This uncomfortable thought line spirits me back to a morning when the sun was a red ball through the mist in the Red River Valley and a coyote paused in yellow prairie grass, her muzzle wondrously sharp and refined, her ears working, dew droplets thrown glistening into the air as her tail switched the grass, her eyes intense and boring straight into mine. The posing of an ancient question. Then the scene was shattered with a rifle blast and she yelped, spun, disappeared.

The next moment is one of the most vivid memories I have, perfect as a circle in the sand. The sun broke through, and all that had seemed only an instant before wild, romantic, beautiful, dissolved in stop-frame motion into a scraggly pasture littered with cow dung and discarded plastic soft-drink bottles and farm machinery, encircled with barbed wire, truck gears rasping like chalk on slate somewhere off beyond the cottonwoods.

In an instant I had personally recapitulated the whole continental experience. I had destroyed what I'd loved, draining the beauty from the world with a syringe as I looked on, detached and wondering. Why the hell had I done it?

Sometime before 1835 the famous bird painter, John James Audubon, wrote that in Kentucky he'd become acquainted with a man who had just returned from the country in the neighborhood of the headwaters of the Arkansas River, where he'd obtained from the Osages a recently captured, four-year-old wild horse. While the animal in question was by no means handsome and had cost only $35 in trade goods, Audubon was intrigued enough to try him out, and he proved to be a delight. He had a sweet gait that covered 40 miles a day, leaped over woodland logs "as lightly as an elk," was duly cautious but a quick study in new situations, and strong and fearless whether swimming the Ohio River or in the hunt, paying no attention as Audubon collected his birds from the saddle. And he left a superb $300 horse in the dust. Audubon promptly bought Barro for $50 silver and decided that "the importation of horses of this kind from the Western prairies might improve our breeds generally."

In his day John James Audubon was usually on the cutting edge of things, but not this time.

Fifteen years before Audubon discovered the Western mustang, in 1820 to be exact, a young native son of the eighteenth-century Spanish settlement in western Louisiana, one Pedro Flores, came knocking on the door (or perhaps he scratched on the hide windows) of a cabin belonging to the oldest Euro-American settler along a stream called Bayou Pierre, the little Red River tributary that trickles out of the hills behind

today's Shreveport. Engulfed as a young man by the would-be revolutionaries and real estate piranhas flocking to Texas as the Spanish Empire collapsed, Pedro Flores and his siblings were of a century-old Spanish family the Crown had tried to shunt out of Louisiana to San Antonio
two decades before his birth. They'd refused, going only as far as East
Texas. Now they were part of a generation that would lose their father's
expansive Rancho Tortuga (Turtle Ranch), an 18,000-acre granted empire straddling the Attoyac Bayou near Nacogdoches. So Pedro Flores
was on the move.

His future as a landed *rico* looking shakier by the year, maybe young
Pedro saw a return to his Louisiana roots as a way to slow the spinning
wheel. Perhaps that's why, at the age of 24, he'd come to seek the hand
of 20-year-old Marie Lafitte from her father, the frontier settler Pierre
Bouet Lafitte. Or maybe they had been smitten with each other since
childhood. I do not know. But I do know that he turned his back on
Texas and decided to follow the fortunes Marie's father had been refin-
ing along Bayou Pierre for 35 years—running hogs and cattle and barter-
ing butter, cheese, and butchered meats, but mostly trading with the
Indians and breaking the wild horses fresh from the western prairies that
milled in Lafitte's corrals along Bayou Pierre. The young couple even
named their firstborn Pierre, although whether after the old patriarch or
the stream (or as a French version of Pedro's own name), no one in my
family can say. But Pierre and Valcoure and other names from those old-
time Frenchmen (as my grandfather always called them) continued in
use in my family. And not just the names. In those same western Louisiana hills 140 years later I watched my grandfather still performing
Pierre Bouet Lafitte's tasks, a master of gardens, hogs, and butchering,
and five generations later he still kept, worked—and swapped—horses
and mules. As a Louisiana piney woods adaptation it probably would still
work today, but not across the old Bayou Pierre country, much of which
in this century has passed into the hands of timber and coal companies.

According to a census he signed before his neighbors Pierre Dolet
and Luis Procela in 1809, Pierre Bouet Lafitte was a native of Natchitoches who had settled among the wilds and the Indians along Bayou
Pierre in 1784. Although he didn't mention it, that happened to be just a
year after Governor Miro in New Orleans had appointed him and Louis
de Blanc (the grandson of Natchitoches founder St. Denis) official traders to the Caddo and Kichai Indians. Lafitte's move from Natchitoches

up Bayou Pierre undoubtedly had everything to do with that appointment. It took him closer to the Indians, whose main villages were 50 to 100 miles north and west. And the grassy river bottoms above Natchitoches were some of the best horse pastures in Louisiana. So Lafitte built a house and cleared pasturage to become a *grazier*, and sometime before 1800 he married. Her name is listed in the census as Feliciano Gane, and for what I think was cause Lafitte made sure that the authorities recorded that both he *and* his wife were apostolic Catholics. Cause, since those who had reason to be jealous had made sure the authorities knew that Lafitte had sought his wife among the Caddos, and only heaven knew what their spiritual practices might be.

By 1809 the Lafitte family totaled seven. The eldest and only daughter, Marie, was nine and the youngest of her brothers only four months, which I interpret to mean that Feliciano must have been 10 to 15 years younger than her husband. As he did with the census takers, my great-grandfather four times removed seems always to have insisted that his contemporaries use his middle name, although it appears in various documents across the years as Bouet, Bouvete, Bobet, and Boit. I doubt if he cared about that. He just wanted to make sure that no one mistook him, since the famous privateer Jean Lafitte had a brother also named Pierre.

It was horses, mostly, that brought Pierre Bouet Lafitte to Bayou Pierre. You do not today look at Louisiana and automatically think horses. Neither did horses. Brought by the early European settlers, they did poorly, susceptible to diseases and hoof rot in the wet setting. But as a frontier colony Louisiana needed a constant supply of mounts, and every Creole quickly came to understand that only a tantalizingly few days to the west, horses were not only thriving but literally taking over the bluestem country. Who knew how many millions lay beyond? So in Louisiana interesting places nearest this source saw possibilities for the main chance. Cobblestone-streeted Natchitoches on the Red River, with its unpronounceable-looking name (and unlikely pronunciation) is just a slow-down Southern college town these days, known recently as the setting for the play and movie *Steel Magnolias*. But the quaint little town is in fact the oldest European settlement in the Louisiana Purchase territory, and a principal reason it was founded was because of horses. Its founder and earliest hero, Louis Juchereau St. Denis, was immediately sent to Texas to open a trade in horses and mules and told to try not to bring them back unladen.

So Pierre Bouet Lafitte and his contemporaries were but a bead on the string—and somewhere in the middle of it—of a mushrooming economy that linked groups as disparate as Comanches, Caddos, Hispanic mustangers, and traders on the Louisiana-Texas frontier in a horse funnel whose wide mouth lay on the prairies of the Horizontal Yellow and whose narrow throat pointed into Louisiana and eventually (via the Natchez Trace) at the enormous appetites of the advancing Anglo-American frontier. What got Pierre Bouet Lafitte noticed was not that he was singular—he was not—but that at the time this trade was making the transition from precapitalist gift exchange and barter to a capitalist market, he and his partner happened to be an annoying thorn to the main horse trader between Texas and Louisiana in those years.

Gil Y'Barbo was the founder of the town of Nacogdoches in East Texas (a bit farther west along the funnel) and appointed by the *Texas* governor in 1780 as principal trader to the Indians of the area. Two things especially outraged Y'Barbo about his Louisiana competitors, and the worst of them was not that de Blanc and Lafitte were underselling him by two to one (they were offering the Indians 10 lead rifle balls for a deerskin rather than the five Y'Barbo offered). What *really* infuriated Y'Barbo was having the headmen from tribes like the Kichai look him in the face and tell him that the only whites they really trusted were the sons of St. Denis and Natchitoches!

Moments like those must have been sweet ones for Pierre Bouet Lafitte, but they're also why I think he was so insistent that he go on record in 1809 as an apostolic Catholic. Because, you see, Y'Barbo eventually explained the Indian attitude to his Texas superiors by angrily describing his French competition as resorting to the worst kinds of unfair practice. Mocking all that was civilized, he reported in 1792, they went among the Indians wearing breechclouts and tanned buffalo skins. They traveled and hunted with them as familiars, even eating from the same vessel as the savages. And most suspicious of all, these sons of Natchitoches went so far as to dance in the Indian ceremonies and sing their songs.

And they even took them as their wives.

I shouldn't romanticize this trade my ancestor promoted. For one thing, it indulged as a side feature an Indian slave trade, sending captives (mostly Apaches) from the tribal wars into Louisiana as household servants. Although none of us knew it at the time, since the places whose histories we learned had names like Jamestown and Boston, I went to high school and had as friends assimilated Apaches (Louisiana versions of the *genízaros* of New Mexico) with names like Procella and Meshell, whose ancestors were brought to Louisiana by mine. And more pointedly, Pierre Bouet Lafitte's trade established the inertia and thinned the viscosity in that great horse funnel, so that a century after he set up his pastures and corrals, almost all the pretty horses had been drained from the Southwestern prairies where for 200 years they'd thrived so splendidly.

Whatever you can say about them, though, Pierre Bouet Lafitte and his contemporaries had an effect that resonated. I've long wondered if my family's penchant for horses, particularly paints (my boyhood ponies were bays and roans, but my older brother—whose horses our grandfather helped select—had a fine paint colt), hasn't come down through some ancestral imprinting, along with the squirrel gumbo and the hot peppers. But there's also this, a far larger issue: When Philip Nolan, the apotheosis and teacher of all the later Anglo mustangers on the Horizontal Yellow, was killed by a Spanish patrol in 1801, more than a dozen of his horse catchers were residents of Bayou Pierre. Cogitate on that, for I should point out in its connection that the principal modern historian of American stock-raising culture, Terry Jordan of the University of Texas, goes so far as to assert that the techniques of working the wild horses and cattle of the western prairies were first taught to advancing Anglo-Americans by the early French-Louisiana mustangers.

I've grappled ever since reading Jordan with a little ancestral guilt over that.

There is plenty of mesquite in this western Oklahoma country, I'm noticing as I loop the car back west toward my homestead along the Llano Estacado. Plenty. And as across much of the Southwest, where the perception is that the choking spread of mesquite and junipers is a recent phenomenon, the Oklahomans are obviously enjoined in a war on it, with mesquite corpses in the pastures showing all the signs of chemical strangulation. Almost everyone agrees now that the cessation of the old Horizontal Yellow fire ecology is to blame for letting mesquite and junipers swarm up out of the draws and across the open prairie, but I'm wondering as I drive and look what role horses played in that release. Various early Spanish travelers, particularly Pedro Vial and Francisco Amangual, noted in their journals that mesquite seemed to increase as

they approached the heavily used horse pastures around Indian settlements and campsites. It's almost if as horses went feral by the millions
across their ancestral home on the American prairies, their effect on the
country was to re-create a shrubby facsimile of the woodier Pleistocene
landscape, which a warming climate and 10,000 years of Indian fires had
nearly banished.

So far there's very little cactus here in the Arkansas River drainage
compared to farther south, I noticed, my idle driving speculations beginning to nibble at the other end of the time spectrum. I wonder what effect another half century of global warming will have on cactus spread?
The High Plains gradually coming under the sway of the Chihuahuan
Desert? Those thoughts get interrupted momentarily, for with the nose
of my Jeep now pointed due west and the last of the mountains dropping
into the horizon behind, before me is the great, sweeping scarp of the
High Plains—heralded, I'm stunned to see, by a gigantic, lit *cross* planted
atop the Llano near Groom, Texas. The intent, I suppose, is to alert
travelers along old Route 66 and I-40 that they're entering God's country.
The actual effect is of an annoying, illuminated eyesore. I do my best to
ignore it and return to speculating on the march of the Chihuahuan
Desert north to Saskatchewan.

Imagining the future is made possible, of course, by the human ability to think in analogy: known pattern extended like a stem from a root,
with the variables like branches, as many of them as possible projected
in all the thicket of ways the brain can visualize before settling on a likely
path for it all. Unfortunately, looking for the base root in the past isn't so
cut-and-dried. History is no science but art, and an art confronting not
one root but a whole tangle of them, a chaos of growth welling up out of
the past that has to be made sense of. Figuring out where we've come
from seems to make some difference even if you tell yourself you're only
concerned with present and future, simply because thinking in analo-
gies doesn't work so well if you've got the basic premises—the foundation
rootstock—of your past all wrong.

Further back in time along that great horse funnel that with my ancestors' help emptied the Near Southwest of wild horses, there was the
rootstock moment, the point at which the historical stem line leading
to *now* first stirred. Of course it started with a horse, head up, bright
eyes searching the horizons nervously in the manner of all prey animals

evolved to openness. But I don't think the proper rootstock moment was synonymous (as we've been taught for several decades now) with the Great Revolt of 1680, when Pueblo Indians sickened by years of zealous Christian attacks on their religions drove the Spaniards out of New Mexico and traded much of the abandoned loot (including horses, burros, and tack) to surrounding tribes. I don't believe the foundation moment came the century before, either, with black-bearded Spaniards riding their Barb and Arabian stallions onto the yellow prairies of 450 years ago.

It was the Yale paleontologist Othniel Marsh who happened upon *the* moment, sifting through fossils taken out of the bone beds of Nebraska during the last century. So grasping the real meaning of the horse in North American history involves looking at the intersects of deep time. There are first the external causes, the changing climate of the earth as it is influenced by sunspot storms and comet and meteorite strikes. Then there are the causes internal to the planet, like its climate-altering wobble as it orbits, the drift and collision of continents like pieces of bark on the surface of a pond, the creation by all these of opportunities for life and of corridors for life's migrations from spot to spot, the flowering of diverse habitats, and the actions of biogeography. And then there is the great miracle, unfolding evolution within all that context, riding along on time's back. The result of all this is what Othniel Marsh saw when he brushed the silt and sand off the horse bones collected from the Nebraska and Dakota badlands.

Marsh was stimulated not only by bones but by a famous lecture in New York in 1876, when Thomas Huxley had taken Yale's horse fossils as the first proof for Darwinism, the direct line of descent of an existing animal, with the further irony that this was an animal whose ancestors seemed all-American even though everyone knew that no horses had existed here when Europeans had arrived. So Marsh went on to assemble a chronology of the evolution of horses. *The* moment appears now to have taken place some 57 million years ago, during the Eocene, with niches opened (in places like present New Mexico and the San Luis Valley of Colorado) for new forms by the recent extinction of the dinosaurs in a cometary winter. But Marsh went on to track many more moments, showing changes in hooves and molars from the little striped, foot-tall animal we now call *Hyracotherium* to much larger beasts with high-crowned teeth layered with cement for munching abrasive materials on the spreading grasslands of the West over the next 25 million years. In Marsh's day these later horses were mostly coming from bone beds in the badlands of West Texas and New Mexico, at least five to six species of them.

More recent horse taxonomists like Gaylord Simpson, Bruce Mac-Fadden, Richard Hubert, and many others have pursued those moments to the ground, tracing (and noting many radiating dead ends and extinctions along the way) what started as a sort of three-toed rabbit down to the modern family, Equidae. The argument now is that for the last 15 million years right down to 10,000 years ago, horses entirely dominated the fauna of North America. By the Miocene there were often as many as a dozen species of three-toed horses on the continent at any given time, sharing resources in some kind of complex partitioning. Most of these spread eastward across the Bering bridge into Eurasia more than 10 million years ago, although the best specimens in the world come out of the Texas Panhandle. But when the climate cycled into the glacial/pluvial stage about 6 million years ago, with an intense spread of pure grasslands, three-toed horses began to disappear, the last of them becoming extinct 2 million years ago in America and about 400,000 years ago in Africa.

The survivors of this new climate regime in America were very special equines. They came mostly from the arid country of the Far West, where nature had pushed their adaptations not just toward high-crowned teeth for eating sand-covered grass but toward hard, single hooves (monodactyly) so that they could surge at high speed across rocky landscapes. Depending on how you divvy up the fossils, the genus *Equus* that possessed these traits appeared either 8 or 4.5 million years ago. Early forms (not yet true *Equus*) crossed into South America when the Panamanian land bridge formed 2.5 million years ago and into Asia via the Bering bridge slightly later, where they diversified rapidly into the zebras and quaggas and asses of Africa and Asia and the true horses of the more northerly plains. At least 60 species have been named from North America.

They formed in a close association with the cool-season stipa grasses, like the needle and thread that in wet years still waves so luxuriously across the Southwest today. As the stipas spread, so did the horses. They multiplied into great herds over the American steppes during the Pleistocene of the last 2 million years. Ten thousand years ago they constituted perhaps as much as a third (by number, if not biomass) of North America's large fauna. And every last one of those animals was as native

American as it is possible to be. So wrap your mind around this: All the equids of the world, all the horses and asses and burros, all the zebras of the African plains, all the great arch-necked ponies painted with obvious religious awe 25,000 years ago on the cave walls of Lascaux and Chauvret, all these are the spawn of the herds of the American Horizontal Yellow.

The horse that we know and love today—the representatives of them that streamed through the great horse funnel of the last century—is *Equus caballus*, an animal domesticated and bred by humans for at least 7,000 years. The wild form from which it springs, Przewalski's horse (*Equus przewalskii*), still lives in wild bands on the Asian steppes, although there aren't many. The basic wild markings are a deerlike dun color with black mane and tail (what we call buckskin in domestic horses), with a black dorsal stripe and faint zebra stripings on the legs. Left to themselves, horses today can breed (and some have done so) back to those original wild markings.

If all the world's horses, even zebras, are more or less American tourists who forgot to go home, then where are the American progenitors? What happened to the *Equus* herds that unquestionably were still in the Americas right down (some believe) to 8,000 years ago? The answer, bizarrely, is that while horses did well abroad, in their home of native origin and after 57 million years, too, they quite suddenly died out. All of them. Paleontologists still don't know quite what to make of it, since the stipa grasses they grazed haven't gone anywhere, and particularly given the horses' apparent joyous response when humans returned them to the continent of their nativity 7,500 years later. But along with nearly three-quarters of their fellow large mammal and bird inhabitants of Pleistocene North America, in a span of less than 4,000 years, all the horses disappeared.

To most of us the argument that the ancestors of the American Indians were responsible for this holocaust seems more than a little farfetched. How could a few tens of thousands, even a few hundreds of thousands, of hunters have dismantled so much of that rich, Serengeti-like ecology on the Pleistocene plains? With the elephants—the grazing mammoths and the browsing mastodons—the process doesn't seem so impossible. Such large animals were limited in numbers and had very long gestation periods, and these, coupled with hunter preference for females, could have made a population rebound difficult. With the climate warming and suitable habitat disappearing as the most recent ice age ended, the elephants could have been easy pickings for the extraordinary flint technology of the Clovis people. But horse herds? Horse remains *are* found in Paleo-Indian kill sites, but horse jumps—analogous to bison jumps that killed hundreds—aren't in the record. And if horses were especially susceptible to human hunters, vulnerable like so many species on the world's islands that went extinct soon after humans arrived, how and why did the horse herds survive in Asia and Africa?

If not human hunters, then climate, other paleontologists argue. Yet even if the end of the Wisconsin Ice Age favored shorter grasses more suitable for bison, stipa savannahs hardly disappeared in the Americas. Besides, horses aren't rooted like trees; they had those marvelous legs to carry them where the grasses were. Horse scholars like Bruce MacFadden may satisfy themselves by referring to the whole range of Pleistocene changes—climatic and vegetative as well as prehistoric overkill—and it may be that in the absence of another explanation, however unlikely what remains as an answer is, it must be true. Personally, unable to fold this scenario so comfortably into my own view of the past, I'm left dissatisfied and suspect that with horses there's something big we're leaving out of the Pleistocene extinction story.

The explanatory problem is exacerbated by what happened 75 centuries later, when horses were returned to the Americas from their Old World refuges 500 years ago. Nature's response to the great ecological simplification of the Pleistocene had been to evolve from large Eurasian bison that had crossed into the Americas a smaller, short-grass-adapted buffalo. In the absence of competition from other ungulates this dwarf bison had blossomed across the American plains like dandelions in a spring pasture. By 5,000 years after the Pleistocene extinctions a great bison belt had emerged where horse herds once had ranged, a bellowing brown mass of beasts that in times of favorable climate must have swelled to 25 to 30 million animals and drifted like summer clouds across the immense oval of grama, buchloë, and fescue grasses stretching from Chihuahua to Alberta. In the absence of hoofed competition the bison herds of the Horizontal Yellow became something phenomenal. When the early Spanish entradas first saw them, in present eastern New Mexico, they reported the *Llanos del Cibolos* to be one of the wonders of the world.

*Not statues but living beasts, still here on the Horizontal Yellow at places like the
Wichita Mountains National Wildlife Refuge. But where are the horses?*

Those horses that now danced beneath the Spaniards onto the buffalo plains were not quite the same animals that had vanished so myste-
riously from the Horizontal Yellow. They were what biologists would
call a different taxon and ecologists would call preadapted. Since their
American diaspora, horses had continued to evolve in Eurasia. The Barb
stock that made up the bulk of Spanish horses had for centuries been
bred in the Islamic world for the desertlike conditions around the Mediterranean. Too, the ecology of North America was different in A.D. 1500
than it had been 8,000 years before. So the horse fit back into the
American West was not an exact return of a species to its long vacant
niche. Not exact, but close enough. In southern Africa, where the Pleistocene had produced nothing like the wave of extinctions it had in the
Americas and the veld remained fully stocked with wild grazers, the
Boer and English settlers struggled to introduce horses. In the Americas
there was no struggle at all. More like release, an opening of a floodgate.
In a fraction of an ecological instant, those preadapted desert horses that

were unlike their ancestors but not so very much took a look at the western America that was now unlike what their ancestors had known but not so very much and went kicking, galloping, and whinnying their way back in. It was in every way a remarkable and (I can't help the impression) *joyous* homecoming, as the many stories from the historical literature make so clear. The account of how horses diffused across the West after the Pueblo Revolt of 1680 has been told often but is only one for-instance. In Texas, for example, the early Franciscan missions founded in 1689 were initially stocked with a horse and mule herd of only about 500 animals total, augmented by another 50 horses in 1691 and a few handfuls of animals abandoned by subsequent supply trains. Due to lack of Indian interest, these missions were abandoned in 1693. Spaniards did not geld their stallions, and when they returned to Texas in 1715, they found that the stock they'd left had increased to thousands and covered the whole countryside with animals.

By the next century, traveling through South Texas, Bishop Marin de Porras wrote tersely (1805): "Great herds of horses and mares found close to the roads in herds of four to six thousand head." Four to six *thousand?* Two decades after that the French scientist Jean-Louis Berlandier, exploring the region west of San Antonio where the hills were so high that the entire region had a mountainous aspect, found that wild horses were everywhere on the hills, inviting his animals to enjoy the freedom of that wilderness. By that point the Mustang Desert in the shrubby plains south of San Antonio was so filled with bands of wild horses that traveling through that country today, the stories strike one as unreal, unconnected to the view through the car window. Like Thomas Dwyer's description near present Corpus Christi in the 1840s that as far as the eye or telescope could sweep the horizon, the whole country seemed to be running. And John Duval's that as far as the eye could extend, nothing over the dead-level prairie was visible except a dense mass of horses, and the trampling of their hooves sounded like the roar of the surf on a rocky coast.

J. Frank Dobie thought—and after looking over the papers and materials for his book *The Mustangs*, I've realized it was only a guess, although no one's could have been more educated—that by 1800 the number of wild horses south of the Arkansas River exceeded 2 million animals. That's called an ecological explosion.

Texas and New Mexico weren't the only places this phenomenon happened. In California in 1775, horses were so few that droves were being purchased in Sonora for import into the settlements. Six years later feral herds of abandoned or escaped animals were reported to be growing numerous along the route between the two provinces. By 1794 the California missions and presidios, starting with virtually no horses in the 1770s, found themselves surrounded by such growing bands of feral animals that beginning in 1806 in San Jose, and then in Santa Barbara in 1808 and 1814, in Monterey in 1812 and 1820, and generally throughout the California settlements by 1827, large numbers of horses in the surrounding countryside had to be slaughtered annually as nuisances and threats to the grass.

Heads up, nostrils flaring at dimly recalled scents, *Equus* was back.

What you will always understand from the back of a horse is that as with all us animals, horses are individuals. Perhaps being an individual is special compulsion to a horse, whose natural life is to be a member of a small and usually kin-related social group. We humans are social, and socialized, enough to understand that. Enforced conformity often seems to produce the most blatant compulsions of self-expression in us, too.

On an early West Texas morning after I've returned from my trip to look in the Wichita Mountains for the wild horses I knew would not be there, I walk out into fine sunlight to slip the hackamore over my 10-year-old paint gelding. For a few minutes we circle the corral as I put him through his gaits with voice commands. As individuals, horses like their particular routines, and Skatopah and I have been doing this since all he could carry on his back was a cheap Mexican blanket. Unusual name for a horse, I know, but it relates to his origins. Supposedly he's descended from the pony herd Sitting Bull's Uncpapa band brought back from Canada in 1881, a really good story that got the North Dakota rancher who sold him to me at least another 50 bucks just for the telling and Skatopah his name (Badlands Paint Horse) in Siouan.

The Southern Cheyennes, one of the most skilled horse people of the old Horizontal Yellow, have many bits of horse wisdom distilled in axioms, one of which is: The best horse for you is one you've raised as a colt and whose idiosyncrasies you know intimately; the next best is a grown horse someone else has raised and trained but whose individuality you'll have to learn; the worst is a grown wild horse you've captured, an animal you don't know at all who is plenty big enough to hurt you. Having a horse for the first time since I was 13, I figured I needed all the help I could get. So I bought Skatopah when he was five months old.

Most people who've only casually encountered horses tend to think of them as the biggest animals that have ever bitten them. Closer acquaintances with horses brings you all kinds of other intimacies. When I trailered Skatopah down the great sere bulge of the plains to Texas in 1987, he was bulking up for the North Dakota winter and of the size and general presentation of a shaggy brown-and-white goat. I turned him out on my little canyon *ranchería* and thought, Shit, I have a horse that looks like a goat. What next? I knew absolutely nothing about training a horse, or a goat for that matter, but I had introduced a few big dogs to at least the outlines of proper behavior and figured I'd just extrapolate. It's not a technique that's seminar-ready, but the horse, being a particularly smart one, helped a lot. The somewhat peculiar end result is that I have a horse that's trained like a dog. Not that he sits or shakes or fetches, but he does come (at a gallop) when called, and ridden, he responds to voice as much as touch. He's got his idiosyncrasies, of course. I let him keep his stallionhood until he was two, and as a friend who knows horses observed, "He got a mite frisky, didn't he?" Too, a dog chased him through barbed wire soon after that little trip to the vet, and a horse sense connection formed. He's chased dogs relentlessly since.

Skatopah has also, shall we say, exposed my verities to the world on occasion. Once when he was a two-year-old and I'd been swinging up on his back for only a few weeks, a friend who is an African historian came out and brought along a Ugandan on his first visit to the States. I rode up to say hello and was in the midst of formal introductions when, for cause that only green broke two-year-old horses will grasp, Skatopah shied and I suddenly found myself, hand extended in greeting, mounted on aught but air particles. Newtonian physics being what they are, in the next instant I was horizontal in the prickly pears. When I peered up at Ed and his friend, the African's startled expression gave way at once to a delighted clap of his hands and (in his Brit Africa English): "Yes! Yes! I have always *wanted* to see a real cowboy!"

This splendid summer morning, with the bobwhites calling and the sky that topaz blue that's so routine in the Southwest it gets taken for granted, I walk Skatopah out of the corral and lead him down my dirt driveway. His hooves raising little puffs in the sand of the road, we cross and I push open the gate that will take us into the ranch across from where we live. We walk through and close the gate behind us. Before us is several hundred acres of June green West Texas canyon—Yellow House Canyon at the head of the Brazos River, specifically—a place rife with horse history, from three-toed horse fossils embedded in the out-crops to a horse-saturated cowboy and Indian history. But who cares about history in the promise of such a morning with the sweet scent of a horse in your nose?

I drape the reins of the hackamore over Skatopah's neck, grab a hank of mane, and throw myself onto his back, pivoting on my stomach to swing my right leg over, then straighten as my knees lock into the sweet spot between his shoulders and rib cage. Head and ears up, nostrils working like bellows, he skitters lightly under me. Both of us are almost naked, I in shorts and sleeveless T-shirt, Skatopah wearing nothing but his hackamore. It's not always practical, but it's the way we both prefer to do this timeless thing that humans and horses do together. So Skatopah dances, shivers a bit, ears working back toward me now, eager to hear me say the words that will set us in motion through the morning and the canyon. I have ridden him only sporadically of late, and he is excited to be doing this.

I cannot penetrate my horse's mind to understand what he thinks of this act. Perhaps by raising him and training him I have socialized him to regard it as a thing that pleases me, which I think he likes to do. He is a spirited and alert horse, interested in the world, and that I do not think I have socialized into him. However infrequently we ride, I do know what I feel on his back, though, and every time in our decade together that we've performed this union of horse-man, I've felt that I've understood something that no amount of reading or observation could ever give me.

The intensity of Skatopah's listening is now almost comical. He seems about to erupt, his muscles flexing and glistening in the raking angle of the sun, every nerve on high alert. He is coiled energy, a laser beam awaiting leap, and my voice is the trigger. My strength, stamina, and speed are magnified tenfold when I am on his back. My ability to touch the world has grown exponentially merely because I have swung myself across him.

The horse cannot be understood fully and certainly not properly by resorting to anthropological language like domesticated work animal, beast of burden, new form of harnessed energy, or cultural amplifier. What it is that so transcends that kind of analysis is not, as the cliché goes, that the horse made humans godlike. Rather, the horse made us truer animals, magnified versions of the runner, the leaper, hyperath-letes of the old world of panting exertion and the pure beauty of refined and reflexive coordination. And speed, of course. Horses gave primates propulsion at the anciently envied acceleration of the gazelle. Only if the horse could fly would it have made us happier.

I slowly lean forward, tighten my grip on Skatopah's ribs, and in the instant before he goes crazy with anticipation, I whisper the word into his cocked ear.

The New Mexico *cibolero* Gambino Rendon was right: Horses remind us that we are wild.

There is a line of argument in cultural anthropology that goes this way: Great ideas and great innovations are relatively rare events in human history, but once exposed to the world, the really valuable ones have a life of their own and cannot be contained. They spread—*diffuse* is the term of art in anthropology—from person to person, group to group, little packages of new information capable of transforming reality.

From their several points of introduction across the West, particularly East Texas and northern New Mexico, the horses escaped, were abandoned when lame or missions were closed, or were confiscated by native peoples a lot happier about the arrival of the horses than about the Spaniards who rode them. The Pueblo revolutionaries in 1680, seizing so many animals when they captured Santa Fe and Taos that they had no use for them all, true enough acted as the diffusers and teachers of stock lore to tribes northward up the spine of the Rockies. But on the Horizontal Yellow between New Mexico and Louisiana, the process had already begun by the time of the Pueblo Revolt. At some bead along the time continuum, for which there is no record but a good imagination may conjure, Indians who knew the animals and all that was necessary about them—how to ride horses, how to train and breed and care for them, how to replicate the tack necessary for it all—appeared on the plains of New Mexico, or outside El Paso del Norte, or rode up out of Mexico, where Aztec war captains had been riding horses since the Conquest. At the point when that first Indian handed the reins of a horse to another, who mounted and then flew, a new reality—and a new economy—came to the Horizontal Yellow.

Good ideas don't require wired computers to spread fast. In an unwired world, this one spread very, very fast, and one of the hacker groups seemingly at the source of it was the so-called Jumanos living in their several villages along the Rio Grande from El Paso to Big Bend, the same people Cabeza de Vaca had found so numerous and civilized the previous century. In this northern arc of the Chihuahuan Desert, droughts often pushed agriculture over the edge, and a major one in the 1660s drove the Jumanos to raid Spanish ranches southward toward Chihuahua City. Unknown and unsung diffusers among the Jumanos must have performed the act of teaching horse lore to one another again and again. By the 1660s these Jumanos were not only riding; some of them were reining their horses into the buffalo herds farther north and studying the situation with a shrewd eye. Others, like the famous Juan Sabeata, were testing the outlines of what would very soon become the Great Horse Funnel by driving a few horses eastward to the Caddo towns in East Texas and fixing up the various members of the Caddoan aristocracy with a possession that, for a few years, must have *really* set them apart from the masses.

Not for long, though. Horses begat other horses, and the idea of what to do with them carried no patent. After the French put ashore on the Texas coast, Father Anastacio Douay says that on April 22, 1686, he left with La Salle on a trip to the northeast and after three days found the most beautiful plains and many people, some on foot and others on horseback, with boots and spurs and seated in saddles, who came toward them at a gallop. Continuing on into the Blackland Prairie, they found more people with horses, even some—the Quaquis the French called them—who had an abundance of horses to sell. Among the Hasanai Caddos five years later, expecting to find pristine New Worlders with no inkling of the industrial order, Fray Francisco Casanas wrote with some astonishment, "The *Sadammo* nation is very large; their houses are all covered with buffalo hides; they have many horses, mules, much clothing, and many iron implements." The Caddos, indeed, were already planting extra corn for their horses and fired the prairies for them. It was a story that was repeated endlessly as seventeenth- and eighteenth-century Europeans confronted Indians they assumed would be innocent and awed, only to discover that the Indian trade network had long before set them up with metalware, fancily tooled bridles and Moorish saddles (or native-crafted knockoffs), and often the latest in European fashion—top hats, canes, double-breasted blazers.

And, of course, horses. Always horses. More of them on the Horizontal Yellow than anywhere else, since it was here they'd first returned to their nativity, here they'd first run off into the far-distant hills, here they best survived the winters, here they'd successfully occupied some rough equivalent of the Pleistocene horse niche, eating almost the same grasses as the swarming buffalo herds (an 80 percent overlap, in fact) and competing successfully enough to shrink the 8 million buffalo on the Horizontal Yellow by (probably) 25 percent by 1800. Enough animals, indeed, to create an *economy* around them.

We've had sufficient examples of that situation here by the beginning of the twenty-first century to know what the outcome was likely to be.

With wind-whipped tears streaming down my face and this marvel of life beneath me, his pounding at the earth reverberating through every connecting tissue in my body, I want to know one thing, goddammit. If my horse is an individual, different from every other horse that ever lived because of the wholly unique juncture between his genetic history and the circumstances of his raising and experiences of his conscious life, then does he also have a soul? And if he does not, then as another animal shaped by the same forces of time and evolution, why do I? Because God is a man and not a horse? Because I can anticipate my death and require a soul to make my ending palatable, and death is not a thing his species has dwelt upon enough to develop an equine philosophy, a religion of horse celestial eternity, or an orthodoxy he feels he must acknowledge?

What happened to the horses of the Horizontal Yellow says a lot about what we humans think about animals. Horses, as everyone involved in the Southwestern horse trade, from Hispano *mesteñeros* to French middlemen like Pierre Bouet Lafitte, from Anglo traders to the Indians, appear to have thought . . . well, horses are just tools. They have no eternal souls. Elite Euro-Americans may have thought of them as Descartes's empty, instinctive vessels made flesh, essentially machines to which humans owed nothing other than decent maintenance. To the mass of American folk, for whom science was the religion of educated fools, Christianity essentially taught that like all other animals, horses were made for humans to use as they would.

The Indians? The role of the horse in Indian cosmologies depends on just which group you're talking about. The Navajos, the Apache bands, peoples like the Lakota and Blackfeet incorporated horses into their sacred panoplies of animals that instructed or healed. But interestingly, the Comanches, the premier horse people of the Horizontal Yellow, who owed their presence on the Southern Plains, indeed their very existence as newly created Plains Indians, to the horses they acquired, never developed a way of looking at horses that made them sacred in the way a wolf, an eagle, a bear, or a bison was sacred.

In their earliest stages of horse acquisition, when the ancestors of the Comanches were still gatherers in the sagebrush deserts of the north, they were so awed by the possibilities horses offered that they were willing to trade their children for them. And when they got horses, they not only abandoned their homelands to be near more, they shaped their entire existence around their herds, moving their camps to accommodate horse needs, retaining young human captives and slaves to use as herders, organizing acquisition and wealth—status, classes, and marriage—around them. Horses shaped gender relations (read: set them back) among many Indian groups, the Comanches notably, since by acquiring a horse herd of 300 or more animals, an enterprising Comanche man was in a position to arrange multiple marriages for himself. Comanche ethnobotany altered to become a medicine chest of what horses needed, and Comanche material culture (adapted from pack saddles, girths, and travois already in use with dogs) flowered, adding picket pins, puzzle hobbles, and the like to their toolbox.

Comanches developed an entire taxonomy all their own of different horse types. And at least according to a couple of early observers—John Sibley and Jean-Louis Berlandier—they bred their animals, probably for conformation, heart, speed. But certainly for aesthetics, too. Frank Roe once demonstrated that there were many more paint horses in Indian herds than would have been the case without conscious breeding for them. Among the Comanches a rich symbology of artistic horse decoration for tipis, bags, and shields sprang into being like some kind of stylized Plains Expressionism. Eventually Comanches came to hunt *everything* from horseback, even flocks of turkeys and herds of deer. From the moment they merged horses and bison in the hunt and discovered how hungry the whites were for bison robes, a shadow fell across the buffalo herds that never lifted, and the shadow was the form of a horse. The Comanches even came to rely on their pony herds as human fodder. They considered the flesh of young mustangs a delicacy, and (so the English traveler William Bollaert says) as a people consumed more than 20,000 horses during that initial, 1840s decade when drought and overhunting were sucking the bison herds into their long night of near oblivion. And last, as an anthropologist friend remarks to me one day, looking around to see that no one else is listening, the Comanches have also preserved stories of horses that became (how shall I put it) . . . uh, substitute girlfriends.

Yet astonishingly for an animal that so fundamentally shaped the Comanche world that it could even serve for the random transspecies tryst, the horse remained a tool, an appliance. Comanche horse traders like El Sordo, a noted contact for the American mustangers in the early nineteenth century, were proud of their horses and recognized how central they were to Comanche self-definition. But in the newly minted Comanche culture that flamed across the Horizontal Yellow in the eighteenth and nineteenth centuries, horses remained a form of living legal tender. And if others, like the Anglos with their guns and lead and fabrics, wanted them in trade, then the Comanches were entirely willing to provide them in volume.

By giving them names and addressing their relative merits as buffalo runners, war ponies, and draft animals, everyone recognized that a horse is an individual, and who with a heart could miss that horses are self-aware enough to experience joy, love, pain? But some set of innate rights of existence? Radical idea. Because horses nickered at you in recognition, looked you in the eye, carried you on their backs, they weren't quite the same as beavers, gold, trees, grasslands, cows, sheep, coal, oil. But close enough.

If you looked away at the proper moment, horses worked just fine as resources.

The Great Horse Funnel worked like this. There were the horses, a real example of American limitlessness, feral horses begetting horses across all the immense curve of the Southwest, horses raised so plentifully on the ranches of Texas, Mexico, New Mexico, and California that they had to be shot as nuisances. There was the need, in the form of the American homesteader frontier forging westward between the Appalachians and the Mississippi. The trick was to get the horses from the deserts of the Southwest to the farms of the southern woods and to make the whole lucrative enough to get the various peoples of the Southwest interested. No problem.

Mustanging (catching wild horses) and the horse trade between Indians and Euro-Americans was in one sense just one more variation of the fur trade that so demolished wildlife populations across the West in the nineteenth century. The horse trade is in no wise as visible a part of it as the trade in the skins ripped from the backs of slain beavers and bison, maybe because it wasn't a pursuit of the big corporations. No matter. The endgame was the same.

Out on the open end of the funnel were the procurers and initial processors. The Comanches were one of the most visible examples, but there were many others—Kiowas, Apaches, particularly the Southern Cheyennes, whose Hairy Rope band became one of the famous catchers of wild mustangs in the nineteenth century and whose horse trade was usually with Bent's Fort on the Arkansas. The Comanches sometimes dealt with horse traders directly but most often preferred going through middlemen, particularly the Wichitas, whose towns were agricultural and fixed and easy for traders to find, becoming (in anthrospeak) gateway communities.

As for the supply, just based on the wild herds it seemed limitless. But there were other aspects of procurement that complicated things. There were plenty of ways to catch wild horses, but it was work, and processing (breaking) them for the market was even more. The Comanches bred and raised horses, but according to the Cheyenne axiom I've mentioned, those were the animals you least wanted to trade away. If not wild ones and not ones you've bred and raised, then what?

Anthropology has a wonderful way with jargon and once again has a term for exactly my meaning here. Ever heard of optimal foraging theory? Fancy way of saying that all of us strive for maximum input for least effort. Indian horse traders were not exceptions, and the mass of horses out there that required the least effort to procure and process just happened to be the horses that already belonged to someone else. What I'm describing, then, is the catalyst to the raiding culture that looms so large in the mythology of Plains Indian history. Need horses for trade? How about the embarrassingly large pony herd owned by that band of Comanches that camps along the middle Pecos in the autumn? Need well-broken horses for traders with specific requirements? How about the Spanish ranches outside Taos? Need *lots* of horses for volume trade to finance a campaign against the Osages? What about all those ranches down in Mexico?

This kind of enterprise, well conceived, often dramatically executed, and undoubtedly loads of fun, carried different names at different times in history, and sometimes (especially if you happened to be a horse) it got a little absurd. There are records, for example, of horses stolen from Spanish ranches in California that were then traded along the Old Spanish Trail to Pueblo groups in New Mexico, who were in turn raided by Cheyennes who traded the stolen animals to the white traders, who then hauled them across the plains to Saint Louis and traded them to emigrants heading out on the trail . . . to where else but California. So long as it was an economy that largely left the Spanish settlements on the suffering end, Anglo-American farmers who ended up with horses carrying Spanish brands chortled into their corn whiskey. As soon as Texas was settled and the trade switched directions, sending Anglo stock into New Mexico and acquiring the name Comanchero trade, Americans screamed victimhood and outrage over savages who couldn't be taught proper respect for private property.

It was yet another of those worlds we create based on a kind of gamble with fate and possibility (and Indians of that day no less than this loved to gamble). A form of obsession, but one centered on an animal and a lifestyle, really, as one Plains Indian, Apauk of the Blackfeet, seems to have understood:

Nowadays everyone is crazy about horses. Our warriors, young and old, think only about going to war and taking horses; they will not take the time to do anything else. Horses we must have, of course, but why any man should want ten times as many horses as he can use, that is what I do not understand.

For reason—but for reason that yet remains beyond reach of my understanding—I am not content with the world I find myself in, this modern Southwestern world of internal combustion conveyances and satellite-beamed information and shopping malls, and sprawling human population attracted to the heat and the sun and the gangbusters economy produced by so much growth. I function in it, but it is a world where the experiences of nature have been so generally deplenished that I wonder if it suits me.

In the reality that my mind sketches from the sensory input I feed it, exactly where the lack of wild horses fits into this dissatisfaction I cannot entirely say. But I think the missing horses are central, right there with the missing grizzlies (the last one seen in Texas, in the Davis Mountains, was shot dead in 1892; New Mexico's last grizzly fell to a bullet in 1932), the persecution of wolves into oblivion, the still bizarre (to me) sight of immense, Horizontal Yellow plains as empty of bison as if you opened your eyes to a night sky forever wiped clean of stars.

I don't in fact buy that this has anything to do with timing. Wild horses, grizzlies, wolves, free-roaming bison—they all still exist in the America of the turn of the twenty-first century, and their return to parts of the Southwest is only a matter of time. Alive *now*, though, I grapple with whether I have a right to demand wild horses in my life, or whether we should all merely be content with the world we've inherited. The one, indeed, we've created.

I have no inkling, none, about whether Pierre Bouet Lafitte would have enjoyed the life he helped fashion for his descendants two centuries farther down the continuum. Perhaps, like me, he'd have enjoyed some of it but raged at the astonishing losses and the general retreat of nature to the distant margins. That's what I like to think of him, anyway.

The young New Mexican woman watching my horse graze against the mesa told me the story with blank eyes that glittered in the sun. She said she couldn't remember where she'd heard it. She thought it was a story of general knowledge among the Hispanos who'd settled eastward from Santa Fe out on the plains.

It had happened long ago, before the Anglos came. A handsome young *mesteñero* coveted a particular wild horse he was sure would impress the senoritas and devised an elaborate plan to capture it, which God allowed to unfold with apparent seamlessness. At the critical moment, his horse badly lathered but alongside the tiring *cimarrón*, the *lariata* secure to the horn, he uncoiled a noose. The wild one dodged but little and he was in the act of furling the loop toward its head when his laboring mount stumbled, pitching him forward. Headfirst and directly into the loop suspended there in midair, which tightened as his horse rolled and broke his neck.

"Hoist with his own petard," I said. She looked at me. "He roped and killed himself trying to own something. For no good reason," she said simply.

West of the bayous and south of the Comancheria but still in the core of the mustang country of two centuries ago, the finest masters of the craft of catching wild horses had been honing their skills for generations. This was in a part of Texas that today bids fair to rival the coasts for urban sprawl, population saturation, and the highway spiderwebs that carry the insect activity of modern life. Today, sometime, driving the interstates and looking out through windows sealed against the cacophony of sound and the frenzied anthill of movement, think horses. Beautiful horses grazing an empty Blackland Prairie. Same sky. Same clouds. Just earlier in the process of space into place. It was only a wink of an eye ago.

Once wild horses multiplied into staggering numbers on the Central and South Texas prairies, to settlers of the early Spanish towns—with real estate, oil, country music, and computer chips undreamed of down the time line—the beasts seemed the most obvious form of wealth in the province. So individuals with an eye toward advancing their station began to figure out how to possess them. An idea of the possibilities can be gleaned from a 1778 roundup in the vicinity of La Bahia, on the Texas coast. When the tally was finished, more than 15,000 horses, mules, and wild cattle had been skimmed off the countryside in one flurry of gathering.

Political life in the Southwest has been colorful from the start, albeit a bit more autocratic when Spain ran things. Caballero de Croix (Horseman of the Cross), an eighteenth-century commandant general of the Provincias Internas, stands as a fine early example of the Texas political type. Convinced he knew how to reform Texas of its backwardness, in 1780 Croix laid down a bit of law. In addition to various decrees requiring that the people be instructed in love and reverence for king and government, that pure Spanish become the only language, that gaming be outlawed, that dangerous books be gathered and celebratorily burned, Croix decided that freelance mustanging was one of the province's vices. He thus declared all the countryside the king's domain, *mesta*, and all wild herds the king's property, or *mesteños* (to Anglo-American ears used to the Germanic chop of English, the word when they heard it sounded more like "mustangs"). Those who wished to catch them—*mesteñeros* as they were soon called—forthwith (or words to that effect) had to fork over a tax of six reales per head to the king. This was a Keynesian miscalculation on Croix's part, since captured wild horses were only worth three reales at the time.

But Croix was nothing if not a reformer, so the next year he reduced the tax to two reales, a mere 67 percent rate designed to grow the economy. And the King's Order of May 1, 1780, gave blanket permission for Texas horses to be rounded up and taken to Louisiana whenever the governor in that province requested, so a market existed. A typical year was 1784, when *mesteñeros* around San Antonio caught and paid taxes on 423 mustangs. The following year was even better: 828 mustangs were captured, and people like Felis Ramon, Domingo Peres, and Salvadore Rodriguez had emerged as professional mustangers. As one San Antonio official put it in 1785:

> The number of mustangs in all these environs is so countless that if anyone were capable of taming them and caring for them, he could acquire a supply sufficient to furnish an army. But this multitude is causing us such grave damage that it is often necessary to shoot them to assure that they do not lead away some of the tame ones that wander through these ranches.

By January 1, 1787, after seven years of experimentation with the policy, 17 *thousand* captured wild horses, along with nearly 24,000 wild cattle, had netted the Texas government 8,805 pesos. And not only that. By making mustanging a regulated, official economy, the policy had so cranked open the mouth of the Great Horse Funnel that a living river of horses now began to flow off the Southwestern prairies and into the American market.

How were the Hispanic mustangers of Central Texas able to catch so many and so easily that, as explorer Zebulon Pike remarked in 1810, "For this business I presume there is no nation in the world superior to the Spaniards of Texas"? One of the remarkable treasures of early Texas, the journals of the French scientist Jean-Louis Berlandier, has left us a vivid description of exactly how they did it.

First there was the apparatus of capture. *Mesteñeros* like Domingo Peres and Felis Ramon found that a spiral-shaped pen built of mesquite posts lashed together with rawhide thongs made an elastic but strong fence whose spiral would sweep a running herd into a mill in its center. Two brush wings fanned out half a mile or more from the corral. It took experience to learn how to situate such a pen strategically in the land-scape and experience to master moving mustangs into it. In fact, Tejano mustangers eventually developed a set of specialists to facilitate the process of capturing wild horses. But let Berlandier tell it.

The common occupation of the lazy people of the countryside is not without dangers. When the *mesteñeros*, gathered in a large number, have prepared large traps built of thick posts and propose to enclose in them some large herds, they divide themselves into three bands with totally different roles to play, called *adventadores*, *puestos*, and *manganeadores* or *encerradores* respectively. Before giving an idea of the manner in which these men capture such a large number of horses, I shall describe the places called corrale[s] where they gather them. These are immense enclosures situated close to some pond, in the midst of a thicket in order that they will be less exposed. The entrance is placed in such a way that it forms a long corridor, and at the end there is a kind of exit whose use we shall explain.

Berlandier seems to be relating his remarkable story from firsthand experience. So picture in your mind the scholarly Frenchman observing, at a safe distance and a little distastefully, what happened next:

After reconnoitering a large herd which they desire to trap, a certain number of well-mounted horsemen position themselves in the environs of the large gate of the enclosure in order to guide the leaders of the herd there and to close the gate when the animals have entered. It is undoubtedly the most dangerous role and one which is only entrusted to excellent riders. The *puestos*, also on horseback, are the *mesteñeros* posted at intervals along the stretch which separates the herd from the place to which it is to be guided. Their role consists of conducting that dreadful mass of living beings by riding full gallop along the flanks and gathering there, in the midst of an atmosphere of suffocating dust, the partial herds which sometimes unite at the sound of the terror of a large herd. The *adventadores* are most often very few. It is they who are charged with startling the horses, which ordinarily are grazing and for which it is necessary to set a convenient course so that they will not escape. It is therefore the *adventadores* who begin the task of startling the horses, which once in flight are under the care of the *puestos*. These, spaced at intervals, gradually increase in number, riding at full gallop along the flanks.

And now the moment of truth:

When the herd arrives close to the ambush, the *encerradores*, who are lurking there in the greatest of silence, will startle the animals should they veer off course. Some *encerradores* take pains to shut the gap. Often some *encerrador*, placed at the gate at the end, opens and shuts it, according to circumstances, to let out the stallions and mares. Forming a first herd, they have entered in the lead, and, being of minimum utility in the country, they are allowed to escape in order that a greater number of young horses can be captured.

What followed were scenes of such emotive power that the *mesteñeros* who participated in this economy developed a specialized vocabulary to describe them. On finding themselves shut in, the Spanish historian Father Bernabe Cobo wrote of wild horses he'd seen captured, "They squeal terribly and rage like lions." That's not all they did. Mustanging aimed at live capture, of course, but Hispanic horse-catching jargon was rife with the terminology of death: death from *sentimiento* (brokenheart-edness over capture), death from *despecho* (nervous rage over capture), and the evocative *hediondo* (stinking) to designate a pen ruined for use from having been too often clogged with panicked and dying animals.
Berlandier's description concludes this way:

When these animals find themselves enclosed, the first to enter fruitlessly search for exits and those in the rear, terrified by the horsemen, trample over the first. It is rare that in one of these chases a large part of the horses thus trapped do not kill one another in their efforts to escape. . . . Although it is not common, it has happened that the *mesteñeros* have trapped at one swoop more than one thousand horses, of which not one fifth remained. . . . The most dangerous moment for the *encerradores* is when they shut the gate of the enclosure. If by mischance the wild horses lunge to escape, the *encerradores*, although on horseback, can be dragged along in the melee, and both riders and their mounts are often massacred. The trapped animals are not removed from the corral until such time as they are worn out with fatigue from their useless efforts to escape. Then they are lassoed one by one. After some hours of ill treatment, these *mesteñeros* have the ability to render them half tame a short while after depriving them of their liberty.

Berlandier was writing in the late 1820s, 40 years after the Spanish government in Nuevo Santander had tried—in one of the first environmental regulations in the Southwest—to enforce restrictions on mustanging from February and August to prevent the deaths of so many horses in roundups. When the royal treasury had initiated formal horse roundups in 1808, Spanish officials discovered that out of every hundred animals captured, only six or eight ended up getting broken and sold.

By the time of Mexican rule in Texas, Hispanic *mesteñeros* had developed the practice of roaching the tails and manes of inferior horses so they could recognize worthless ones at a distance. The intent was to devote your time only to quality animals, for all across the Horizontal Yellow, from the Blackland Prairie to the piñon foothills of the Rockies, wild horses still seemed as innumerable as the wildflowers of the southern prairies.

The tightening noose in making that kind of scene only a Montana or Nevada fantasy for modern residents of the Near Southwest commenced when a young Irishman named Philip Nolan appeared before Spanish authorities in Texas in 1790 and requested permission to supply Louisiana with horses from the wild herds in Texas. At that time in New Orleans wild horses brought from $15 to $50 apiece. The trick was to get them there.

In an effort to control the mustang trade, the tax on which was all too easy to avoid in such a vast landscape, the Spanish government had granted trading monopolies to certain traders—the House of Barr and Davenport is the most famous but there were many others after Gil Y'Barbo, among them men like Antonio Leal, Marcel Soto, and Vicente Tejeiro—to permit horses to be taken out of Texas. What Spanish officials called the Nolan problem is exemplified for us by the view from the opposite sides of the Horse Funnel. Officially Spanish records showed 1,187 horses going from Texas to New Orleans in 1802. But on the other side of the funnel, John Sibley in Louisiana figured the volume of horses that *arrived* from Texas was closer to 7,300 animals in that same year!

What the Spanish Southwest—and the wild horses—had now come face-to-face with was the Anglo-American frontiersman become cognizant of the possibilities for wealth. To proffer regret that the monopolies, or the officials, were incapable of stopping what was coming is a bit like raging against the laws of thermodynamics. The market even for green broke wild horses on the advancing American frontier was a mind-less, yawning mouth; outstanding horses from the plains could bring $100 and more in Saint Louis, Natchez, and Lexington. Between New Orleans and Saint Louis were a vast number of Indian trails radiating from the plains. It was impossible for Texas troops to guard all of them.

And oh, some of the scams! In addition to the straightforward contra-band horse trader, Spanish officials kept encountering individuals like Francisco Roquier and his 10 companions in 1805 and Juan Carlos Cash-ily in 1806, who posed as prospective Spanish colonists and then re-quested they be allowed to return to Louisiana with droves of horses to bring their families west. Right.

Although few but J. Frank Dobie have seemed to take cognizance of it, until the opening of the Santa Fe trade in 1821 the horse trade was the most important economy in the Southwest. For three decades after Philip Nolan's first forays for horses, scores of almost unknown Ameri-can trading parties probed the Southern Plains, returning mustangs to the American frontier, making geographical discoveries, and extending American interests among the Plains tribes. It was the still mysterious Nolan, though, who established the pattern. Nolan began his mustang-ing ventures in 1791, and before antagonizing the Spaniards with his intimacies with Americans (he was a protégé of General James Wilkin-son), he and a group of associates made five expeditions into the South-west, trading, catching horses, loving Indian women, and (so Nolan says) impressing some tough connoisseurs of the masculine virtues with *los Anglos*. No doubt for all the reasons above, he described his adventures as a life of extreme fatigue and reportedly said that mustanging could only be effected with success by those used to the practice. But he made money, probably over $25,000 from the 2,500 horses (Spanish letters speak of as many as 8,000!) he brought back from the prairies (with a $7,000 trade goods investment) in 1798–99. Maybe jealousy over that as much as anything is what got him a bullet in the forehead two years later.

Nolan was taught the practice by the old Spanish/French mustangers, particularly those from Bayou Pierre, Louisiana. The prescription was simple: (1) Get financial backing from merchants who carried English or American goods, (2) recruit active young hunters from the frontier farms and ranches, (3) take along French or Spanish guides/interpreters, (4) go overland, using packtrains, (5) trade guns and powder but take a variety of merchandise, (6) live among the Indians. As Pierre Bouet Lafitte did.

These traders who helped clear the Southwest of its pretty horses scarcely even exist as names in our stories anymore, despite their visible effect on our world. Who in the modern Southwest has ever heard of John Calvert, Andres Sulier, and Henrique Visonet, Southern Plains horse-trading contemporaries of the mountain men? Or mustanger John Davis of Natchez, who appears in the old Spanish documents so frequently (usually as Juan Debis)? Alexandro Dauni or Edmund Quirk, poking around the Wichita Mountains as early as 1803–4? John House, a 25-year-old who drove horses back from the plains in 1805? The William C. Alexander and John Lewis party, which actually made an official report to the Jefferson administration? Daniel Hughes, who somehow got all the way back from Chihuahua with a drove of horses in 1807? The Anthony Glass expedition, which traveled widely with the Wichitas and Comanches in 1808–9 and left a journal describing how difficult it was to catch wild horses about where Fort Worth now stands (buffalo kept getting in the way, Glass says)?

Or George Schamp and Ezra McCall, who made at least two horse-trading forays from Natchitoches around 1809–10? Ever heard of John Maley? (No one else at the time had either; apparently he interviewed other horse traders and wrote a bogus account of the life of a plainsman, circa 1810). Alexander McFarland and John Lemons, whose mustanging party was plundered by the Osages in 1812? Auguste Pierre Chouteau, Jules DeMun, and Joseph Philibert's horse trade with the Comanches and Arapahoes between 1815 and 1817? Jacob Fowler (who left us one of those marvelous frontier journals written in phonics) and Hugh Glenn, trading among those same Indians on the plains of present southern Colorado in 1821? What about William Becknell, the Missouri trader who opened the Santa Fe trade in 1821? Becknell could do that because he was an old Comanche horse trader who had been making mustanging expeditions since 1811. Caiaphas K. Ham, who joined up with the Penateka Comanches to facilitate a horse-trading venture to Louisiana? David G. Burnet, who became modestly famous as a horse trader to the Comanches in the 1820s? You've driven the Austin thoroughfare named for him for years.

These Anglo-American horse traders—and there were undoubtedly hundreds more who left no trace at all of their experiences—are entirely lost to the history of the Horizontal Yellow today, but they shoulder a share of the burden for why no horses gallop across our Southern Plains.

Who were they? Think of them this way: They came from the same Southern classes that in our time produce redneckery and militia sympathizers. A few were educated; most thought the earth was flat, and the leap from that to New World Order conspiracies is nothing. They were essentially the foragers of their time, living off the land, although middle-class merchants financed them and occasionally led the parties. As mustangers, few of them could hold a candle to the Hispanos or Indians; horse catching was less familiar to Americans than trapping and apparently harder to learn. So they were content to let the Indians harvest the resource and to trade for it—and of course the Indians were only too happy to oblige. William Bollaert estimated that the Plains tribes obliged to the extent of liberating 10,000 horses from the Spanish settlements in 1818. Twenty years later George Ruxton was crediting the Comanches with similar numbers taken annually out of Durango and Chihuahua. Perhaps this is what the modern anthropologists mean whey they describe the great value old-time Comanche culture placed on the redistribution of wealth.

What these Anglo mustangers were, then, were white Comancheros, and if you seek to reconstruct their lives in the imagination, the best place to go is to the memoir one of them left in the 1840s: Thomas James's *Three Years Among the Indians and Mexicans.* The Missouri judge to whom James dictated his experiences described James as an ordinary-looking man, six feet tall, muscular, and of the pioneer or coon hunter type who actually had been a mountain man, ascending the Missouri River to the Three-Forks (the Garden of Eden, James called it) in 1809–10. James didn't make his first expedition to the Horizontal Yellow of the Southwest until 1821, riding from Fort Smith to the Salt Plains of present Oklahoma and ultimately viewing the Shining Mountains (which turned out to be the Caprock Escarpment and its mesas) before he was confronted by Comanches under orders not to allow Americans to approach Santa Fe. Eyeing those splendid Comanche horse herds appreciatively, Thomas James got a sense of the possibilities.

Invited to return the next summer to trade for horses, James did, and the result was a three-year expedition (1822–24) financed with $5,500 in goods. Ascending first the Canadian and then the North Canadian, James's party of 23 finally met the Wichitas under their headman, Alsarea, and the trading commenced. Four yards of British strouding and two yards of calico, along with a knife, a mirror, flint, and tobacco, was the going rate for a well-broken horse, and James quickly bought 17 that he knew would fetch $100 apiece back in the settlements. So far, so good.

Eventually the Wichitas introduced James to the Comanches, a Yamparika band under Big Star, and James got his first taste of a neat little twist the Comanches put on horse trading: They were perfectly willing to trade their best horses since they had every intention of stealing them back! James watched, amazed, as the source was replenished, too. At one point the Comanches drove a hundred wild mustangs into a ravine and at the end of the day were riding them about the prairie. Judging from Thomas James, the life of a nineteenth-century horse trader on the Horizontal Yellow was equal parts exoticism, frustration, and excitement tinged with a hint of danger, and to his credit, he seems to have relished the moment. I've always loved these lines in his memoir: "I began to be reconciled to a savage life and enamored with the simplicity of nature. Here were no debts, no Sheriffs, no Marshals; no hypocrisy or false friendships. With these simple children of the mountains and prairies love and hate are honestly felt and exerted in their full intensity."

James departed for the settlements once he had assembled a drove of 323 high-quality animals, but not before Alsarea made a present of his own fine warhorse, Checoba, and urged that James return the next year to the three big mounds on the headwaters of the Red River, where the Wichitas grazed 16,000 fine ponies. In the old horse trader's memoir, that was the promise of the Golden Fleece. But he never returned. Pushing his drove back through the Blackland Prairie, he lost all but 71 to stampedes and what must have been a biblical attack of horseflies. More attrition followed as he penetrated the woodlands. When Thomas James finally reached Saint Louis, for his $5,500 he had just five horses to show. That happened to be precisely the number he'd started with.

This time it is no mere glimpse of wild horse, no look-so-quick-it-seems-a-dream experience. Nor is it something my imagination has conjured from having read too many old stories. It is the mid-1990s, and that is a real band of wild horses trailing single file, stallion in the lead, down to a salt lick less than a quarter mile from where I sit in the sagebrush. It's a small band, six mares—one a black with a blaze-faced, bay colt glued to her side, another with a swaying belly, seriously pregnant here in mid-April—plus two yearlings just showing some independence. And there's the stallion, a horse as *negro* as a black hole, so dark he has to turn at an angle to the sun before I can see the muscles rippling across his sleek torso.

These horses are not a group of new colonizers making a magical appearance in the Horizontal Yellow after a century of absence. To find wild horses in numbers I've had to journey far to the north and west of where Hispano *mesteñeros* once built their corrals, to the humpbacked pine and sage ridges of the Great Basin in Nevada, the nexus state for the whole wild horse controversy of modern America.

Despite the war waged against them, when the twentieth century opened, there may have been as many as 200,000 wild horses still left in the West, including a few Near Southwest bands (mostly in the deserts of Trans-Pecos Texas and southern New Mexico). Over time, Americans had come to look upon mustangs and Indian ponies roughly they same way they viewed Tejano and New Mexican culture—a little bit of grudging admiration mixed with lots of derogation. After the Civil War there was a flurry of roundups that sent the wild horses of the Texas mustang plains to slaughterhouses on the Texas coast. Or (as happened to the last few bands in southwestern Kansas) the Near Southwest's last wild horses were simply shot down as vermin.

Thus in the twentieth century mustanging in the West shifted to the northern plains and the Far West. During the wars of the turn of the century—the Spanish-American War and particularly England's Boer War and World War I—the market for wild American horses was still a strong one. Miles City, Montana, for example, famously furnished Allied buyers 32,000 wild horses that sold, green broke, at between $145 to $185. In fact, the United States exported almost 375,000 horses in 1916, a significant percentage of them from wild stock. After World War I's tank technology changed military tactics forever, most of the wild horse capture and trade in the West fell to twentieth-century mustangers with contracts courtesy of modern America's love affair with poodles and kitties. Pet food quickly became a billion-dollar-a-year industry after World War II, and since any horse at all brought $50 to $60, mustangs once again became the target of an economy, only this time the *mesteñeros* herded them to capture with pickups and planes. Between 1945 and 1963 more than 100,000 were caught in Nevada alone. Estimates in the 1950s were that only 15,000 to 20,000 wild horses remained. But thanks to a Californian named Velma Johnston (Wild Horse Annie)—

and an exposé in the form of the Marilyn Monroe–Clark Gable movie, *The Misfits*—the Wild Horse and Burro Conservation Act of 1959 finally brought an end to the brutal practice of airplane mustanging.

That, of course, didn't end the story, which strings out in front of us yet. At least three steps have been taken since. One involved the creation of wild horse refuges, the first of which was created here in Nevada in 1962. Next came the Pryor Mountains Wild Horse Range in the Martian red canyons of a mountain range in southern Montana, 32,000 acres set aside in 1968. In the early 1970s, when there were an estimated 26,121 horses and 10,581 burros on Western public lands (18,000 of the horses in Nevada), Richard Nixon took the second step by signing the Wild Free-Roaming Horse and Burro Protection Act of 1971, which recognized wild horses as "living symbols of the historical and pioneer spirit of the West [and] . . . as an integral part of the natural system of the public lands."

Wild horses now had a legitimate place—and a new refuge, the Book-cliffs Wild Horse Range in Colorado, created in 1974—but what kind of place was it? A determination that horses were true wildlife seemed essential, and in 1976 horse activists got it with a Supreme Court case over the status of New Mexico's few bands of horses and wild burros. *Kleppe* v. *New Mexico* ruled that horses were wildlife and the property of the public. *Kleppe* didn't douse rancher outrage at wild horse competition for grass and water on grazing leases but at least gave the horses some legal standing. Despite the court's ruling, the Park Service in particular—committed to an idea of restoration to a wilderness ideal of America as it existed at the time of first viewing by whites—has refused to allow wild horses or burros in parks, monuments, and wildlife refuges and has systematically removed them (for example, from Bandelier and Big Bend) when they were there. And that is why places like the Wichita Mountains National Wildlife Refuge in Oklahoma today has bison, Rocky Mountain elk . . . but no wild horses!

So here I am instead in Nevada, which grudgingly allows wild horses their old niche in the American West. And where the war wages on. Lacking their predators—grizzlies are gone from this country, big cats are hounded, and wolves have yet to recolonize these desert ranges— wild horses are still up to their old trick of reclaiming their Pleistocene niche. Here and elsewhere where they still exist in the West, roundups and Adopt-A-Horse programs (at an average cost to taxpayers of $15 million a year) are necessary to keep their numbers in check. In 1993, in fact, the Bureau of Land Management took the first steps toward inject-ing Nevada's wild mares with the immunocontraceptive vaccine PZP. Even winnowed down to these remnants of fewer than 50,000 animals, wild horses still eye the West as home base and seem bent on exploding across it.

But Christ, what a sight to see a sagebrush desert with the horses still in it! Instead of a landscape dead under the sun, emptied of its life, this one crackles with drama. As I watch through binoculars the black stal-lion abruptly throws his head erect, ears cocked, muzzle pointing like a setter's. He takes a step, another, half a dozen more in the direction he's looking. I lower the glasses and draw a tangent from his muzzle across the sagebrush, and after half a mile of scanning I spot what has him mesmerized. It's another horse, a striking bay with a white blaze and three white stockings.

At once I understand the game. The bay is another stallion, a bache-lor now, but given that bay colt, perhaps only recently the stud of this band, and still hopeful. I am struck by the thought that what I am watching is no one-act play, that this no doubt is why the black herd stallion seems lean and fit as a greyhound. For when I turn back for his reaction I don't have to track nearly so far across the hills. At a double-time trot the black stallion has already closed the distance to the bache-lor bay by half, and as I pick him up in the glasses he breaks into a canter and I can see his astonishingly long tail snagging the sagebrush as it plumes into a bluish cloud behind him. Now, as he breaks into a clear-ing with his head high, he suddenly accelerates, puffs of tan dust erupt-ing from the rhythmic gathering of his feet beneath him, and as he gains speed he begins to lower his head to within inches of the ground, ears so flat that as I watch he transforms into a black snake extending out of a chariot whirl of churning legs, and in this incarnation he disappears from my view into a ravine.

In a clumsy excitement I swing my binoculars to the point where I think he will emerge. But he never does. Instead, from the far end of the ravine the bay stallion bobs to the surface in an obvious panic, head and tail up and eyes rolling so that I can see them in the glasses from more than half a mile away. He is scared shitless and seems to be heading for downtown Ely. Turning back once again to the black stallion I am astonished to find that he has done a 180 and is already emerging from the ravine and heading back to his band at full gallop. He never once glances back at his rival. But when he arrives among his band, he rakes the flanks and takes the names of every mare that had dared glance in the bay's direction. Popping his teeth and in a really bad mood, he herds them over the ridgeline and out of my sight.

Where I ride Skatopah out in the heart of the Horizontal Yellow, there are of course no wild horses at all now, but a bit more than a century ago it's estimated there were 50,000 of them—the number of wild horses across the whole American West today—just in the hundred miles of country between Yellow House and Palo Duro Canyons. The pet food industry was still a couple of decades in the future then, and the automotive age was at hand. Wild horses had gone from being a resource to being pests, and what happened to those 50,000 horses is a fitting finale: Ranchers paid their cowboys to shoot them on sight. It was merely another detail in the policy of eradicating all the bison, poisoning all the wolves, blowing up the eagle roosts, erasing the prairie dogs (and with them the 160-odd species dependent on dog towns). This ancient natural ecology was a waste of space. Everybody could see that what the country needed was *cows and cotton.*

As they grew scarcer, special animals were seen more than ever as individuals by their pursuers. Sifting through J. Frank Dobie's papers in Austin one afternoon, I come across this story, told by Frank Collinson, one of those who participated in this systematic unraveling. It attracts my attention because the setting is local and familiar but also because since I first found it, it has become emblematic to me of the senselessness with which we've used up this country and made it less than it was or could have been.

In the 1880s there still ran free on the Llano Estacado a particularly fine band of wild horses whose stallion was an incredible white animal that some thought descended from horses stolen by the Indians off a pair of big ranches in Chihuahua known to have imported Arabians. The white stallion was given the fanciful name Ghost of the Llano Estacado, and with a Melvillian plan for possessing him, in March 1882 Collinson arranged to meet the famous New Mexican mustangers, Celedon and Pedro Trujillo, on Blackwater Draw, the stallion's home range. They jumped the band northwest of where Lubbock is now, stuck a pole with a red flag in the ground to mark where they started the run, and commenced the pursuit with fresh horses and riders brought up to restart the chase whenever the pace slowed.

Take a moment to spread out a map of West Texas. Find Blackwater Draw. Trace your finger north to Running Water Draw (near Plainview) and then farther north to the Tulia Draws (west of Tulia) before circling back again to Blackwater. That's how far he ran the first day, an 80-mile loop with first one mustanger, then another pushing him, giving him no rest. Back in his home range the white horse found no respite, for the run began again at dawn. This time he turned south, to Yellow House Draw (due west of Lubbock now), and as his mares dropped behind in singles and pairs and were caught, the white horse seems to have come to some decision. Or maybe—probably—he was overtaken by panic. In any case, when he galloped down the slopes of the Yellow House, he ran without hesitation straight into the alkali bog of a lake bed, floundered in a spray of mud and hooves and lunging desperation, and then suffocated in the stinking mess before the riders could get to him.

It had all been for nothing. And now the world—in one more tiny increment that added up—was less than it had been.

4 The Long Shadow of the Desert

The Chihuahuan Desert may be defined as the warm desert of North America east of the Continental Divide. . . . It is also the least known desert region of North America.
SYMPOSIUM ON THE CHIHUAHUAN DESERT REGION

There are hundreds of millions of dollars in Texas for the promotion of right-wing political and educational programs, but not many dollars for private ventures to save pieces of our outdoor heritage. . . . A park is socialism, isn't it?
WILLIAM O. DOUGLAS

Why does every American with any sensibility and wit despise Texas?
EDWARD ABBEY

It's 3 a.m. on January 1 of one of the last years of the twentieth century, way down on the Mexican border outside the crumbling rock ruin dirt street town of Terlingua just west of Big Bend National Park. Post-New Year's Eve, in other words, and the party that never ends is holding forth tonight at the refurbished old Terlingua Bordello, basically an adobe cavity with a cement floor and tin roof topped off by a red signal light hijacked from a train crossing. This is New Year's in Trans-Pecos Texas, and the euphonious names and sensations of the previous several days seem to be running together into a kind of jumbled desert chant in my brain—South Rim Santa Elena *para* Marathon, Solitario, *y* alpine Lajitas grilled with Mariscal *y* Boquillas *con* creosote agave, followed by Starlight lechuguilla over *montañas de* Christmas *y* Davis to the sweet serenade of Chihuahuan La Kiva Las Damas Tejanas. The chorus appears to be, "Yes, with salt, *por favor.*"

Interesting crowd for the middle of nowhere. Real old Texas rangers in string ties and there's a trio of characters covering the cultural range, one a Buffalo Bill Cody clone, the others decked out in Cactus Ed Abbey and Freewheelin' Franklin costumes, all *dos* stepping alongside redneck hippies from Austin, river runners out of Montana, Mexicans slipped over from across the river, Park Service grunts in partial uniform, a delicate New Ager or two, local artist wanna-bes, a photographer from *Texas Monthly*, the cowboy flotsam of a slew of local bunkhouses, and several women so beautiful that the pure, freshly distilled *so-TOHL* we're all sipping must be involved in the perception. Or else somebody's down here shooting a beer commercial. In any case, as a friend puts it with true Texas elegance, "Just a whole buttload of people," and all reduced to a democratic humanness by the scene. The music? It's loud, joyous, distinctively regional and a good bit drunkenly awful. The whole, I am thinking, is the purest expression of the unredeemed soul of Tejas—what Texas can be, ought to be, ought to *want* to be—that I've witnessed in 20 years of living in the state and with more than one Willie Nelson brainfry and ejacorama in my past. Unlikely situation for a Big Insight, I'll admit, but there you have it.

It's either too late or too early to think hard about, but I can't help wondering: What is the base source of this Terlinguian interpenetration of peoples? Is it the shared Mexican culture that Edward Abbey, who would never visit any part of Texas but this, believed the animal-ignorant and dollar-godded Texans (as he characterized us) crushed and then co-opted? The distinctive food and distinctive drinks that reduce us all to the same level and whose origins lie in the Indian past across the river? Something else?

I think it's all those, but the something else choice may be the explanation most worth examining. For however near to the source we are in Trans-Pecos Texas, Hispanic culture is an influence virtually everywhere in the Near Southwest. The real power of indigenous release and commingling we're experiencing tonight springs, I think, from another pervasive agent in this part of the world, one like Hispanic culture that extends northward out of Mexico and lays an enormous (and ever lengthening) shadow across the whole of the Near Southwest.

It's the desert. Of course. The desert and all the things that follow from a condition of desertness is what has set us loose tonight, what has made modern Terlingua and Big Bend National Park and this eclectic assemblage of souls in Way Outback Tejas possible. We are joined here together, drinking the desert's juices, ingesting its flesh, agog at its stars, telling its stories, dancing to music inspired by rock and sun because desertness has left this place one of the free landscapes for human adventure. This desert, its animating spark, has always been and is especially so now one of the Great Gods of the Near Southwest. Its existence places an imprimatur on the region that's partly threat, partly symbol. The desert—and I mean to be specific, the *Chihuahuan* Desert—is the bass note across this world. And if I seek to understand even the nondesert parts, I have to start here or the world makes no sense.

We are living in an age of a desert aesthetic and even a desert chic. Many of us grow up now with romantic notions about cactus-studded landscapes lit by neon sunsets, notions some scholars think may be the emerging landscape stereotype of the American West in the eyes of the world. But of course you know in your heart that the desert aesthetic must be a very recently acquired taste, for its opposite—a revulsion and even fear at its barrenness and screaming heat—flirts about the edges of the mind. In fact, the desert is the landscape equivalent of the film star as cultural hero, and sometimes you have to think it's just as much a product of the capitalist genius for turning every rising tide in social life into stock shares. It was after all only a century ago that the film or rock star was unimagined (military men were our premier heroes then), and thanks to the artists of the romantic age, the green Alps of the

Desert wasteland as preserved national monument—New Mexico's White Sands, near the northern terminus of the largest desert in North America.

Rockies were our ne plus ultra landscape. The desert was still a repellant wasteland.

No need to analyze this transformation play by play. The end-run version is roughly this: By the 1880s the desert wastelands of America, with their sun and dry air, were becoming destinations for those suffering the lung diseases of the industrial age. Ten years later the painter Joseph Henry Sharp discovered Taos and the Pueblo Indians, and within another 10 years the railroads had recognized how to market the deserts as tourist destinations using Taos Society of Artist paintings as advertising. Automobiles turned what had once been a real horror—crossing the desert on foot, horse, or wagon—into scenic weekend outings. It's no coincidence that the first literary naturalists of desert celebration, John C. Van Dyke and Mary Austin, wrote *The Deserts* and *Land of Little Rain* at the same time the Model A appeared.

A decade later, just before the Grand Canyon became a national park in 1918, Georgia O'Keeffe fell for West Texas. And in two more decades, after Roger Toll of the National Park Service first saw Big Bend and

Piñons and century plants and broken white limestone can mean only one place:
the island mountain ranges of the northern Chihuahuan Desert.

around the time (it was 1942) that Forrest Shreve first recognized a distinctive desert in the Near Southwest he called Chihuahuan, O'Keeffe crystallized her desert vision of New Mexico. The Sierra Club had a tough time breaking with green mountains, but David Brower finally got the desert religion as a result of the flap over dams on the Colorado River in the early 1950s. Then came Wallace Stegner's evocative depiction of the arid lands in American history in his biography of John Wesley Powell that same decade. In 1967 Edward Abbey published *Desert Solitaire,* and via Abbey the counterculture collapsed into ecstasy over slickrock and cactus. By the time American auto ads started putting Jeeps atop rock pinnacles, Thelma and Louise sailed into the Utah ether, and young Californians put Moab and the mountain bike together, the world had flipped over. We were in love with the desert. And it had all taken just a century.

The desert's power to affect the human psyche has always been there, of course. It's just that technology (or the lack of it) and cultural preparation (or the lack of it) until recently mostly got in the way. Although we didn't evolve in deserts, the desert was always out there on the margins, resisting us with its aridity but compelling us with the strange music of aridity's effect on topographical architecture. In the Euro-American memory the desert is lodged like a knot in wood as the sacred setting of the Bible, the ultimate unconquerable wilderness waste, the antipodal antithesis of the Garden of Eden. Rippling out of North Africa across the Mediterranean, the sun and dry air and blue skies of the desert have long called northern European writers and painters desertward. Van Gogh and Monet and Rimbaud, after all, were reviving a tradition stretching back 500 years, and the muse of nature they sought was the same one that drew Blumenschein and Fechin and O'Keeffe and Dasburg to New Mexico and Bywaters and Hogue to Trans-Pecos Texas.

There are dozens of true deserts—that is, landscapes getting less than 10 inches of precipitation annually—across the planet, and depending on who is doing the counting, either four or six deserts in the United States, each as different as siblings. All of them have intriguing human histories primarily because we aren't by nature a desert species and have never found them easy to live in until recently. In North America, desert most classically dominates the *Far* Southwest beyond the Continental Divide, and the names are names we know: the Sonoran in Arizona, the Mojave in California, the Great Basin Desert and Colorado Plateau farther north, and beyond those still more, like the Big Horn Basin, the Snake River Plain, the deserts of eastern Oregon, and the scablands of Washington.

But in the Near Southwest *the* desert—and by proximity of birth and residence my personal desert—is the Chihuahuan. Except for a piece of the Colorado Plateau exposed by the Chama River west of Taos, the Chihuahuan is the only large American desert lying east of the Rockies. Startlingly, given its huge size and lurking presence in this Age of the Big Warm-up, the Chihuahuan has almost no name recognition; in fact, it's probably the last desert most Americans might list in a North American drylands litany. Perhaps this is because the Chihuahuan is mostly a Mexican desert. Its foot lies near San Luis Potosi, and it drapes languidly northward across six Mexican states and almost a thousand miles of continental landscape before its effects finally dim between Socorro and Albuquerque, in central New Mexico. Where it laps across the Rio Grande into Texas it roughly follows the Pecos River north, but it casts

High Chihuahuan Desert of the famous Jornada del Muerto, southern New Mexico.

a shadow nearly 400 miles wide northwest across Texas and much of southern New Mexico.

In the last century the Chihuahuan's northern perimeter has been extremely dynamic, a taste of what's to come, many of us think, for much of the Southwest east of the Rockies. On the Southern High Plains, Chihuahuan vegetation and Plains vegetation are presently jousting for dominance in the vicinity of Roswell, on the perimeter of the Llano Estacado. West of the Sacramento Mountains the desert entirely blankets the immense basins and bony mountains of New Mexico, extending its longest arm up the Rio Grande from El Paso northward along the river in the form of the legendary Jornada del Muerto of New Mexican colonial history. West of the river it lays a patchy hold on the country to the Continental Divide and slightly beyond, where it confronts the Sonoran Desert at Texas Pass.

At this juncture in time the Chihuahuan is a much appreciated and loved desert by those who know it. But my experience and yours of the Chihuahuan Desert at the turn of the twenty-first century only *appears* to us the obvious one. What inhabitants of the Near Southwest think of the Chihuahuan Desert a century from now is certain to be different, and for causes just as good. What we thought of it a century ago . . . well, what we thought of the desert a century ago, perverse as it was, makes the song of the desert as we hear it possible.

"So far as man's conception of time is concerned, the American desert is, always has been, and always will be." Not a bad opening line from an engineer, but on the other hand, Robert Hill was not ordinary. Neither was the place he was describing. Since I took the time to dig it up several years ago, I've been thinking that for an on-the-ground example of an American mind caught in the crossfire of changing ideas about the desert, Robert Hill's account of the first official exploration of the canyons of the Rio Grande through the Chihuahuan Desert is almost too good. A protégé of John Wesley Powell, conqueror of all those stupendous canyons of the Colorado River, Hill was dispatched by the United States Geological Survey to investigate stories that the middle Rio Grande contained canyons as frightening as those of the Colorado. The year was 1899, just before Van Dyke and Austin published, while they were out in their own deserts farther west, engaging in some serious new arid lands appreciation. The image of deserts was on the cusp of big change, but the ancient revulsions held by Anglo-Americans were yet very real.

Take Hill's "Running the Cañons of the Rio Grande" into the Chihuahuan Desert sometime. (It's in a 1901 issue of *The Century Magazine*, illustrated with seven halftone plates of lovely drawings by the famous painter Thomas Moran—among them *View of the Grand Cañon de Santa Helena from the Beach near the Mouth*, a piece that fairly hums with the kind of grandeur Moran put into his magnificent Yellowstone and Grand Canyon paintings.) Settle in against an alligator juniper and flip it open. But dig your feet in the ground for balance: Severe cerebral whiplash looms.

Hill's party of six, loaded into three johnboats, started their "long journey into the unknown" at Presidio on October 5, 1899. Hill was not the first to descend these now familiar canyons of the Texas-Mexico border. The famed artist George Catlin, during a low ebb in his career, apparently floated the canyons in 1855. Texas Ranger Charles Nevill ricocheted through Santa Elena barely in one piece in 1881–82. And James

Exiting Santa Elena Canyon, Chisos Mountains in the distance, on the Wild and Scenic stretch of the Rio Grande, one of the great river floats on the continent.

MacMahon, Hill's guide, said he'd previously done three trips. But after having its boats destroyed in Mariscal Canyon, the International Boundary Survey of half a century earlier had pronounced the canyons impassable. Officially they had never been explored.

The whiplash? Well, from his mystico-appreciative beginning, within two sentences Hill reverts to the classic nineteenth-century American take on deserts: "Every . . . aspect of the Big Bend Country—landscape, configuration, rocks, and vegetation," he wrote, "is weird and strange and of a type unfamiliar to the inhabitants of civilized lands." The great basins between the mountains were covered by "a spiteful, repulsive vegetation." Today's much admired ocotillo waved its fronds above the desert floor "like serpents rising from a Hindu juggler's carpet." The local residents suffer from stereotype, too. A reputed Mexican bandit named Alvarado, notorious for his bicolored mustache, lurked in Hill's nightmares, compelling the party to spend nights secreted away in the canebrakes. Alvarado turned out to be a rancher and a family man who happened to live on the wrong side of the river and didn't suffer the Americans to push him around.

By the time they'd reached the first canyons on the river, the present Colorado Canyon stretch through the Bofecillos Mountains, Hill is still writing of the "mocking desert flora," which he finds "shocking and repulsive." But experience was starting to bring him to the point of seeing the desert differently, so he could speak of coming to "a valley which presents a beautiful panorama of desert form and color. The hills are of all sizes and shapes . . . dazzling white, chalky rocks . . . [with] vermilion foot-hills of red clay." When the river entered the "Grand Canyon" (Santa Elena) "in a narrow vertical slit in the face of the escarpment," he concluded that the "solemnity and beauty of the spectacle were overwhelming."

In spite of his shock and alienation, Hill's soul was capable of being moved by all the same scenes that move desert visitors to these places today. From the top of the rim, looking into Santa Elena, Hill couldn't help himself: "The view is grand beyond all conception." At the one major rapids in Santa Elena Canyon, the famous Rockslide, Hill's party decided to portage, which took them three days of misery yet left an impression "of unusual beauty," especially during "the glorious moonlight which is one of the characteristics of the desert."

Exiting beneath 1,700-foot cliffs through the mirrored staircases of

Santa Elena Canyon's mouth, Hill was now back in what he called the
"Terlingo Desert." Dig your feet in and do a few neck rolls, 'cause we're
back to the "weird." Out in the high desert again, Hill resorts to a neat
combination of superlative negatives. Now the desert was "one of the
most bizarre pieces of landscape that can be imagined" and "one of the
hottest and most sterile regions conceivable." But there were compensa-
tions. Looming against the sky now were the Chisos Mountains, and like
all nineteenth-century Americans, Hill was prepared to see mountains
positively, in the case of the Chisos as "a group of white-clad spirits rising
from a base of misty gray shadow and vegetation."

So it went on through Mariscal Canyon, where "the river presented
the appearance of apparently plunging into a seething hole without visible outlet," past the hot springs on the approach to Boquillas (in this age
of pre-adobe appreciation Hill describes the houses as "dirty adobe").
But however unsettling the desert, Hill likes canyons; he *gets* canyons.
He thinks "Carmen Canyon" (Boquillas) better deserved the appellation grand than Santa Elena, as it was a place of "remarkable forms of
rock sculpture." "The moon was full while we were in this cañon," he
writes, "and the effects of its illuminations were indescribably beautiful. . . . Language cannot describe the beauty of such nights."

Good thing for Hill, for now the course of the river was nearly due
north and they were into the stretch of the Rio Grande known as the
Lower Canyons, today one of the major stretches of water in the National Wild and Scenic River system. Hill writes that this "lower course is
almost a continuous cañon to Del Rio, and from an esthetic point of
view is even more picturesque and beautiful than the portion of the river
already described." In the clear air they guess the cliffs below the Mar-
avillas Castle Butte are 500 feet high; an actual ascent proved them to be
1,650 feet. They find more hot springs and many "forms like the Bad
Lands of Dakota." In the last run before the Devil's River were "some of
the most beautiful and picturesque effects," in an entrenched canyon
where the walls were "purest white, which weathers into great curves."

It had taken a month of exposure, but eventually the words *weird,
repulsive, spiteful, bizarre, sterile* all disappear from Robert Hill's vocabulary. In that subtle and simple alteration in language, Hill symbolically
vaulted a gulf. The Chihuahuan Desert might remain a difficult place
for Americans to imagine as home, but Hill's experience showed that it
was a place you could think about in another way entirely. The desert

was a landscape fully capable of moving the American soul, even a hard-bitten engineering soul, to marvel at beauty, form, nature, wildness.

Robert Hill was onto something important.

What is it, exactly, that defines the American West in the modern mind? "Where there was a frontier" no longer works and is ethnocentrically disastrous in any case. Where people live rurally, drive pickup trucks, wear shitkicker boots, and listen to country music sounds operable but describes the South more than the West. Two other definitions do work, though. The West is a place we all recognize when we're there, but you don't have to cast eyes on cowboys, miners, or even Indians or Hispanos to know, because the West is all about the imprint of external impressions through our senses. Drive up out of Houston or Tulsa three or fours hours toward the sunset, stop to gas up the car, and you step out into air that is fundamentally different, light that is brighter and more transparent, skies of an icier blue, stars that are polished and enlarged, ground no longer covered by a mat of green but exposed as hard edges in pigmentations of off-white, buff, red. The farther west you go toward the mountains, the greater the combined effect of these changes seems to be. Elevation is not the cause, although it contributes and you *are* climbing into more rarified air as you ascend the Rio Grande or Canadian. Aridity, the elemental Big It at the heart of the West, is the cause. What makes the West almost everything it is, is the result of dry. And what enough dry creates is deserts. Add mountains that stand like gushing moisture islands in the deserts, and you've described the Western landscape.

Despite its marvelous effects on air and light, plants and animals, the fundamental of aridity is no longer all the West is. A century ago, at the same time Robert Hill was discovering the desert's potential, the federal government initiated a plan to identify lands that aridity made particularly environmentally sensitive or literally worthless economically—or that might be significant as badges of national pride. This big story is in danger of becoming a cartoon unless I provide some detail, but the final result was the creation of the National Forests (all the original ones in the mountains of the West), later on the National Grasslands (several out on the Horizontal Yellow), and the monuments and parks in the National Park system. Much of the West—most of the deserts—not homesteaded by the 1930s ended up in the hands of the Bureau of Land Management.

A plot foisted on innocent Americans by an international conspiracy? Not exactly. Deserts and arid-lands mountains planetwide have always been landscapes that human societies across time and space have left as commons, open to regulated use by the public. Rather than privatizing them, the fed of a century ago followed suit and has managed them since as a kind of national commons. The moral of this simple little story is that in addition to aridity, the existence of a national commons in the form of the public lands has defined what the West is for a century now. Of the states carved from the Near Southwest, Colorado and New Mexico are public lands states, where the federal commons make nature a major player in human life. The forested Rockies south of the Arkansas and Rio Grande headwaters are mostly managed as national forests. Where the effect of the desert surmounts the island ranges, the mountains have largely ended up in the hands of the BLM. Ditto for the desert in New Mexico. Where the Chihuahuan hasn't been deemed too worthless for anything but being bombed to rubble by the military, extensive BLM lands checkerboard the landscape. And a pair of high-drama parts in New Mexico—the limestone caverns of Carlsbad and a kind of ultimate desert essence place, the brilliant gypsum dune fields of White Sands National Monument—are part of the National Park system.

Cross the desert south from Albuquerque sometime into Mexico or, better yet, Texas. The desert of course is oblivious to our petty human boundaries, so what you're reading in the landscape is purely cultural, an impress of history as vivid as a curtain. Texas, as its residents are so fond of pointing out, is different. What I have been preparing to say here is that while Texas's 20 million residents may not realize it yet, their state's historical trajectory and the Chihuahuan Desert have long been caught in a dance of fate, a kind of desert fandango. Over the long haul, it's a dance that will give Texas a sounder claim to being a legitimate part of the West than all the cowboys or frontier Alamo heroes Texas flag-waving could ever hope for.

"I think a century ago this is what they'd have called looking for the elephant."

I straighten up from behind my tripod-mounted camera and in the process abandon a precious but tiny slice of shade, cast by a grainy purple mound of mud as tall as a *T. rex* and (since this is Cretaceous dirt) just as old. A windlike belch as if from a volcano slaps me across the face, and I am certain I can literally feel desiccation operating. *The crow's feet*

Painted Desert of Big Bend Park, Texas.

at the corners of my eyes just cracked to my earlobes, I'm thinking. But what I say is, "Hey! You within hearing?"

Eyes shaded with my hand, I scan the scene in front of me. Earth, all right. Not, as I could be tempted to think, deep in that ultimate desert of the solar system, the five-mile-deep canyons of the Valles Marineris on Mars. But maybe this is one of the closest places to it on this planet. Chihuahuan Desert. Summer, a day that started at 78 degrees at sunrise, was 92 at nine, 96 at 10:30, 98 at 11, a hundred by 11:45, 103 by noon. Last time I looked, maybe an hour after straight-up noon, it was 108. I'm in what the old-time silver and mercury miners of Terlingua used to call the Painted Desert, a compelling stretch of badlands humping in rolls and folds scarcely above the elevation of the nearby Rio Grande's polluted gurgle. The blast furnace wind and the fearsome, singsong buzz of the cicadas are absolutely the only sounds. Except for two whiptail lizards that dashed madly for another shade when I kicked over their rock and the infrequent salvation—a cloud shadow riding over the striped mounds around me—there is absolutely no movement, either.

In the early afternoon of a June in Texas the badlands of the Big Bend are direct contact, the full sensory experience of earthly desertness. It's the penultimate desert, the desert squared (my God, what must Mars be like!). Exploring the Painted Desert at this time of year and day is the flip analogy of taking a mountain stroll during a subzero Montana blizzard in February, which I've also done. A profundity from such experiences? Well, you don't have to elbow anyone else out of the way for a view.

I balance the camera and tripod on my shoulder and step out through the sumptuous and downright sexy terrain. The 40 granular acres immediately in the line I pick do not appear to have a speck of green, but I am pretty sure that this is where my companion was headed. If my ability to see through these heat waves is trustworthy, last I saw of her she was in fact *running* with outspread arms through this Martian surface.

As is the situation for many Texans, among them my hiking partner and me, for half a century now the Chihuahuan Desert has served as a kind of grand nature touchstone and spiritual mecca for Texas. Shocking to me when I think on it, by dint of a part of my education (a close encounter with real hullabaloo Texicanism) and 20 years residence in the state, I find myself as an adult at least nominally a Texan. So I come now to do what Texans do so well: I come to praise Texas. Not Texas history and culture so much, for raised in the milieu of the Deep South I recognize Texas for what it is: the South's West, the piece of the western prairies, deserts, and mountains that Southerners almost entirely innocent of enlightened motives managed to wrest free of every other government's influence for a while and leave indelibly marked.

The result of that—virtually all the Indians driven from the state and almost all the landscape locked up behind fences in Western history's great experiment with privatization of nature—keeps giving me reasons not to be moved to flag-waving by the general arc of Texas history, past or present. Yet like a few others (too few yet), I am a committed partisan of the Texas soil, and what I come to praise is Texas *nature*. In fact, I eat the place up, even the famously flat and unloved parts that still exist beneath the overgrazed, overcropped, strip-mined, strip-malled wallpapering of posted signs and exotic animals that is modern day Texas. Hot, polluted, posted, and raped, I still love the place.

Ascending a smoothly eroded mound striped like Neapolitan ice cream, I finally catch a glimpse of tanned legs churning up toward the rimrock 250 feet above me. If anything, the heat seems to be even more ferocious near the rim than in the full badlands below, but after a few minutes of climbing I make it to where my companion sits, queen of all she surveys. Hell of an overlook. In the typically translucent atmosphere of the hot months (pollution from power-generating facilities in Arizona and Mexico has become a regular summer feature in the Chihuahuan Desert) blue horizons pile atop one another westward in the direction of Lajitas. The improbable V where Santa Elena Canyon saws through the fault block ridge shimmers in the distance to the south. The Chisos rise like chalk blocks to the east.

"Did you say something back there a bit ago? Or were you just having a heatstroke and blathering unintelligibly? Sounded like you said you'd spotted an elephant."

I'm swilling down a quart of her (hot) water in reckless gulps and fantasizing about margaritas on the rocks in the dim cool of the Starlight in Terlingua, so it takes a minute to reply. It's clear that the desert regards us as big ugly bags of mostly water that it would desperately love to suck to raisins.

"I think I said this would have once been called looking for the elephant. You know, doing something a little nuts for the sheer experience of stomping on the terra, knowing you're alive. Stuff like that."

She looks at me with a cocked eyebrow and then asks, very patiently: "Your vision getting blurry? Need to lie down in the shade? For someone who's been coming here for twenty years, floated these canyons, pointed out to me last winter the map of the continent from the South Rim in the Chisos, single-handedly keeps the Mexican agave-farm economy ship-shape, you don't have a clue why you're here, do you?"

"Huh?" Heat, as is well known, slows synapse connections.

"Listen. I mean I know you *love* the desert and think it has magic and

power, but you know we're here because in the whole grand state of
Texas, this and Guadalupe and a couple of other spots are the only
places you *can* go. This desert has power because you can stop on the
side of the road, like we just did, and do something as idiotic and wonderful as walking right off into the country with a canteen and a map and
never look back. Can't do that very much in this state."

She is right, of course, and good thing the desert is a potent place,
because in Texas it's the only part they've let us have, and you cannot
overemphasize being able to get into your landscape. There is no way to
go native without it, no way to develop a sense of place centered in the
fundamental world, no way to imagine yourself a part of the natural
community of plants and animals and the regional forces around you.
For that you have to have the full, five-sense experience of direct and
repeated contact, experiential immersion with nature. That's what the
Chihuahuan Desert offers.

How that came to be in a state like Texas is a story with a moral fiber
richer than Dallas.

Texas loves its vital statistics and likes to trot them out: second-largest
state (600 miles on the diagonals from border to border), second-largest
state population (20 million), etc. But try this one you rarely hear about.
The state famous for having been an independent republic for a decade,
which negotiated a bargain that got it title to a huge sweep of the Southwest when it entered the United States, had the presence of mind to
preserve only 3 percent of that 172 million acres as public land. This is no
breakthrough story if Texas history is your forte, although outside the
state the situation puzzles. When Texas was a republic, it went hor-
rifically into debt, primarily because of Mirabeau Lamar's costly wars to
run off all the native peoples. The annexation deal left Texas with title to
the lands the Republic had claimed so their sale could retire that debt.
But five years later, in 1850, Texas got $10 million from the United States
to relinquish its spurious claim (to 67 million acres of the Southwest)
based on the premise that the western boundary of Texas followed the
Rio Grande to the river's headwaters in present Colorado. So the Republic's debts were paid off by 1855, and the state at that point still had 98
million acres left. With the kind of deal no other Western state got,
Texas's subsequent history stands as a lesson in what could have happened to the whole West, for Texas proceeded to hold a clinic in privat-

ization and property rights. State politicians and real estate interests went on to massacre the part of the Near Southwest that Texas folded into its boundaries.

Twenty-six million acres had already been granted under the governments of Spain and Mexico, and the state built its infrastructure by cashing in on the rest. It granted 36.2 million acres to railroads and irrigation and canal companies. Rather than retaining them for mineral revenues or as seeds for a wildlands or parks system, it privatized almost all its school lands, 44 million acres of them, in fact. Three million acres—most of the Texas Panhandle—were given to a Chicago firm to build the present state capital in Austin. Another 3 million went to Texas Revolution and Confederate veterans. Only 4.8 million actually ended up going to homesteaders.

Today the State Land Office considers 20.6 million acres to be public in Texas, but to anyone looking to get at the Texas natural world, that's the unfunniest joke in the Southwest. In addition to highway corridors and bomb plants, 4 million of it is submerged tidelands in the Gulf; another million is "public" riverbed lands, much of it under fence and unconceded by gun-wielding private landowners. The state park system? Those little parcels have saved my sanity plenty of times, and as I write this there are 132 of them, which seems like a lot. Yet until 1984 Texas ranked forty-first in the nation in per capita state park acreage. Two recent acquisitions, Devil's River State Natural Area and Big Bend Ranch State Park, have doubled the size of the system to 433,908 acres, causing the state to jump in national ranking to twenty-sixth. But for perspective, wrap your mind around this one fact: Six private ranchers each own more of Texas than is in the state park system. Extrapolate those ranching families at 25 people each, and 150 people in Texas get access to six times as much land as the other 20 million people in the state. In 1995 then National Forest Service Chief Jack Ward Thomas captured the situation perfectly: "I was a Texas boy. I hunted and fished and roamed around on private lands, begging access or sneaking in and out when I wanted. When I grew up, moved away, and discovered public lands, I thought I'd died and gone to heaven."

With 80 percent of the state's population now living in urban areas, the old saw that Texans don't need public lands because most everyone lives on or has relatives who live on a farm or a ranch doesn't work, if it ever did. Yet environmentalism still seems to strike many Texans even

today as a foreign idea hatched by people with strange accents, berets,
and granny glasses. When endangered black-capped vireos and golden-cheeked warblers ("yellow-assed *what?*") were first beginning to threaten development in the hills west of Austin, a friend who holds an environmental law degree from a Texas university told me in a crowded Austin bar one night that he thought the developers' best strategy might be to air-drop leaflets with the birds' pictures on them across the countryside in Mexico where they wintered, with an offer of a quarter a carcass. I laughed, then scanned the papers for months scared to death someone had overheard us and run with the idea.

If you get the sense that environmentalism hasn't exactly caught on in Texas, you'd be getting the picture. It seems to limit the economic possibilities, and Texas has always had problems with that. Austin's *Texas Observer* may be a liberal gadfly, but it was never more right than when it editorialized in 1967 that "the unenlightenment, the callous indifference, the selfishness, the Neanderthal nature of Texas government is nowhere more clearly apparent than in this state's reprehensible record in conservation." Throughout the 1990s the League of Conservation Voters has located wealthy and populous Texas in the bottom five states in the nation in environmental affairs, right there with cultural pacesetters like Mississippi, Alabama, and Louisiana. When the Davis Mountains, the most scenic mountain range in the state, once again (as it had in the '30s and '50s) attracted the attention of the National Park Service in the early 1990s, a vocal minority went into property rights hysteria before the rest of the Southwest even knew another park was being considered. When Richard McLauren and his "Republic" group papered the mountains with its "Republic of Jeff Davis" (the range is mostly in Jeff Davis County) claims, the NPS backed off, and the place that Roy Bedichek and William O. Douglas tried half a century ago to get us to recognize as a national ecological treasure is yet hay-baled with barbed wire and posted signs and saddled with a ridiculous little 1,800-acre state park.

All of us advocates of nature and the wild who engage the myopia of Texas economics and politics desperately need heroes. We have them, too, although they aren't the bit players of Texas history—the Crocketts and Travises—that get the Daughters of the Texas Revolution and the war buffs wet and squirmy. I'm speaking here of people whom history will judge as having produced tangible benefits for millions of people, countless hundreds of species, and ecologies that were thousands of years in the making. Participants in overrated battles are not in this class.

Except for Lady Bird Johnson, that sweet partisan of a peculiarly Texas kind of environmentalism (wildflowers viewed from the highway)—but of the Chihuahuan Desert, too—you have to reach back a ways to locate those heroes. Earth saint Roy Bedichek, the best literary naturalist the state has produced in 160 years of existence, has to be our patron. His friends, J. Frank Dobie and Walter Prescott Webb, weren't shabby as nature champions, either; indeed, the ranch-bred Dobie was the first Texas literary figure to call for a national park in Big Bend (in *Nature Magazine* in 1930), the most "Texan part of Texas," he thought. And in 1937 that proponent of history as high adventure, Walter Webb, became one of the first to run Santa Elena Canyon—certainly the first to do it in a bow tie and with Coast Guard planes buzzing overhead—even if he spray-painted his name on the rocks and his instinct on seeing the mouth of the canyon was to want to *buy* the place. (When he realized the national park was a go, he bought his Friday Mountain Ranch in the Hill Country instead.)

But the author of *Adventures with a Texas Naturalist* was something special, in good part because of the inspired role model he presents. In a state wild against liberals and crazy for growth and sports, Bedichek was a kind of Indian in the cupboard, quietly pointing out what was really important. Like the state's finest range, the Davis Mountains, which he was still climbing in his seventies. Or the simple animal passions, like sitting around a fire before sunrise or shitting out-of-doors from a natural squat (johns always gave him trouble because of the difficulty of balancing over the throne on his feet!). The love of golden-cheeked warblers and mockingbirds, of course. Bedichek liked to "cook outdoors, eat outdoors, sleep outdoors, look and listen outdoors." One of the mottoes he lived by was Only Nature Is Normal. "He was a renowned naturalist but we didn't love him because he was a naturalist," Edmund Heinsohn wrote, "but because of his naturalness. There was something earthy about him. . . ."

Bedichek was a class act on behalf of Texas-wide nature inspiration and has been much celebrated. But he was preceded by an individual who Texas history has taken no cognizance of at all. Nonetheless, Roger Toll ought to be known as one of the founding fathers of Texas environmentalism. Those of us alive now who have Chihuahuan Desert fever have Toll to thank in part for making it possible. I am convinced that Roger Toll, who has a mountain in Big Bend named for him but is otherwise a nonentity in the state, will have more long-term significance for modern Texas than any one of the Lone Star icons who committed hari-kari at the Alamo. In fact, like Davy Crockett, Toll gave his life to Texas, dying in a car accident in Big Bend in 1936.

Who was Roger Toll? Truth be known, Toll was a fed. He was a bureaucrat, actually, an experienced National Park superintendent who'd previously headed up Yellowstone, Rocky Mountain, and Mount Rainier National Parks. He'd been born in Denver, and with public lands out the door he climbed mountains—50 peaks in Rocky Mountain National Park alone. But Toll understood other kinds of landscapes, too, and when he eventually got selected as a one-man new-park evaluator for the 1930s National Park Service, he did nothing for Texas he didn't also do for places like Utah and the Dakotas.

Who was Toll? It was Toll's 1932 and '34 surveys and recommendations of potential park sites in Texas that fueled the initial Washington interest in what eventually became the Near Southwest's two big desert parks. In 1924 Congressman C. B. Hudspeth of El Paso had first drawn attention to Trans-Pecos Texas by introducing legislation to create a national park in the Davis Mountains. And in 1931 two state representatives, R. M. Wagstaff and Everett Townsend, had begun work on bills to create "Texas Canyons," a state park, in Big Bend. Now sent to Texas to evaluate seven sites for *national* park or monument status, Toll resolved that five out of six—in rough order of their consideration then, they were "Texas Canyons" (Big Bend), the Guadalupe Mountains and/or McKittrick Canyon (these were treated separately), the Davis Mountains, and Palo Duro Canyon—should either become parks or, in Palo Duro's case, be considered for national monument status. Roger Toll, in other words, took a look at the Near Southwest and picked the spots that he thought would become our regional sacred places.

When it first sent Toll to Texas, the NPS operated under the assumption that this was mostly a political visit, that actually no unknown areas of national park quality existed in the United States in the 1930s. Because of Texas's history of privatization and because many of the places on Toll's list were in the "desert wastes" of the state, not even Texas residents had seen much of its landscape. Let's just say that the NPS turned out to be badly mistaken. Toll's reaction to Big Bend is an example. Thirty

The writer-historian Walter Prescott Webb's first thought on seeing the truncated canyon mouth where the Rio Grande breaks through the Terlingua anticline was to buy it. He later supported creation of Big Bend National Park.

years before, when Robert Hill had floated the canyons, he'd been told
that horizontal plains so dominated this part of the world that there were
neither gorges nor mountains in Texas. But as Hill had been, when Toll
first saw the Chisos Mountains and those astonishing 1,700-foot-deep
slots the Rio Grande had sliced through sheer rock, he was flabbergasted
and wrote his superiors that the place was "one of the noted scenic
spectacles of the United States." And like Glacier Park in Montana,
perhaps this border region could inspire a twin park on the other side of
the international boundary, in Mexico.

In the case of Big Bend, everything appeared at first to line up like
dominos. The image of deserts as wastelands bereft of any economic role
in modern life still lingered powerfully in America; it's an idea that can't
be understated in creating Big Bend, a large park in a state with no federal lands. There was also Lone Star pride, never a factor to be taken
lightly in Tejas. Steven Mather, the first director of the NPS, had cleverly
advertised national parks as patriotic creations throughout the '20s, and
plenty of Texans urged parks out of state pride. As early as 1930 the Texas
Democratic Convention had made it part of their platform that the
state's delegation in Congress seek at least one park for the state for
that reason. Equally critical in the Great Depression was that creation of
a park around Big Bend would serve as a federal bailout of pioneer
ranchers, whose cows (30,000 of them in Big Bend by 1891) had devastated the fragile desert grasslands in little more than three decades of
grazing. In the midst of the Depression, some owners were ecstatic to
have someone—anyone—actually interested in buying up country that
could scarcely support a few herds of goats anymore.

Then the Texas bottom line set in. The New Deal represented a first
rising of the tide of conservative distrust of the fed, and it began to play
out with respect to all these Texas and Chihuahuan Desert places the
NPS coveted. *Maybe* one park, but five? The wild, volcanic jumble of
the Davis Mountains, whose 8,382-foot Mount Livermore was the second tallest in the state, was more valuable as ranch country than as a
silly nature preserve, local ranchers shouted. The same was said of the
Guadalupe/McKittrick Canyon region to the north, which held the
tallest mountain in Texas and one of the geologic wonders of the world
in the exposed Capitan Reef. Wallace Pratt, who owned much of South
McKittrick Canyon, was uninterested either in donating or selling, and
Toll decided that the Guadalupes would have to wait. Up in the Panhan-

dle the proposed 135,000-acre national monument in Palo Duro Canyon disintegrated, too, when neither Texas nor its citizens mustered any enthusiasm to acquire the lands for transfer to the NPS. This in the decade when citizens of places like Tennessee, North Carolina, and Maine all scrambled for money and created Great Smoky Mountains and Arcadia Parks.

In Big Bend, where the NPS planners wanted a 1.5-*million*-acre park, where ranchers were letting their depleted lands go back to the state for taxes (but still demanded—and got—three to five dollars from the fed), where unsold Texas school lands were going for one copper penny an acre, the total purchase price for Big Bend was a measly $1.5 million. Yet the Texas legislature and Governor James Allred refused throughout the late 1930s to appropriate money to acquire the land! A statewide volunteer effort, led vigorously by Amon Carter and the *Fort Worth Star–Telegram*, netted all of $8,346.88. Of all people, it took governor/country radio personality Pappy Lee O'Daniel to respond to President Roosevelt's entreaties and persuade the state legislature that acquiring what is today an International Biosphere Reserve just might be an act of statecraft. Finally, in 1943, Texas transferred 708,000 acres to the NPS, and after an estimated 25,000 cattle, 8,000 sheep, 18,000 goats, and 1,000 horses were evicted, Big Bend opened the next year. Thank Pappy, or Roger Toll (my choice), or Davy Crockett if you have to—whoever—because this is the wild soul of the Near Southwest.

In Texas, at least, the Big Bend debacle almost ended Chihuahuan Desert preservation. (The caverns at Carlsbad had become a national park in 1930, and in 1931 Toll also recommended national monument status for the White Sands gypsum dunes in the New Mexico heart of the Chihuahuan, and that state was comparatively prompt in transferring 143,000 acres of the dunes to the NPS.) But Texas produced other environmentalist heroes who through tremendous, sustained effort made sure that the Chihuahuan Desert and subsequent society got their due. Of them, none played quite the all-encompassing role on behalf of nature that East Texas's Ralph Yarborough did. Twenty-first-century Texas ought to carve his visage into the pink granite of the state capitol or at least name a wine or a beer after him, because Ralph Yarborough transformed Texas.

Yarborough became a U.S. senator in 1957, and a boyhood of hunting, fishing, and hiking instantly transformed itself into a legislative agenda. In his first session he introduced a bill to protect whooping cranes and in his second (June 1958) a bill to create a national park on Padre Island, then the longest undeveloped shoreline in the country. Padre became a national seashore in 1962, the same year Yarborough got golden eagles protected from harassment and for his efforts got hung in effigy by West Texas ranchers. Despite the incomprehension his stand generated in Texas, he also became a cosponsor and one of the chief supporters of the Wilderness Act, which established the world's first wilderness preservation system in 1964. The Alibates Flint Quarries/ Texas Panhandle Pueblo Culture National Monument was another success. And it was Yarborough who got the Wild and Scenic Rivers Act of 1968 amended so that the Lower Canyons below Big Bend qualified. In 1965 he introduced the bill to create a national park around the Big Thicket country of his childhood. Passing it required the creation of a new category of parklands—national preserves, which allow more economic use than parks—but four years after Yarborough was defeated (by Lloyd Bentsen) in his 1970 bid for a third term, the 84,550-acre Big Thicket National Preserve was added to the park system.

As for the desert by this time, twentieth-century events had made deserts seem less like wastelands every decade and more and more landscapes of striking ecological adaptations. Since the 1940s the Texas/New Mexico desert had had a name, too—the Chihuahuan—and naming is a first step in understanding. Led by writers and artists, many Southwesterners were now coming to see their deserts as mystical places, the natural symbol of their special immersion in place. For a whole new set of reasons, the time for preserving another part of the desert was at hand.

In creating the second great Chihuahuan Desert wildlands park, NPS officials at first reacted with caution. They pointed out that Roger Toll had thought the Guadalupe Mountains scenically inferior to Big Bend in 1932 and implied that the Capitan Reef might be insufficiently monumental and too near existing Carlsbad Caverns National Park, anyway. By the 1960s, however, Park Service criteria had shifted from monumental scenery to values like geology and ecology, and here these mountains with their great canyons—the two McKittricks and Upper and Lower Dog—full of relict and endemic species, began to shine in a way they hadn't in 1932. And this was, after all, the largest exposed Permian-age fossil reef on the planet.

Guadalupe Mountains National Park is one of those cases, and there are plenty, where the ranchers were heroes for nature, too. Or at least most of them were. (One, Walter Glover, pointedly placed a .30–30 on

El Capitan and Guadalupe Peak of Guadalupe Mountains National Park as seen across miles of Chihuahuan Desert.

his café counter and ran NPS representatives into the street. He's become a poster boy, too, but for the property rights movement.) In addition to Wallace Pratt, whose 1930s opposition had postponed the move for a park, Judge John C. Hunter owned more than 70,000 acres of the Guadalupes. An individual with a love for the desert and a great heart for society at large, Hunter had been amenable to a park from the first, and his position eventually won Pratt over. In 1961 Pratt decided to donate 5,600 acres of McKittrick Canyon to the NPS to create a core area for a future park. Hunter and his son had operated their own ranch more as wilderness hunting lodge than as working ranch, leaving the relict forest uncut and back in the 1920s introducing Rocky Mountain elk to replace the extinct Merriam's elk native to the range. They feared developers and were looking by the 1950s for a conservation-minded owner to purchase the whole 72,000 acres, including El Capitan, Guadalupe Peak, the "Bowl" with its relict subalpine forest, and a chunk of South McKittrick Canyon, with the only trout stream in Texas.

Hunter and his realtor, Glenn Biggs of Abilene, in 1961 decided to see how interested the NPS really was and invited a survey. By now a full team of evaluators did the job Roger Toll once commandeered. When that team reported to Secretary of Interior Stewart Udall in 1962, they recommended acquisition based not just on the range's prior selection but on its ecology and geology and also on a new value, its splendidly preserved wilderness character. Yet once again, as had happened in the 1930s, efforts to persuade a Texan philanthropist like Amon Carter, Jr., or the Rockefeller Foundation, the Moody Foundation, or the Robert Welch Foundation to purchase the mountains for transfer to the NPS came to naught. Fortunately Frank X. Tolbert, the desert-happy columnist for the *Dallas Morning News*, refused to let go of the idea, and he brought the matter to the attention of—who else?—Ralph Yarborough.

No conservationist hero with credentials like Yarborough's could have been unaware of Roger Toll's 1930s recommendations. So despite his interest in East Texas, it was Yarborough who in 1963 introduced S. 2296 to resurrect the 30-year-old plan to create a second Chihuahuan Desert national park in Texas around the Guadalupe Mountains. To deny Texas's millionaires yet another public opportunity to snub their own landscape, Yarborough also became an ardent supporter of the Land and Water Conservation Fund of 1964, which half a century after the creation of the National Park Service finally gave the agency an acquisition budget! The Guadalupes became the first large national park acquired with those funds. Fortunately desert land prices still prevailed in Texas, and the entire extent of 76,293 acres cost only $1.8 million. Lyndon Johnson authorized Guadalupe Mountains National Park in October 1966, and the park opened in 1972. Most of it became official wilderness in 1978.

Stewart Udall, the secretary of interior under Kennedy and Johnson, visited in 1964. A couple of years ago over breakfast I asked him his reaction. "That place just bowled me over," he said. "That transparent desert air. El Capitan looming like the prow of a ship and visible from a hundred miles away. All the geology. And that canyon—what is it? McKittrick? My lord, what a paradise that place is! There was just no question in my mind. It was a national-park-class landscape."

Thank the gods for heroes.

You gotta love the desert. Ten billion creosote bushes just can't be wrong. And you'd better love it, since with global warming it's on the move, aiming roughly at Saskatchewan.

Another desert season—spring this time, one of the great times to worship the desert—and with many a "Yes, the desert" and "Holy shit! This desert!" my companion and I are neck deep in an orgy of desert worship. Six straight days of it—so far. A float with Mike Marks of Texas River Adventures through Santa Elena and the maze of the Rockslide ("through the Mexican Gate, down the Center Slot, around the Dog Nose, in front of the Space Capsule, over the Pour Off"). Then the coasting glide on down the canyon slit. A two-day drive along the 51-mile River Road with the peculiar, recumbent face of the Sierra del Carmen range in Mexico as destination object. Everywhere volcanic rubble and pastel badlands and bestial shapes (the Mule Ears, the Elephant Tusk) surfaced like atolls in an ocean expanse of spaced creosote bushes stitching out across pebbly desert pavement. The world both fore and aft an interleaving of blue planes stretching into opalescence. Now the South Rim Trail through the High Chisos, three days' worth as we start down from an evening of communing with Emory Peak. Tomorrow the Davis Mountains and looking with lust in my heart from the highway over Wild Rose Pass at country I've seen up close only once, by slipping over a fence years ago and outlawing my way through the hills like an Apache. Then the Guadalupes the next day. And White Sands the next.

A desert tour, for sure, but not just any desert, and not indeed the more famous deserts of Austin or Van Dyke or Joseph Wood Krutch or even Abbey, although Abbey did come here for a quick adventure or two. This desert exists unto itself, a specific, never a generic thing. It's the desert of the Comanche moon, of the Seminole patriot Gato del Monte (Wild Cat) who led his people in a nineteenth-century exodus to Mexico, of John Glanton, the fundamentalist preacher, archetype racist and onetime Texas Ranger who killed Big Bend Indians for fun and sport (his gang once slaughtered 250 Apaches near Santa Elena Canyon) and the profit of any nation that would pay him for scalps in the 1840s. It's the desert of the military's great camel transport experiment, whose animals went feral so well we'd have replicated the Pleistocene with horses *and* camels except for the shootists who couldn't resist them.

With its rippling mirages and preternaturally calm serenity, is it a mystical desert? Well, it's certainly a desert full of ghosts, even to the names of the landforms, like the Chisos themselves, a word suggesting danger with a hint of Apacheness about it.

And everyone who comes here knows it as a desert teeming with spirits and devils of every form—ridges, rivers, and mountains, all named

Love your desert: from none to 10 billion creosote bushes in 8,000 years.

devil from the time when good Christians were convinced that nature was the shrine of paganism. Then there are the dancing jackrabbit devils (maybe it's the methyl parathion pesticides stored up in their brains), the tailless burro devils, the rumored devil who appears as a hog with the face of a seductive woman—devils mustered when the unwary drink too much tequila, smoke too much marijuana, eat too much peyote. Then the devils that saturate the desert come and pull at you with their little devil hands. Or *loan* you their hands for a night, as one did me when I committed all those sins and one or two others the first time ever I sat beneath the Sierra del Carmen in my personal year of the devil, which was 1981.

After six nights, or better a few weeks, of sleeping in the Chihuahuan Desert you will realize that this desert is a form that nature has taken to express entire individuality. Poets, philosophers, and recreation professors have all tried to figure out why some of us are sick unto death without nature, some of us ambivalent to it, and some despise and fear it as the ultimate evil. There is no real logic in loving nature and hating civilization, and even less in the reverse and for the same reason: They are not two things but merely one. E. O. Wilson and Stephen Kellert must be right, then, when they argue in *The Biophilia Hypothesis* that there is an evolutionary hardwiring in the human animal to dispose us to love nature and diversity. This they call *biophilia*, a legacy of millions of years of gathering and hunting that has led directly to tree hugging. But our genes gave us an inherent fear of nature, or *biophobia*, too, as in the effortlessness with which your dweeby cousin learns to recoil from snakes and spiders while continuing to stick his fingers in the electrical sockets. We are hardwired for both delight and revulsion. It is cultural context—education, society's values, and access or lack of it—toward nature that creates John Muirs or Woody Allens.

I am a sort of quasi-ethnic redneck from the bayous, but something in the way I grew up nurtured the John Muir rather than the Woody Allen. Since my education and the values I absorbed must be only minimally different from those of my fellow inhabitants of the Near Southwest, I conclude that the reason Texas, particularly, seems so full of Woody Allens must have to do with the success with which Texans as opposed to the rest of us have managed to beat the natural world to submission and to the margins. That has to be the explanation, for how else can you explain ambivalence toward the Chihuahuan Desert? It's a place to go mad for.

It may be, as the title of a recent book on this desert suggests, that even at the turn of the twenty-first century most people continue to think of the Chihuahuan as "barren, wild, and worthless." Wild, yes, but that's high praise. The rest is lunacy. The Chihuahuan Desert is rife with your *paisanos*—your countrymen—those entities with whom anyone claiming nativity to the Near Southwest ought to feel a genuine sense of familiarity and community. On our Chihuahuan Desert version of an Australian dreamtime walkabout, for example, my companion and I are making right-neighborly house calls on literally hundreds of different desert dwellers, every one with a story of migration and survival that outdoes our own.

What I want to say is that those of us who are repeat devourers of the Chihuahuan Desert recognize it as the living refutation of *deserted*. Hot and beautiful, it is spare only to forest-trained eyes. Looking out from the highways across the endless creosote bush flats is to misapprehend. Ignore economics and this desert is a paradise, the most ecologically rich and diverse desert in the United States. Part of the reason is a topography formed both by volcanics and by fossil limestone reefs exposed by intense canyonation. Then there's the wild ride of elevation runs from 1,300 feet (at Langtry) to 9,000 feet atop the Sierra del Carmen. There's also the fact that the northern end of the Chihuahuan hasn't been a desert for very long. Until only 8,000 years ago this country was actually a grassland savannah and a woodland of pines and junipers. Many living relics of that former time remain, along with more than a thousand endemic species across the Chihuahuan that are found nowhere else in the world. Finally, in desert taxonomy this is a moist one, with 10 inches of annual precipitation, the most a country can get and remain a desert.

The short version, then, is that life occurs here in a riotous splendor of concentric patterning based on soil type and slope and the availability of water—naturally—but also on exposure to that broiling sun, perhaps most visibly on elevation. And on history, for Rocky Mountain and Sierra-Madrean floras have warred back and forth across this country for eons, a war that in our time features a Mexican rout of the *Norteamericanos*, who've been chased to the highest mountaintops.

Start, say, at probably the most dramatic spot in Texas, the truncated V where Santa Elena Canyon scallops its way through the Sierra Ponce Escarpment at an elevation of only 2,160 ft. Then by whatever means possible—on foot and with a pack if you can do it, since it's the only way to glimpse more than a fraction—work your way up. Start with the lush thread of the river with its exotic cane and salt cedar and its native willows and cottonwoods. Turn north and enter the bright desert, climb toward the peaks of the Chisos on a trail like Elephant Tusk or the trail up Blue Creek Canyon to join the South Rim Loop. Climb Emory Peak or (because no one else does it and to honor its namesake) Toll Mountain so you're in the 7,400-to–7,800-foot range. Now for a fuller Chihuahuan Desert treatment and because it's there and it's another place in Texas where you *can* climb a mountain, do something similar to what my companion and I are doing on this mid-1990s expedition. Drive 140 miles northwest, to Guadalupe Mountains National Park. Shout a few obscenities and strew a few strategic one-finger salutes at all the posted signs in the Davis Mountains, where a hundred ranchers own 1.5 million acres and the other 20 million of us in Texas own 1,800. When you arrive in the Guadalupes take one of the trails (South McKittrick or Bear Canyon or the Guadalupe Peak Trail) that will get you up to the Bowl or atop Guadalupe Peak, where you'll be above 8,500 feet.

What you've traversed, from the Rio Grande canyons up through the desert to the high country of the Chisos and Guadalupes, are 20 different plant communities. That kind of floristic diversity doesn't happen regionally anywhere else in the Near Southwest, and if you pay attention, it will teach you more about how life finds a way than any book or church that ever existed. That riparian community along the river is an obvious thread of lushness made possible by water. But when you climb away from it, don't take the desert around you for granted: Amidst the rock shrines laid out by New Age desert mystics along the River Road, you'll encounter two different low-elevation desert grasslands—a sacaton community nursed by mesquites and pure colonies of naturally *cloned* tobosa grasses in the basins called Tobosa Flats.

Everything else look like scrub, with only the waving fronds of the ocotillo to spark interest? There are six different desert scrub communities out here, all dominated by a distinctive form of creosote bush with a different number of chromosomes from other members of the genus in the Sonoran and Mojave Deserts. Admittedly any plant that dominates 70 percent of a country is guilty of monotony, but it's *Larrea* that makes the rain-soaked desert smell like a garden of medicinal herbs, *Larrea* that leads the vanguard as the Chihuahuan Desert relentlessly marches northward. Successful as it is, the truly amazing thing about creosote bush is that according to the pollen record, until about 6,000 to 8,000 years ago it wasn't here at all. The genus is South American. The assumption now is that migrating golden plovers ferried its seeds over the Tropics to a Southwest that was drying out and helpless against its invasion.

The additional species that distinguish these desert scrub communities depend on whether the soil beneath your boots is limestone, igneous rock, or sand. Where it's limestone, the additions include lechuguilla, growing like little ground-dwelling banana clumps and diagnostic to the Chihuahuan Desert the way saguaros are to the Sonoran and Joshua trees are to the Mojave. Where there are sandy arroyos or dunes, the additions run to species like the fragrant *Artemisia* called sand sage. Rocky, volcanic canyons add mesquites.

Hike up beyond the alluvial flats, badlands, and bajada slopes into the foothills and you're into another set of communities, beginning with a wonderland of fan-spray yuccas and sotols that are a riot of cream-colored flowers—bouquets on a stick—from March till May. This is the zone where the holy century plants, origin of the liquid essence of the desert (mescal, tequila), commence. For most of their lives the two big

Lechuguillas and an ocotillo, its fronds rising like snakes from a Hindu juggler's carpet out of Robert Hill's "bizarre and shocking" Terlingua Desert.

species of agaves that grow here look like giant, robust yuccas or lechuguillas. Anyone with a lick of curiosity who's even driven through the desert knows the rest. After 40 to 50 years of quietude an agave will evidently develop a tremendous yen for yang and suddenly, almost overnight, erupt a turgid, tumescent stalk that scaffolds garish flowers 20 feet into the air in a kind of trembling, prolonged orgasm. And then they collapse and turn to gelatinous mush within a few weeks. Life's a long, boring summer capped by a frenzied bacchanal, and then you die.

Where water collects belowground, mesquite mottes *(mezquital)* appear as another community, and where it pools in basins and evaporates is still another community consisting of 25 salt-tolerant species (and three genera found nowhere else). Where the soil consists of gypsum outcrops or dunes like those of White Sands National Monument, a community of specially evolved gypsophilous species appears, with four genera and some 70 species that are endemic only to here.

The botanists like to say that the Chihuahuan Desert is dominated by scrub and not cactus, but when you walk, the desert cactus is literally

The life zones of the Chisos Mountains unreel from the floor of the Chihuahuan Desert in Big Bend National Park.

everywhere, from the rivers to the peaks, with almost as many species in the part of the Chihuahuan spilling into Texas as in all the other deserts of the United States combined. Most are low, prostrate, clumped, with many endemic hedgehogs and Turk's heads, claret cups, rainbows, and strawberries, pincushions, and nipple cactus. If Texas has an emblematic cactus, they're the *Opuntias*, especially the prickly pears. I'm of a mind that the otherworldly, many-armed chollas would make a more upright symbol myself but haven't noticed any stampede toward my position. The Austin counterculture might be more inclined toward *Lophophora williamsii* (peyote to the Latin challenged), a species that evidently was introduced here by the Indians. Or maybe the bizarre species called the living rock or star cactus, which remains invisible until touched by moisture.

At about 4,500 feet the great desert grassland zone unfolds, and on igneous slopes and especially igneous mountains like the Davis Mountains it once presented a wonderland that people addicted to hanging out with cows just couldn't get over. That it's a relict community from

the Pleistocene and one that hadn't seen significant grazing for a hundred centuries is the principal reason why putting cows and goats on it
was like adding a bucket of locusts to a flower garden. Unlike the situation on the High Plains, in the desert the 11 grama species that make up
these grasslands lack an understory of buffalo grass as a backup. One of
the modern dramas of the Chihuahuan Desert has been watching desert
species take over the landscape. So look at the cactus and yuccas appreciatively. It's in good part because they're here that you get to hike these
mountains.

On the Blue Creek Canyon Trail in Big Bend the big transformation
begins near the mouth of the canyon; on the McKittrick Canyon Trail in
the Guadalupes it commences within half a mile of the trailhead. What
unfolds as you ascend either are five woodland zones of these desert
mountains. The first change has to be looked for: low sumacs, mountain mahogany, dwarf acacias, and miniature oaks beginning to appear
among the common desert species. They let you know you've entered
what botanists call the montane chaparral. As the trails pitch upward
three different species of junipers join in, along with a startling, silky-
limbed tree that seems to be molting its bark—the Texas madrone, actually a rain forest tree. Another hundred or so feet of elevation gain and
piñon pines, four different ones, begin to dot the slopes, the key species
of this juniper-madrone-piñon community, called the montane woodlands. Pay attention and you'll notice that at this same elevation the
moister, north-facing slopes are now clothed in oaks (nine of them, in
fact, including the chinquapins I grew up with way east in Louisiana)
plus in the Chisos yet another juniper, the drooping juniper, whose
main range is in Mexico. And in McKittrick Canyon, especially, big-
tooth maples, hot red in autumn, join the forest. This is the eighteenth
community you've encountered coming up from the river—the oak
woodlands. In Big Bend it extends right to the top of Blue Creek Canyon
and along the South Rim and in the Guadalupes all the way to the
wilderness boundary.

Two zones remain now, but they occur on only the highest and
biggest mountain masses of the northern Chihuahuan Desert. What you
get in the 7,000-foot-plus range, though, are island relics of trees that
10,000 years ago extended at least 1,500 feet lower down these ranges.
They include the most southerly and most picturesque aridity-sculpted
ponderosa pines in the United States, Rocky Mountain junipers and

white pines, and, at least in the Chisos, towering Arizona cypress. And aspens, like the grove along the west base of Emory Peak. At last, if you top out in the Bowl of the Guadalupes (or get up into the Sierra del Carmen in Mexico), you'll find remnants of true Rocky Mountain forests: Douglas firs and true firs, evergreen Pleistocene pinpricks clinging to the highest, wettest needles of this desert.

Had you seen the Chihuahuan Desert only a hundred years ago, you'd have seen roughly the same floristic world, except far more dominated by grassland. Unfortunately that's not the case with animal life. In contrast to the plants, this is not a desert of large numbers of endemic vertebrates, which must be a testament to its youth. The most typical species represent convergence of animals common elsewhere. Kangaroo rats, pocket and grasshopper mice, and desert mule deer are easterly extensions from deserts farther west. Javelinas and the jaguars that are increasingly showing up in the Chihuahuan these days are Mexican species at their northern limits. Great Plains animals like prairie dogs and antelope were common before the grasslands collapsed, and there are a few Rocky Mountain species (even marmots, once) on the mountaintops. Convergence is the reason the 18 species of bats in Big Bend are the largest bat fauna in North America.

Although the bird life is rich in all these southerly latitudes—California condors nested in the Chisos as recently as 1,500 years ago, and on the South Rim at this very moment peregrine falcons from the largest nesting population in the country are swooping the cliff faces like jet fighters—convergence is true of the birds, too. Only scaled quail, colima warblers, and white-necked ravens are considered characteristic of just the Chihuahuan. Snakes and reptiles naturally are numerous in the desert, and here there are a few more endemics, like the Trans-Pecos rat snake I once tagged along with for half an hour on the River Road. The Texas banded gecko, the greater earless lizard and fringe-footed lizard, and the bolson tortoise are Chihuahuan species, too, although the tortoise is following prairie dogs and other grasslands animals here into oblivion.

What's missing (guess) are the most dramatic species. The naturalist Vernon Bailey closely examined the Guadalupe Mountains, especially Upper Dog and McKittrick Canyons, in August 1901. Among 17 mammal species he noted (by no means a complete list), he found black bears so numerous they'd worn paths to their feeding areas across the highlands. Although he saw neither wolves nor grizzlies, both were there in 1901. Bailey brought in the skull of a wolf and reported the troubles a local cattleman said he'd had with them. He saw grizzly tracks and speculated that they must follow a corridor from the Guadalupes across the Delaware Mountains southward, for the only known grizzly reported from Texas, a whopping male, had been gunned down in the Davis Mountains 11 years before. Cougars were all over the place. The endemic Merriam's elk of the island mountains of the Southwest was then gone from the Guadalupes, although in 1901 there were still white-tailed deer and a few pronghorns.

What the Guadalupe Mountains really teemed with in 1901 were Mexican desert bighorn sheep, probably as many as 300 then, as many as 1,500 across West Texas two decades earlier. Bailey's assistant actually killed a pair at the naturalist's urging. In 1928, about the time the last band of bighorns was seen in Santa Elena Canyon, only 100 were left in the Guadalupes. Twelve years later there were only 25. When Frederick Gehlbach did his survey for the national park in 1960, he found none. Not one. The last two native bighorns ever seen in Texas—two ewes— were glimpsed that same year in the Sierra Diablo range 70 miles south. Thus studies done in the 1970s came up with a total of nine locally extinct mammal species in the Guadalupe Mountains—all (except prairie dogs) the biggest animals around.

What had happened? Everything imaginable. Diseases from domestic and exotic sheep are traditionally blamed as the main cause of bighorn sheep decline and remain a problem in reintroduction, particularly since West Texas ranchers' introduction of African sand goats (aka aoudads)—walking time bombs of pathogens—into the mountains of the region as pay-to-kill targets whose take can't be regulated by the state.

Frankly, though, it was hunting that brought the native sheep to a state of vulnerability. Miners near Van Horn harassed them, and when the bison were eradicated on the High Plains, veterans of the Texas buffalo wars turned their rifles on sheep and antelope, shipping the meat out in refrigerated boxcars. The year Texas finally banned sheep hunting, 1903, Vernon Bailey described how hunters in the Guadalupes crowded 20 sheep against a ledge and killed 18.

As for erasing the other big species, at rancher insistence the fed's Animal Damage Control had mostly exterminated the wolf in the desert by 1945 (the last two were killed in 1970). Gehlbach thinks that "two or three ranch families are responsible for the Guadalupe overkill" of black bears and that the same thing happened in the Davis Mountains earlier. The Forest Service reported that there were still grizzlies in the Guada-

While native desert bighorns struggle to make a comeback in the Near Southwest after being hunted nearly to extinction, introduced aoudads from North Africa not only thrive but are almost impossible to remove now.

lupes in 1909, but in 1931 the last known grizzly of the area was hunted down in southern New Mexico. A remnant of 20 Chihuahuan Desert grizzlies survived in the Sierra del Nido, west of Chihuahua City, as late as 1973. Cattlemen illegally poisoned them with sodium fluoroacetate and wiped out the population.

Thanks to the existence of the parks, since 1990 Mexican black bears have made a dramatic comeback in the Chihuahuan Desert. Desert bighorns yet remain on the San Andres National Wildlife Refuge in New Mexico and in the Hatch Mountains there, and despite all the discouraging setbacks, the desert bighorn reintroduction program started in Texas in 1954 will eventually take hold and return bighorns to the crags of the Texas mountains. Unfortunately, as with the elk herd in the Guadalupes, they won't be the native species, now irrevocably lost. Wolves without doubt are going to lope across the slopes of these desert mountains soon into the twenty-first century.

But someone needs to answer me this question: If private ownership

of virtually all of the world is the grand and divinely ordained thing Texas
has long believed, how could all that charismatic megafauna have disappeared in the first place?

The group sitting around the rising smoke and popping campfire of alligator juniper in the Chisos Mountains in 1928 was mostly from Dallas, and they were heroes of another sort. Young men, they'd found this place a decade before the rest of the Southwest knew it existed, and as artists they intuited that it was something special. One of them—his name was Jerry Bywaters—had recently been in Mexico and had been swept up in the heady regionalism of Diego Rivera and the Mexican muralist movement there, which sought to ground Mexico in its indigenous place and deep-time history. Now he was proposing something similar for Texas and the Southwest. Not an art for elites and the East Coast but—as their literary friend Henry Nash Smith would phrase it—"of the Southwest, for the Southwest."

What began as a discussion around a fire under the wheeling, blazing stars of the desert became Texas Regionalism as it was practiced by Bywaters, Alexandre Hogue, William Lester, Otis Dozier, and many others since. The most interesting thing about it was its distinctive vision. Unlike regionalism in Mexico, which was steeped in class struggle, or regionalism in the South and Midwest, centered on agriculture, the Texas form evolved (and has remained) an art of nature, of landforms, quite specifically and deliberately an art of the desert and life in the desert. That campfire discussion of three-quarters of a century ago has generated a body of wonderful work—Bywaters alone produced 15 major desert paintings between 1934 and 1944—that has come close to making the Chihuahuan Desert stand in the same relationship to Texas that the Sonoran does to Arizona and the Colorado Plateau to Utah.

Thing is, while the desert's power to mesmerize with a beauty that can break your heart may have been the base ingredient, haunting beauty alone is insufficient to create a set of imagery icons for a society. Texas has come more and more to imagine itself as synonymous with the desert because, simply, the desert is the only big public lands part of the state. The desert is what of Texas us river runners, backpackers, nature freaks, artists—all us partisans of the big and the wild and a world left free to run on its own—can get at. The much maligned Texas Parks and Wildlife Department (once infamous for racially segregating its parks and more recently for unwillingness to pursue park acquisitions) has come to shine

Thousands of people a year today experience what Robert Hill struggled to describe in 1899, here near the mouth of Santa Elena Canyon—nothing special amidst the many spectacular canyons downriver, Hill thought.

in one area: taking the desert off the hands of ranchers. So in our own time we get to combine Big Bend National Park's 775,000 acres with the adjoining 99,920 acres of Black Gap Wildlife Management Area to the east—a less scenic part of the desert essentially managed for hunting— and the nearly 400,000 acres of two recent state acquisitions in Big Bend Ranch and the Chinati Mountains natural areas to the west. That's almost 1.25 *million* acres of wild desert before your boot. Add to them the 192-mile Rio Grande Wild and Scenic River and 73,000-acre Guadalupe Mountains National Park. In New Mexico add Carlsbad Caverns National Park, with 40,000 more acres of desert atop the caverns, and White Sands National Monument, with over 145,000 acres of the most beautiful pearly dunes on the continent.

And now, compliments of the UN and the University of Chihuahua, add this: Mexico is working out a plan for a continuous reserve on the south side of the river, El Proyecto Reserva de la Biosfera Santa Elena– Sierra del Carmen, 1.5 million acres extending in a 200-mile strip that will front the complex of preserves in Texas and will include Chihuahua's Sierra Rica range, said to be the Mexican-side version of the Davis Mountains. If we can someday add *our* Davis Mountains to these desert jewels and maybe figure out a way to string them all together with connecting biological corridors, the northern Chihuahuan Desert will be ours again. Not just the biologists' to study but ours to walk, camp in, be moved to rapture over.

Now you understand how and why desert regionalism has succeeded even given Texas's history and politics. Why excellent little art galleries specializing in bioregional art can be found in tiny crossroad towns like Marathon and Marfa. Why in places like Study Butte and Lajitas you can find writers with astonishing libraries living in (more or less) restored adobe ruins indigenous enough to lack running water. Why, if you wish, you can float the Rio Grande Canyons whilst being serenaded by Texas folk singers like Butch Hancock, Steve Fromholz, and Bobby Bridger. Why many Texans know this part of the state better than any other and participate more in its care.

And why Terlingua on a New Year's night captures more of the genuine, source-point, sensuous essence of what Texas is and ought to appreciate than any other place in the state. That's the way public lands work. So *viva* Terlingua. *Viva* the desert. And *muchas vivas* to the public lands, amigos.

5 Sky, Mesa, and Merging with the Llano Estacado

The sea, the woods, the mountains, all suffer in comparison with the prairie. . . . The prairie has a stronger hold upon the senses. Its sublimity arises from its unbounded extent, its barren monotony and desolation, its still, unmoved, calm, stern, almost self-confident grandeur, its strange power of deception, its want of echo, and, in fine, its power of throwing a man back upon himself.

ALBERT PIKE, *Journeys in the Prairie,* 1832

I cannot see a plain without a shudder; "Oh God, please, please, don't ever make me live there!"

W. H. AUDEN

[Opposite: Yellow House Canyon, remnant of the natural High Plains landscape. The place I sought out as home on the Horizontal Yellow.]

During all those inexpressible eons when the snows fell on the mountains, then—melting—dripped and cascaded and surged toward the sunrise, the rivers they formed had no names. Neither did the mountains, the plateaus, the mesas. The mountains and plains throbbed with life and animals then, but none were the naming kind, so that what transpired to shape the landscape proceeded as an undifferentiated flux of processes. One more example that the world scarcely needs *us* around to operate. Self-expression may be another matter.

Namelessness had absolutely no effect on how the rivers did their work, and in their flood times they proceeded to lay sediment loads down in great sheets that splayed 500 miles toward the unending rhythm of the dawns, the sediment layers smothering already existing and older ones until at least six different blankets of them lay in a tilted pile on the sunrise side of the mountains. Linked to the planet's spinning journey around the sun, years certainly had meaning (if no numbers), and roughly 2 million of them ago an interesting thing started to happen. Because the pile of sheets was soft, pooling rainfall along their lower edge began to eat gullies into them, and as the gullies lengthened they began to crawl westward up the sheets. Up, leaving chewed rubble behind them. Up and toward the mountains.

Eventually the walls of some of the different gullies linked, creating an escarpment—for which there was still no name—that gnawed relentlessly westward on the sunrise side of the pile. Other gullies, confronting softer parts, made open-field dashes for the mountains, chewing long trenches up the pile of sheets. Some of these gullies made fairly direct links with the nameless rivers that still dripped the snows off the nameless mountains. By about 100,000 round-the-sun journeys ago, two of the fastest gullies—one dashing directly into the sunset and one that looped up the sheets from the south—had chewed long trenches in the great blanket literally to within sight of each other at the base of the mountains, intercepting all the snowmelt along a 200-mile stretch of upthrust blocks and rounded volcanic cones.

Behind them now the largest remaining slice of the ancient sheets stood walled off and isolated, immense and horizontal. But hardly awaiting a name, or awaiting anything. Just being.

A farm-to-market back road, West Texas, September 1978. Without consulting a map, I am not sure just where I am. It has been two days since I

left the oak savannahs bordering the Texas prairies, gathering up and
moving my paltry possessions to alight 450 miles farther west and 3,000
feet higher up, atop a country like no other in my experience. It is not
the featurelessness of the surrounding plains I find so disorienting. In
fact, the plowed ground stretching away everywhere like a corduroyed
sheet to the curve of the earth is not devoid of features. The surface,
green with crops, seems literally tacked down against the constant surges
of wind by power lines marching away to sink into the horizon. Spindly
silver machinery linked by pipe to industrial-size wellheads crouches in
the fields like an invading fleet of otherworldly insects. Here and there a
tree grove around a farmhouse or the odd windmill futilely challenges
the overwhelming horizontality. It's a scene that probably fills some
hearts with pride and romance. For me it possesses all the appeal of a
parking lot.

Taking in this scene, it comes to me after a moment: What I am
finding so massively disorienting here is the almost total absence of
natural signals. I stand in the grass along a remote highway and listen for
birdsong, look for tracks or trails in the brown dirt, repeatedly suck in
lungsful of air to test for living scent. But except for the keening of the
hot wind surging through a million cotton plants with a sound like surf
and the acrid whiff of ammonia fertilizer, there is nothing, and no
promise of anything. Only the sky, more of it than I've ever seen in my
life, seems natural.

This place I have moved to seems at this encounter a lifeless shell, the
juices and the joy sucked out of it by some immense parasite whose form
is too large to see but whose name I know well. Shocked at this realiza-
tion, I stand in the wind at the edge of the road and spin slowly around in
every direction, like a top, the wonder escalating with each rotation. It is
the vastest country I have ever seen, with the biggest sky, and only the
gods know what kind of power it must have had once. But with its natural
world virtually erased, are vastness and simplicity enough? What quality
can I possibly find here that would make me want to embrace such a
place? How to envision this country in a way that brings me into its
community? How in hell to go native here?

What I moved to in 1978, expecting I know not what, was ground zero of
the Horizontal Yellow. Who knows how many different names it has
been called since women and men first ascended to its slate-top crest,

but for three centuries now it has been called *El Llano Estacado*—the Staked Plain. What little I knew of its reputation in 1978 was linked with phrases like "flattest place on earth," "buckle of the Bible Belt," and "ghastly dust storms." A geographer had described its eastern scarp as a kind of looming shoreline across the plains, and a friend had mentioned the place in connection with the novels of a writer we thought of as a kind of Teutonic Louis L'Amour, the German writer Karl May. But lifeless? National agribusiness sacrifice area? No one had mentioned those. Like most people who come to the Llano Estacado from somewhere far away, I came expecting a West commensurate with that evocative name. What I found was the Ultimate West of Modernist Transformation.

Let me tell you now what I didn't know then. A terrestrial leviathan, the Llano Estacado is too enormous to have its full measure grasped by mere earthlings. But seen from above and from sufficient height, it assumes a recognizable form—the sedimentary version of an irregular, oblong pancake plopped down in a skillet. Look at it on a raised-relief map, and the skillet's left rim becomes the Southern Rocky Mountains. There is no right rim, for beyond the right edge of the pancake the Llano's rivers have eaten everything away. We have names for topographies like this. If they're small enough, in the Southwest we call them mesas. Bigger ones are called plateaus. Huge ones, like this one, can only be conjured by the word tableland.

The Llano tableland's dimensions and vital statistics can be set down on paper easily enough. It sprawls across a whopping five degrees of latitude (from 31 to 36 degrees north) and three and a half degrees of longitude (101 to 104 1/2 degrees west). It is roughly 300 miles north-south by 150 miles east-west, a bit shy of 50,000 square miles altogether. Atop Luciano Mesa on its northwest rim it is almost 6,000 feet above the sea but less than 2,500 feet where the Concho River drains off its southeastern edge. That's a surface slope of only about 20 feet per mile, slight enough to be imperceptible to the eye. Around its wild, ragged perimeter—the rim of the shoreline—the escarpment stands 100 to 800 feet above the surrounding rolling plains, lower along the western and southern scarps, where it's sometimes buried in sand dunes, highest on the northwest and eastern rims, where deep canyons cut the table edge into a wonderland of geology, color, and form.

In the present arc of time the Llano Estacado is not a desert. Just now wild oscillations of climate here in the rain shadow of the Rockies mist it

with an average 16 inches of precipitation a year along the Mescalero
Escarpment (the western escarpment), rising to 20 inches in the Caprock Canyonlands on the eastern shoreline. Four major rivers of the
Near Southwest—the Red, the Brazos, the Colorado of Texas, and the
Concho—gather the infrequent deluges into headwaters atop the table
and dump them through the eastern canyons. Another pair of rivers, the
formative pair, the Canadian and Pecos, skirt the north and west shore-
lines. For most of recorded history the Llano Estacado has been considered ecologically a part of the Southern High Plains, but in our time
Chihuahuan Desert species like creosote bushes and ocotillos are pushing into its sandy southwestern border. Such are the Llano Estacado's
essential statistics in three-dimensional space.

To create the human place called El Llano Estacado requires that
culture and history be added to that space. Who knows what the Clovis,
Folsom, Plainview, and Firstview peoples called the Llano Estacado,
how the Plains Archaics and Plains Woodland farmers conceptualized
it, how much the mysterious Jumano (probably Puebloan) folks missed it
when they were displaced by Athabaskans 600 years ago, whether the
Teyas Coronado encountered (who were likely Wichitas) dreamed of it
as the Eden of the animals? We know it was the heart and soul of the
Comancheria and that as late as the 1920s the Kiowas were still saying it
"comes back to us in wishes." We know that it was named El Llano
Estacado by New Mexicans, who embarked eastward from Santa Fe,
Española, and Taos on trading, hunting, herding, and eventually homesteading expeditions and for 300 years journeyed effortlessly across the
Llano's awesome space, mounting *La Ceja* (the rimrock's "eyebrow")
and confronting without apparent fear the runeless slate extending be-
yond the curve of the earth. And that the Llano was considered a part of
Nuevo México until the Compromise of 1850 accommodated the Re-
public of Texas's pretensions by dividing it between Texas and New
Mexico, a political situation that has existed ever since.

The name *El Llano Estacado* is as satisfyingly mysterious as it is
euphonious. *Llano* (properly "yah-no," a pronunciation downstate Texans need to practice) conveys horizontal earth well in Spanish, but
estacado could refer to anything involving a stake—stakes marking trails
across a featureless surface, the place without trees where horses had to
be staked, a plain pulled so flat it seemed staked at the edges. After
walking 10 miles across a relict Llano prairie on a deliriously hot June

day in 1993, my gut feeling is that the name refers to the Llano's once monotonous prospect of short-grass verdure sprinkled into infinity with the stiff flower stalks of thousands of yuccas. But the truth is that neither I nor anyone else really knows anymore.

The history since 1850 has been a lot less romantic and considerably more coldly calculative. For better than 35 years after the military chased the Comanches, Kiowas, and Cheyennes to Oklahoma and Anglo cattlemen ran the Hispanos back to New Mexico in the 1870s, all this was ranching country and men like Charles Goodnight and C. C. Slaughter were feudal kings. Then from about 1910 until 1930, these last remaining—because they had long been thought the most marginal for agriculture—lands on the Great Plains were privatized through the federal homestead laws and the sale of the XIT Ranch. The big breakout had commenced; row crop agriculture had arrived to the place surveyors only 50 years earlier had pronounced the major uninhabitable part of the Near Southwest.

It's not that the Llano hadn't experienced ecological revolutions before. Many of its animal species, the great Pleistocene bestiary that made the Llano Estacado a form of American Serengeti, had probably been killed off by those first human arrivals a hundred centuries before. Major drought pulses had transformed it into a true desert of drifting sands many times during the long span of time since. And well before the Big Breakout, hunters, ranchers, just plain folks—even the Indians—had engaged in a wildly successful war of obliteration against the remaining bison, wolves, bears, mountain lions, prairie dogs, eagles, and ravens of a 10,000-year-old short-grass ecology.

I've not met many people raised on the Llano Estacado who feel this way, but to someone arrived from another part of the world, if the shooting war was the Llano's nature holocaust, the row crop transformation was modernism's scorched earth mop-up. Since the 1920s, atop its surface the Llano Estacado has lost well over 70 percent of its grass to conversion to cotton, wheat, and sorghum. Particularly on the Texas side of the plain, all that immense carpet of buffalo grass, oceans of blue grama, millions of prairie dogs, and all the community that went with them has been almost entirely erased. From the sacrifice have come cities—Lubbock, Amarillo, Clovis, Portales, Hobbs—universities, libraries, more than half a million people living a pretty well-off American lifestyle, thank you, as the Llano Estacado yields up its life juices to the global market. The general point of view of the present human residents is that the whole enterprise has been a smashing success. The place was resilient enough to survive what was probably a fairly mild drought pulse in the 1930s, although without the grassland community there to inter-vene, the pulse produced a devastating collapse (in human terms) called the Dust Bowl. Those involved in the row crop phase also have been ingenious enough to tap the fossil aquifer lying beneath the Llano, and that Amazonian volume has enabled West Texas and the "Little Texas" Llano of New Mexico to become even wealthier, to survive dry pulses in the 1950s and 1970s, to thrive in high cotton—so long as the water lasts.

Yet the Anglo-American row crop experiment on the Llano has also produced, and as its direct result, an impoverishment beyond measure, one certainly beyond the comprehension of anyone reared to places where nature was never such victim. Simply, few places in North Amer-ica, and none in the Southwest, can match the losses in the natural world that tragically disadvantage the present Llano Estacado. Except along the escarpments and in the canyons, where country too rough to transform has left 10- to 20-mile-wide biological corridors stretching hun-dreds of miles around the plateau's perimeter, wildness has been almost entirely purged from the place.

Perhaps Llano residents, like our fantasy New Yorkers or Angelenos or residents of Mexico City, have spun a way of life that does not need wildness and the native natural world in it. I have often suspected, in my struggle to reimagine the Llano Estacado in a way that could make possible my own allegiance to it, that most of its present natives could care less. Drug them with sports and malls and chain restaurants and you've met the requisites of the good life in Hobbs, Portales, and Plain-view. The problem with such lives is that modernist reality carries with it a future consonant with nature alienation at its core, and here on the Llano that future includes a disappearing aquifer, repeated pounding from droughts and dust, and the return of desert as the global climate warms.

Like much of the world, the citizens of the modern Llano Estacado might find cause to need the old wildness in ways they have yet to recognize.

A century ago a vision quest might have been the only way to grasp the most essential *thing* about the Llano Estacado; today mundane airplane travel will also do it. Fly above the Llano's screaming winds and look down on the toy box geometry of agribusiness's plowed circles and squares or the serrated edges where this plateau breaks off into bright badlands and canyons. From height its historical and cultural ties vanish. What remains is inescapable: This plateau straddling Texas and New Mexico is a distinct entity. Connected to the rest of the world, it nonetheless stands apart. Its topographical life exists in the slow motion of geologic time. It was there long before the two states that claim it existed, and of course it will outlast them, and us.

To employ a new term for an old idea, the Llano Estacado is a *bioregion*, a place where nature has fashioned life-forms and suggestions for living unlike those elsewhere. Having turned the place inside out, we have a long way to go now to re-create an environmentally and humanly healthy Llano Estacado. But there is a philosophy and worldview that might save the place.

I mean the modern philosophy of living in place called bioregionalism. It could be that I am entirely wrong. Perhaps my neighbors in Lubbock and Clovis really don't need contact with the Llano's natural community or a sense that they, too, are a part of nature. The present culture has deeply internalized a conservative and Christian worldview that appears to regard itself as outside nature, with the natural world as superfluous. So it may well be that bioregionalism will play no role at all in Llano Estacado history. But as a 20-year inhabitant who has made a conscious effort to go native here, I have the right to say it: I think, for reason, that the sooner the Llano's Texans and New Mexicans embrace a community sense of place based on the natural world, the sooner this canyonated tableland will regain an ecological and psychological balance dangerously in tilt for three-quarters of a century.

For five years I sought connection to the Llano Estacado through history, and through names. History, particularly the long history of Llano-human interaction going back 11,000 years, gave me a sense of a personal occupation of space as merely a recent bead on a very long string. Which is to say, it inverted any sense of "ownership" between me and the earth. The names were an entry point of a different kind, not just into history, but into familiarity. My names, I realized soon, were not the names that inspired the good Baptists around me, who spoke words like Amarillo, Big Spring, Seminole, Hereford, San Jon, Broadview, Lamb, Dawkins,

A rare native prairie left after the agricultural assault on the Llano Estacado;
native needle-and-thread grasses wave luxuriously in the wind along the rim of
Yellow House Canyon.

Randall, JA, XIT, Bell. Those city, county, ranch names resonated not in
my ears.

But these came to: Running Water Draw, Palo Duro, Courthouse
Mountain, Tucumcari Mesa, Luciano Mesa, Alamosa Canyon, Tule
Canyon, Mulberry Canyon, Indian Creek Canyon, Tierra Blanca Draw,
Dead Negro Draw, Double Mountains, Flattop Mountain, Canadian
Breaks, Yellow House Canyon, Rocky Dell, Landergin Mesa, Mesa
Redonda, Mesa Rica, Cowhead Mesa, Turkey Mesa, Blanco Canyon,
Dockum Creek Canyon, Monahans Sandhills, Blackwater Draw, Sun-
day Canyon, Pease River, Little Red, Wolf Creek, Antelope Creek, Tai-
ban Springs, Permian, Triassic, Trujillo, Dockum, Ogallala.

And these: Side oats grama, sand bluestem, blue grama, buffalo grass,
little bluestem, Tahoka daisy, Indian blanket, basket flower, croton, bee
balm, sand lily, lemon sumac, skunkbush sumac, catclaw acacia, pea-
vine, agarita, mesquite, netleaf hackberry, wild china, Rocky Mountain
juniper, Pinchot juniper, piñon mouse, kangaroo rat, painted bunting,

sandhill crane, canyon wren, scrub jay, yucca, tree cholla, Klein cholla, desert Christmas cholla, stavation prickly pear, candelaria, cougar, bob-cat, coyote, Texas gray wolf, Plains lobo wolf, black bear, bison, and mustang. And Comanche, Kiowa, Apache, Southern Cheyenne, Kiowa-Apache, Pueblo, and Jumano.

But knowing the history and knowing the names are not enough. It has all come to me eventually as this: Knowledge is insufficient in itself to enable humans to open to a place as home. Knowledge is too cerebral. Experiential, sensuous immersion—the way we've always done it—is the path home.

Confronting what seemed a dead world on the Big Flat of the Llano's surface, my only recourse to going native on the late twentieth century Llano Estacado was to go face-to-face with the right-angle verticality of its escarpment. With 750 miles of encircling scarp and hundreds (if someone took the time to count) of canyons and draws trailing down from the bordering rims of the Caprock and Mescalero escarpments, this was where the remnants of the ancient, 5,000-year-old High Plains ecology had retreated to after a century of Euro-American inhabitation. Here, where the horizontal linearity of the plains breaks off into a sud-den, rival linearity of the vertical, what remained of the Llano's ancient natural essence survived in a thin and precarious strip. Having almost all been privatized, scarcely enough of it is accessible to lay a foundation for bioregionalism. But this is all that remained.

Immersion

The top surface of the Llano Estacado is a world where ground and sky constitute the two 180-degree halves of a circle. To approach the edge of the plateau is to effect a 90-degree rotation to the vertical at near warp speed. That first 400 feet of Llano Estacado vertical comes at you in a series of stair steps: across the plain and off the Caprock rim, slide, then off the chalky Ogallala cliff, slide, then off the tan stone of the Trujillo wall, slide, then to the top of the Dockum sandstone, and . . . adios! a final 200 feet of free fall into the abyss, time for a fleeting few last thoughts before kissing the mesquites and boulders down where a stream like the Little Red River flows.

Of course there's a better way to do it, and it's what has brought David Keller and me to this fiery red turreted cliff we call the Big Red Wall,

Caprock Canyons State Park in the canyonlands encircling the Llano Estacado at ground zero of the Horizontal Yellow.

deep in the marrow of Texas's Caprock Canyons State Park, in June 1993. We've come here in the heat and blaze of a summer midday to confront the Llano Estacado as home place. As natives (David was born here; I'm naturalized), we're here for sensuous *inscendance*, spiritual transcendence's opposite. And full inscendance, for us on this day, involves descending that last 200 feet on a rope, our faces inches from the sandstone, acknowledging fully on the level of the senses the way the Llano Estacado stands separate from the rest of the world.

Atop the Big Red Wall there is no mistaking that you are on an edge. Down canyon there is a descending rib cage of cliffs angling into the Rolling Plains, and you know that somewhere out there beyond the curve of the earth the country eventually changes, acquires forests, drains the very waters that spill off these cliffs clear to the Gulf of Mexico. Up canyon the early afternoon backlighting in the Llano Estacado's wettest month gives the country a deceptively green and lush aspect. Now the spires and cliffs seem to be emerging from a spreading green mold. But look more closely and bare rock, bare ground, suspended dust motes in the air all supply evidence of a desert stamp that lies upon the plain above like a lengthening shadow.

The Big Red Wall is actually a fluted sandstone fin with a knife-blade top only about 12 feet across. It grows only a single mesquite and one scrubby sumac, so we drive in two rebar stakes to add an extra margin of safety, do bowline knots around everything in sight, and then toss the rope off into empty space, listening to it *hiiisssss* over the ledge, gaining velocity. David goat-hops around to a point where he can confirm that the end of the rope has reached the ground below. It has, and so it is time to lose elevation. In a hurry.

I am going first. I slip on the harness and double-cinch its belt, loop the rope through the alloy figure eight, and attach the figure eight to my harness with a device rappellers and climbers call a locking D. A raven sails the cliffs, lazing around in the thermals, mustering only a single caw at half-minute intervals. I briefly entertain then dismiss the thought that a harness failure and about three seconds could lift this raven's life out of the doldrums, switch off the depressive and flip on the manic behind its lidded eyes. But actually I've rappelled this and other cliffs here numerous times and know how safe it is.

It is easily a hundred degrees today, and the 3 p.m. wind seems to surge right out of the ground, whining familiarly through the sandstone teeth of the canyon, defying gravity by carrying dust swirls *up* the faces of these brilliant cliffs. To think of heat at a moment like this is diversionary, I have to admit, but it is goddamned hot, almost preternaturally hot, as it seems to be every summer in the Llano Estacado country these days. But I'm all rigged out now, and everything is double-checked, so I back to the edge of the plunge, feel the sun on my back, feel it on my legs and arms. There are three cottony white summer clouds directly overhead. Otherwise the sky is Southwestern blue, the color of turquoise jewelry, and leaning back and trailing my eyes down the long rope as it snakes groundward I am conscious mostly of gleaming, heat-radiating *red*, with a stippling of a strong, pure green that I know is juniper.

The national flag of the Llano Estacado ought to be a tricolor: the deep red of the sandstone escarpment, the deep blue of the blank dome above, and the deep green of the junipers that live here as fulsome adaptation to place.

Then it is into the ether, an extreme interpenetration for the mere
seconds that most epiphanies last, doing the dance that David and I call
"the vertical moonwalk." It is a dance step consisting primarily of great,
hopping, 20-foot bounds in a graced slow motion and in between getting
up close and intimate with rock geology that otherwise can only be
gazed at wistfully, never caressed, smelled, tasted. As I flex and prepare
to spring outward and down the ribs of the Llano Estacado, it comes to
me that our vertical moonwalk is in reality a kind of windup, like a
pitcher's motion.

A windup for what? Why, for stabbing ourselves into that blazing red
earth, of course.

Walter Prescott Webb never used the term *bioregion*, but I have no
doubts that he would have intuitively understood its meaning. With its
chapters on Great Plains literature as well as its well-known paeans to the
adaptive advantages of technology like Colt revolvers, windmills, and
barbed wire to life on the grasslands, Webb's famous classic, *The Great
Plains*, is in some ways a proto-bioregional book. Interestingly, too, when
Webb characterized the Great Plains as a unique North American environment whose defining stamp was its flatness, its treelessness, and its
dryness, he recognized the Llano Estacado as perhaps the supreme
example across the Western plains of all those qualities.

Webb was sort of an academic who, like all of us, was steeped in the
worldviews of the culture surrounding him. And intellectually, that was
a Darwinian worldview that caused him to see human cultures as organ-
isms, shaped by unique environments just as plant and animal species
were. I suspect that Webb would have seen the word *bioregion* as a useful
term for his art. On the other hand, neither Webb nor most contemporary Southwesterners would readily infer from bioregion the philosophy
of bioregionalism. Yet bioregionalism's underlying premises are very old,
because what this late twentieth century American philosophy stands for
is a relationship with nature that links us back to the good green world of
our Paleolithic consciousness. The word's linguistic roots—*bio* ("of life")
and *regionalism* ("of region")—are self-explanatory, but their combination into a philosophy appears to have had its genesis in the early 1970s
with the writings of a Canadian, Allen Van Newkirk. Over most of the
next two decades the bioregional movement has been most closely asso-

Rocky Mountain junipers left over from the Pleistocene beneath the slickrock walls of the Caprock canyonlands.

ciated with California and with the famous poet Gary Snyder, historian Raymond Dasmann, writers Peter Berg and Stephanie Mills, and *Whole Earth Catalog* publisher Stewart Brand.

As set forth in bioregionalism's official publications, *CoEvolution Quarterly* and *Raise the Stakes*, bioregionalism has come to stand for what its head druid, Peter Berg, calls "a kind of spiritual identification with a particular kind of country and its wild nature [that is] the basis for the kind of land care the world so definitely needs." If their occasional congresses, held all over the country (including one in Texas) since 1974, might strike the average resident of the Llano Estacado as a cross between Woodstock and a cowboy camp revival and the participants as a bunch of New Age Pollyannas preaching the jargon of mysti-speak, then reevaluate. Scholar James Parsons, writing in the staid academic journal *The Professional Geographer,* asserted in 1985 that while bioregionalists might *seem* like "misty-eyed visionaries," in fact the movement was attracting "a remarkably sensitive, literate group of adherents" who might well "be the unwitting architects of a new popular geography, a grass roots geography with 'heart.'"

What bioregionalism promotes ought to be attractive, in fact, to anyone on the cusp of the new century who is troubled by the size, the complexity, the sameness, and the impersonal qualities of the world that modernism has built. At bioregionalism's foundation is the argument that humans are after all *animals*, whose evolutionary trajectory for 99 percent of our time on earth has been spent as gatherer-hunters living in bands of 125 to 150 that were deeply conversant with small pieces of the world. Even after the agricultural revolution, generations of related people continued to live in and learn intimately even more limited slices of the planet, and they built up a cultural legacy (primarily transmitted in stories associated with local landscapes) that produced adaptive packages of "captured knowledge" about the settings they inhabited. If our social lives for the bulk of our time as primate species teach anything, it is that staying in place and interacting in small communities is what evolution has prepared us for.

Bioregionalism thus implies that living removed from the natural world, residing in the enormous congregations of people and built environment that are modern cities, eschewing roots in place for endless relocation (20 percent of the American population relocates every year), all lurk darkly in the gut of the modernist psychosis. A fundamental alienation from the natural world that envelopes us, bioregionalism asserts, has controverted human nature as evolution crafted it. Our best chance for animal sanity—and the best chance for the animals, too—is for us to get it back.

Once out of curiosity I asked students in a class in one of the Horizontal Yellow's largest universities whether they grew up thinking of themselves as citizens of the Llano Estacado, citizens of the Great Plains, or citizens of Texas. "Texas," they answered in unison. Just so. In America political boundaries, capitalist consumerism, popular culture, rapid transportation, the disinclination to stay put—and television's tendency to erode regional distinctiveness—have worked hard to scrub clean whatever ecological sense of belonging to place we ever had. And professional history, with its tendency to regard local history as insignificant and interest in place as antiquarian, has contributed to our reduction into a one-shade monoculture where everywhere is like everywhere else.

But think of it this way: "Texas" as an entity may have validity historically, but ecologically Texas is a cobbled-together creation consisting of parts of 10 distinctive bioregions. The Llano Estacado is one of these— the "Texas High Plains Province," as biologists and geographers who have mapped out the state refer to it. The boundaries of these 10 provinces have little really to do with watersheds but with shared ecology and (particularly with one like the Llano Estacado) to some extent physiography. The only real question about the Llano is where the ecological boundaries between it and the Rolling Plains below the plateau occur. Some mapmakers want to include the Llano's canyonated perimeter as a subregion of the Rolling Plains. But the long story of the human animal here argues rather for the reverse, that the Llano and its canyons were always thought of as something like a holistic yin-yang held together by what each contributed. When the Kiowa I-See-O spoke before a crowd of Amarillo pioneers in 1924, he so considered the country: "For a long time it has come back to us in wishes, this great prairie and these beautiful canyons." Note his pronoun: *It.*

A condensation of the ideas in books like geographer Yi-Fu Tuan's *Topophilia* and *Space and Place*, Desmond Morris's *The Territorial Imperative*, Diane Ackerman's *A Natural History of the Senses*, and Winnifred Gallagher's *The Power of Place* explains how affiliations to more abstract political bodies can arise from the territoriality that lies deep in the reptilian cores of our brains. The evidence is that human evolution is so tied to topography, that our multiple senses continue such rich receptors and our brains such vivid recallers of natural signals, that humans in fact react *most* emotionally to smaller and more familiar slices of the world. Our natural inclination of attachments actually occurs on an ascending scale of sizes: to hearth and home most of all, then to locale, and finally to more artificial creations like states and nations. What Tuan calls "topophilia" happens most naturally, given sufficient time and familiarity, in places small enough to be learned well—local landscapes of familiar rocks and soils, the recalled sounds of local birds, the peculiar cycle of seasons, of weather and plants and animal behavior, as we observe them again and again in specific places. A patriotic affection for a historical idea like Texas, New Mexico, or the United States is merely the political and commercial subversion of those kinds of instincts.

Bioregionalists have seized most ardently on what they call "watershed consciousness" as the organizing principle of human attachment to localized nature. They point particularly to nineteenth-century scientist John Wesley Powell's unrealized hopes to organize the American West around 125 to 140 commonwealths based on regional watersheds. In the early 1890s Powell actually produced a series of maps delineating the boundaries of those watersheds, divvying modern New Mexico, for example, into as many as *nine* different commonwealths premised on the way the rivers flow. The country from today's Pecos Wilderness southward across the state into Trans-Pecos Texas, as one example, was designated a potential "commonwealth" centering around the Pecos River and its tributaries. What Powell was attempting to do was to organize the arid West around the irrigation principles that drove Pueblo, Hispano, and Mormon cultures. Even if Congress and the various states and territories were unimpressed (congressmen who heard Powell's presentation on watershed communities called the ideas medieval, un-American, utopian, Russian, communal), he had some valid points. From the perspective of water organization and manipulation, watersheds are crucial in most arid lands, and bioregionalism is probably correct to emphasize them.

But while awareness and care for local rivers ought to be fundamental to the philosophy of bioregionalism, watersheds don't really work as an organizing principle for nature-based community affiliation on the Llano Estacado. The draws and canyons of the Llano Estacado's rivers are powerful shapers of life, but today most of the water that makes human culture possible on the Llano (and, indeed, in Central Texas and many other places in the Near Southwest) comes not from the rivers but from the underground aquifers of the region.

Consider the river that flows by my door in Yellow House Canyon, on the eastern edge of the Llano. The storied stream the New Mexicans named *Brazos de Dios* ("Arms of God") is the third-largest river in Texas. Today's version of it (it was once much longer) is 840 miles long and drains almost 43,000 square miles. To provide a sense of scale, the Brazos is a river twice as long as either the Seine or the Marne and four times longer than the Thames. Down to 1929, when the Brazos River Authority set out to tame and domesticate it, the Brazos *was* the force of an eco-system that in technologically simpler times had tied together the human cultures within its watershed. It did so for the Prairie Caddoans in the seventeenth through nineteenth centuries, and the lower river did so for the Anglo settlers of Texas later on. It was food-giving lifeline, highway, cultural corridor all in one, a connecting ribbon more effective than any artificially drawn border decreed by a state. The Brazos was not only organizing the waters of a vast reach of Texas before we were recording time, it was doing the same with plant and animal ranges and evolution and all the while altering the very shape of the landscape. This force-of-nature Brazos in July of 1899 sighed over its banks to the tune of 9 million dollars in damage and 30 to 35 human deaths and reprised that performance with a flood that in 1915 swept 177 hapless people to their deaths—and, in its amoral way, simultaneously enriched the Coastal Prairie near its mouth with the residue of a broad swipe, like liquid sandpaper, down through the viscera of the Horizontal Yellow.

The reason I am suspicious of watersheds alone as the organizing principle of bioregionalism, though, is that I have some familiarity not just with this river's history but with its spatial and ecological dissimilarities. One part is the Brazos River I left, pretty much permanently, in 1978. This was a Brazos River of fog-shrouded cottonwood bluffs under a moisture-filled steel wool sky, a stream muddy and languid in its Southernness, the ambiance of Tennessee Williams about it. Down at the riverside the banks were rank brown mud and the air smelled like snakes. The bottomlands of this Brazos River were broad, flat floodplains bordered by low, undulating hills. The other Brazos I know is not a single river but a complex of four intermittent creeks fashioning draws and canyons, probably the very "Arms of God" the Hispanic travelers had in mind. This is the Llano Estacado Brazos, and its god must be a very different one from that of the Tennessee Williams Brazos I knew in College Station. Few people pay much attention to this part of the Brazos River: You get the impression that downstate Texans don't really know where the Brazos comes from. But in this headwaters country, the river exhibits a base reversal compared to the lower Brazos. And in spite of the thread of aqueous connection, this High Plains community of life is radically different. Along those 800 miles of river the natural world changes dramatically, from Western steppe to swampy Gulf Coast marsh.

I'm not dismissing watersheds and rivers as ways to imagine ourselves back into Horizontal Yellow nature, but the quintessential land of horizon and yellowed grasslands in the Near Southwest just so happens may be an exception to the rule. Here our best palimpsest for going native may instead be our ecological province, where the connections really exist to what the philosophy of bioregionalism values most: localism (never in short supply in the Near Southwest) wedded to surrounding nature. Or, in other words, ties to a community of nature in a place where the common citizenhood just can't be missed.

A sense of a shared history is supposed to be critical to bioregionalism, but in history as it's been taught and written in the Near Southwest, the fate of the community of nature so far has been virtually ignored. When history assumes that the extirpation of bison, wolves, prairie dogs, and grasslands is an *inevitable* consequence of human existence, then history is acting as a *de*-nativizing process. It does so when it ignores crucial cultural connections as well, such as that inhabitants of the Llano Estacado rightfully owe our allegiance to New Mexico as much as Texas (the downstate Lone Star folks have always smirked just a little too much about the Llano Estacado, anyway). Physiography has something to say as well. By naming the plateau *El Llano Estacado*, seems to me the early New Mexican travelers were using physiography as a basis of uniqueness in a way that makes sense.

Thus the Llano Estacado, a country that physiography and ecology and climate—all the elements that work in nature to create community—as well as the history that connects us both westward and eastward, offers sufficient cause for bioregional identity. Acknowledging that, how then to join up?

Evolution—or perhaps in deference to Richard Dawkins's insights, the *genes* that fashioned me to carry forward their time-capsule messages—

gave me a serviceable body. It does very well all the physical things a male humanoid has been shaped by life in nature to do. Distilled through ancestors carrying my genes, nature has made of me an animal that is light and well-knit, strong, coordinated, quick if not fast as other animals go, but with great endurance. At my physical peak my primate body could run a hundred yards in little more than 10 seconds—fast enough to run down a wounded or injured deer. (I know this because at 17 when I could run 10-flat hundreds I ran one down.) Although my throwing skills were refined by sports, it was a natural primate inheritance that made possible slinging a football 60 yards or hurling a rock-size baseball at 90 miles per hour.

This body that genes made of me interpenetrates the corporeal world and grasps even the abstractions culture teaches me, through the same senses that inform running and throwing. The unmystical truth is that my senses bound what I can know; they define the real edge of human apprehension. My primate taste buds, honed for recognizing toxins in ripened fruits, carry off marvelously the subtle distinctions of an evening in a fine Santa Fe restaurant where a companion and I decadently go through nine courses with a different wine for each on a spring night in 1994. I inhale, in quick burns of neuron sensation that go straight into long-term memory, the split-cucumber smell of a rattlesnake, or like nasal pepper, the expanding oils of a sagebrush frond as I crush it under my nose. The calls of different birds, whose mere voices can summon their images into my head instantaneously, connect me to aural signals that pour in unceasingly. That sense of touch that enabled me to spiral a football is my vehicle to the rasp of Llano sandstone, to the silk of my lover's thigh, to the contours of *aliveness*, delicate but resistant, in the flower top of an Indian paintbrush that I reach down to squeeze of a May morning.

And there is vision, maligned these days as the sense of subject/object (as in "objectification"), the sense that can outrun all the others and thus (so it is said) separate us from nature. Maybe; I have a hard time buying the idea myself. Human vision's apprehension of the world's colors, forms, perspective of distance, its attraction to symmetry and hence beauty—not to mention its response to the holiest of holies, *light*—combine with vision's reach into the world to make it the exalted sense. Its power to evoke, recognized by anyone who has taken a good photograph, exceeds that of any other sense.

One way of saying what I am coming to here is that because the neuron pathways linking the sensory receptors to the brain have a tendency to become "engraved" with habitual use, the visions, tastes, smells, sounds, the very feel of life that enable us to interpenetrate with the world are what make possible going native to place. And because, as Scott Russell Sanders has written in *Staying Put*, "Earth is sexy, just as sex is earthy," this immersion is best felt not just as a neighborliness but as an eroticism, not just sensuous but sensual, too. For those of us living in the Llano Estacado bioregion, an erotic connection to place embodies something like passion for the particular, respect for the familiar, and an unconditional love of the world as nature made it. As with any lover, the key to real intertwining is shared experience.

When bioregionalist philosophers speak about how to go native to place, they often couch their points in questions—as in, "These are the kinds of things a native takes pains to know." These kinds of questions, for example: Where did the water you drank today come from? How many days is it until the moon is full? What are the natural boundaries of your region? Can you name five native edible plants that grow locally? Can you explain the subsistence techniques of at least three of the cultures once native here? What were their populations? What are the different characteristics of the storms that approach from different directions? What are the most common native trees? What are the naturalized exotic trees? What are the common resident, nesting birds? What primary geological events or processes created the landforms? What species have become extinct here, and what happened to them? What are the major native plant communities here? What spring wildflower is consistently the first to bloom? What geological epochs are exposed in the rocks? Were the stars out last night? When is the summer solstice? What does winter solstice mean? What are the plans for massive developments here? Have there been any massive ecological breakdowns in the area in the past century? What caused them? What is the largest wilderness in the region?

About half of these were adapted from Bill Devall and George Session's 1988 book, *Deep Ecology: Living as if Nature Mattered*. I made up the rest to fit local conditions. My gut intuition from living in this part of the world for almost two decades is that put such questions, the huge bulk of modern residents of the Llano Estacado would likely perform pathetically.

Badlands, the landform Georgia O'Keeffe first encountered in Texas and later made the iconic landscape of the Southwest.

Going native to North America is a process that for various reasons has frightened Euro-Americans for 500 years. On the Llano Estacado we have telescoped into a century's time the entire Euro-American experience, and a part of that has been fear of being possessed—possessed by the Indians, possessed by the wilderness, possessed by the animal instincts within ourselves. It is a fear that still resonates and is used here: In a regional TV ad in the early 1990s a local minister exhorted Llano citizens not to stray from their Protestant roots lest they become "just like the animals." The implication is that the religions we brought to the Americas remain a force for extracting us from the natural community rather than healing our alienation from the continent.

If mainstream religion on the Llano Estacado—not only one of the strongest shaping forces here but also an extremely conventional and conservative one—isn't likely to help us in creating a nature-based society, perhaps local stories can. There are stories of people going native here, of course, stories of Llano Estacado seduction—like that of 18-year-old Doak Good, who in 1879 was discovered living the wilderness life in a pole and buffalo-hide house in Yellow House Canyon and who was so compelled, he said, because it was such "a wild, dreary place"; or about Georgia O'Keeffe thrilling to the great forces of Llano thunderstorms and dust storms; about Dust Bowl artist Alexandre Hogue loving the Rocky Mountain junipers as if they were his own kin, which of course they were; of Frank Reaugh painting every grand scene along the Caprock at the turn of the century. What we need are contemporary stories like these, of people who've collected rocks from every canyon around the perimeter of the tableland, or rappelled all the 150-foot cliffs in the Canyonlands, or turned away in disgust from water-devouring manicured lawns and exotic trees and embraced Llano nature by planting native species in their yards. We Llaneros ought to hail as a local hero any poet or musician who writes verse or songs to all the waterfalls along the Caprock, plays a flute or guitar from atop all the mesas, does fasts and vision quests at solstices—or something as simple as chasing a lover through crunching buffalo grass under silvery Llano moonlight.

Quitaque, Texas (that's "Kitty-Kway" to you Yankees), a bleak and snowy January day in 1997, smack in the heart of the country of which New Jersey geographer Deborah Popper (of Buffalo Commons fame, as in returning the buffalo herds to the Great Plains) is supposed to have said:

The Ogallala Aquifer still leaks enough water out of the edges of the Llano Estacado to create springs and flowing water, as here at the falls on Quitaque Creek, but irrigation may kill the Ogallala in less than half a century.

My camp in the canyons of the Llano Estacado, one of the places where the wild survives on the High Plains of Texas/New Mexico.

"This is un-country. It shouldn't be allowed to exist!" Actually, if the Poppers had paid more attention, they'd have recognized Quitaque as an example of exactly the kind of nature-based Great Plains future they're advocating. It struck them as just another bleak and dying farming town. But partly from its own efforts Quitaque is now the headquarters of a small-scale industry of nature-tourism centered on the jewel of a state park in the nearby red rock canyons and a recent rails-to-trails conversion that routes a new, 64-mile Caprock Trail directly through town. It and the nearby burg of Turkey now have bed-and-breakfasts and 50 jobs based on tourism.

On this winter day my companion and I return from the canyons that for two decades Marlboro made synonymous with the mythic, masculine West and search out Quitaque's main eatery. Inside we grab plates and a couple of "Kers" from the serve-yourself bar and settle in around the woodstove with the locals beside an old one-armed farmer sporting a pink cowboy hat, who to establish bona fides points us to a likeness of himself done by Bob Wills's daughter. While we eat and imitate an audience the assemblage grows, and we listen to their stories for hours.

Quitaque represents the vanguard of Llano Estacado bioregionalism in practice, with its own stamp of localism. It even has a controversy: To mounting animal rights activists' dismay, Quitaque celebrates the anniversary of the Caprock Trail by . . . well, by dropping guinea fowl with $100 bills attached over the town from an airplane (it's a bird, it's a plane, it's a bird dropped from a plane). Some of the farmers and ranchers gathered round the stove this afternoon are cashing in on the new thing—one or two offer fee camping on lands alongside the trail, and there are some dismayed references to various experiments on the Llano with organic dry farming. But most of the talk is about how the Ag Department for years has encouraged them to plant fence-to-fence even though everybody with shit-for-brains knows the Ogallala Aquifer is a well that the bucket's already hit bottom in. Farmers on the free-enterprise Texas side of the Llano Estacado, with "right-of-capture" guarantees to use up every drop of water under their land without state interference, have clung to farming the Llano a lot longer than those on the New Mexico side, where pumping limits and wellhead meters were imposed by the State Water Engineer in the 1960s. The result is that one farming area after another on the Texas Llano has used up its water and now depends for survival on the Conservation Reserve Program: your tax dollars paying farmers to do something that shocks even them—returning their farms to grassland. This January of 1997 the future of the CRP is in doubt; our friend in the pink hat assures us that without its continuation, they will all be destroyed.

The future of the Llano Estacado? These grandsons of the farmers who broke out the tableland are still shocked and unbelieving at how it has all happened, and they are still pissed at the rest of the state for refusing back in 1978 to fix the whole shebang up proper by pumping water up from East Texas, building big storage reservoirs in the canyons of the Caprock, and making sure that the Llano Estacado Ag Empire lasts at least as long as the Roman Empire.

On this snowy day in Quitaque, though, as the beer flows and the fire pops, there are other things to think about than where to go from here. As we rise and say our good-byes a quiet fellow who'd been listening and watching and catching pure hell most of the afternoon for his Elmer Fudd hat delivers this bit of sum-up, earthy bioregional wisdom.

"Boy, I was you I'd say to hell with all this crap and take her home and rear up on her and snort in her flank."

Who cares whether a bunch of Republican, fundamentalist farmers and ranchers on some remote plateau out in the middle of the plains ever takes to heart a weird environmentalist credo? Perhaps finally becoming true natives of local places, learning (and learning from) the local plants and animals, feeling some religious tug toward the diversity of life as it evolved regionally, creating art and cultures and economies that are different from those elsewhere and as local in feedback loop as we can make them won't have anything to do with the future of North America at all.

Perhaps, but I don't believe it. And the reason the Llano Estacado is important to this process is because this is *the* ultimately marginal country, the place where modernism's and capitalism's assault on nature and localism has become more apparent more quickly and more completely than almost anywhere else. Mechanized agriculture has used the Llano Estacado up in only a single century. Then there's this: If the Llano Estacado—a place presently so alienated from nature that its major city (Lubbock) once advocated to the EPA that the local feedlots clean up their stench by wiring Re-Newz-It air fresheners to the fence posts, canceled Earth Day festivities in 1996 as trumped-up scare tactics, regularly darts and removes *deer* that wander into the city, and cannot grasp the simplest of ecological connections (with its vast, surrounding farmlands lying utterly bare and exposed in the spring, it is still de rigueur in West Texas to blame dust storms on . . . New Mexico!)—if *this* place can embrace bioregionalism, then there's hope for America after all.

There are ways to shift toward bioregional thinking, and despite Lubbock, some are already under way on the Llano Estacado. Since the early 1990s a pair of progressive Catholic priests in Hereford, Texas, Fathers Daryl Birkenfeld and Jerry Stein, have held annual bioregional conferences on the Llano through their Promised Lands Network. There is more appreciation recently of regional writing and art about nature and place; because of its healthy traditions, music is probably the best venue for a Llano Estacado sense of place. But despite all the singer-songwriters famously emanating out of Lubbock, there is only the barest beginnings of nature-based folk music from the region. Problem is, there's some urgency. With its natural world sacrificed to the national market, today 55 Great Plains species are threatened or endangered in the United

States, with a whopping 728 grassland candidates up for those listings! Plains bird species suffered a sharper population decline (25 to 65 percent in the 1980s) than any other single group of continental species. Modernism's war on the Horizontal Yellow is not just a thing of the past. It continues.

Don't misunderstand. This is not an idea for substituting one kind of *political* layer for another; I'm by no means advocating a "Republic of the Llano Estacado." But fully expressed bioregionalism does imply significant changes, not just in mind-set and education but in fundamental terms like land ownership, public access, and nature restoration. Given the agricultural fact of the modern Llano economy, the best basis for the Llano Estacado bioregion to develop as an environmentally grounded society is to push hard for more public wilderness preserves to restore the natural diversity of the plains. In other words, the Llano needs what conservation biology calls "a regional network of preserves"—a mix of small and large ones and as many as possible—linked by connecting corridors into an encircling ribbon of wildness all the way around the rim of the tableland, where the old plains natural world can flourish once again. And where more of us can experience and be motivated by what is, after all, a spectacular country of stupendous natural forces.

It was a tragedy of regional history that the National Park Service in the 1930s failed to get either a national park or a monument established around Palo Duro Canyon. In a 1991 study, though, Oklahoma historian Dennis Williams demonstrated that such a wilderness park aimed at returning the extirpated large animals native to the Llano—bison, mustangs, wolves, bears—is still a feasible, if difficult, $10 million project. Llano Estacado society is truly crazy if it opts for a Disney-type Wild West theme park in Palo Duro rather than an authentic and noble project like a Palo Duro wilderness park. It's a decision that will be a measure of the maturity and intelligence of the place.

Bioregionalism on the Llano Estacado has to aim at little targets, too. More New Mexico and Texas state parks here—like the 70,000-acre one Texas Parks and Wildlife may be able to get spanning the High Llano down to the Canadian River along the New Mexico line—beg regional activism. According to TP&WL officials, citizens of the Llano Estacado are right now more favorably disposed toward parks than Texans anywhere else in the state—pretty faint praise, of course, but something to act on. Playa lakes critical to migrating birds need designation and

protection. The Conservation Reserve Program should be a permanent policy to continue the restoration of the grasslands, but in native grasses only, the ones that evolved and work here. And since the bulk
of the Llano is going to remain in private hands in our lifetimes, the
region literally cries out for land trust activity in establishing conservation easements.

To be loose with an Aldo Leopold idea, of what avail is a land ethic
and bioregional attachments unless there is some remaining natural
community to which we can attach ourselves?

June 21. Summer solstice, one of those infrequent ones when the life-
generating force of this longest day of the year is converging with the
power of a full moon, which this raucous crowd of 50 or 60 people ex-
pects to see drifting up over Turkey Mesa in Yellow House Canyon
within minutes. We've just finished a free-form sunset dance around a
circular rock medicine wheel perched up on the lip of the rimrock, properly setting the sun back on its northward course across the horizon and
ensuring that the earth continues to cycle through the seasons—a heavy
responsibility. We've read a bit of poetry. And we've conducted an infor-
mal Llano Estacado Council of Beings ceremony, with various folks
speaking on behalf of various regional constituencies—mesas, rivers,
rattlesnakes, tarantulas, coyotes, the unceasing wind—that normally get
neither representation nor respect on the Llano. Who knows whether
the snakes and spiders approved, but midway through David Keller's
evocation of "Coyote del Llano," the local coyotes chorused in with
what was widely taken as an amen.

Now that the ceremonies are over, it's time to break out the tequila
and the regional wines, marvel at the geometric canyon silhouettes—
circles, planes, triangles—just now washed in the blue glow of lunar
twilight. And at the striking vision my companion cuts in her red velvet
dress, cowboy boots, and summer-brown skin. All manner of entertaining weirdos are here, too. Over there is a famous good old boy nature
photographer who lives in a West Texas jail, holding forth to a couple
from down the canyon who make fine regional furniture. The folks all
bent over at the waist are from the local native plant society, and the
lanky fellow in the duster is spiritual adviser to a contingent of native
artists who've done the typical self-exile to Austin. The guy with his
hands on his head, Aggie style? He's the winemaker at Cap-Rock Win-

ery, and who he's lying to so expansively is the editor of a magazine about the Llano Estacado and the local priest who earlier blessed our medicine wheel with Cuervo holy water. Over there, in boots and underwear, is the legendary sculptor of bronze shamans based on the rock art of the Pecos River, who's most notorious among this group for being the co-inventor of the Go-Cooker ("a baked chicken in just 50 miles, courtesy your own muffler!").

We've also got your marketers of organic cotton tampons, and those are your employees in the local health food industry who are manning the margarita keg. The undifferentiated ones are mostly Lubbock Lake Site archeology grunts, along with a few academics coaxed out of the local suburbs. Hard to keep 'em straight, of course, with everybody wandering about from fire to fire, listening to Andy Wilkinson sing about Rayado, the famous New Mexico racehorse, or the Yellow House Ramblers evoking Georgia O'Keeffe in West Texas, or Eddie Beethoven do one of the best songs ever written about the Llano, "Blame It on the Wind." But down in the draw, where the sweat lodge is covered, the rocks are glowing, and the tub is all full of cold Ogallala water that's reflecting the stars? Just a local museum curator, seeking recruits for a sweat and maybe a little innocent naked campfire dancing.

Who knows whether such earthy celebrations, which have been going on for close to two decades now in Yellow House Canyon, have any impact on Llano Estacado bioregional sensibilities. When I bought this little slice of the canyon in 1983, I'm certain none of us had ever heard of bioregionalism; few of us had any idea what the summer solstice was, either. It's all been pretty much instinctive, propelled by the alienation from nature so visible everywhere in modern life on the Llano. Yet however marginalized this crowd of lovely eccentrics might seem, they're a core of Llano Estacado partisans. Change from within has begun this innocuously more than once.

One ringingly clear winter predawn in the 1990s, with Jupiter a spinning, molten throb in the southern sky and the slate-smeared moon listing into the rimrock, I am awakened by a feeling as sharp as a knee in the gut. Shamans and artists have forever known that it's the moment at which light lasers over the horizon that the sun is god, but fear of missing the divinity of the sunrise is not what has roused me. I have been dreaming.

My personal spot for going native to the Near Southwest, in Yellow House Canyon at the head of the Brazos River, near Lubbock, Texas.

Outside, I set a bowl of smoking coffee on a banco and sit, leaning my back against the sandstone scratch of the adobe walls. Sunlight rolling up over Texas seems to gather into a point behind the mesa that dominates the sky east of my house, obliterating its familiar angles in suffused yellow halo, and something in the coloring suddenly brings back my dream in a rush of images, snatches of thoughts and reactions—the subconscious anguish that awakened me.

Two decades of simultaneously marveling at the power of the Llano Estacado while hating what has been done to it have put me in a strange and complicated position. I have never experienced a part of this earth where the emotional content of nature's forms and colors is so simple and elegant and direct. And yet, to anyone for whom the excitement of a *complete and accessible* natural world is rudimentary, necessary the same way that beauty and sex are necessary, the privatized Llano Estacado of the contemporary agribusiness experiment is the most endlessly frustrating and depressing region of the Near Southwest. In my time, knowing Thoreau's entire heaven and entire earth on the Llano requires too much imagination and too much exorcism of the ghastly. Too much trespassing. Too much anguish for wolf howls, the visual rapture of bison overspreading a canyon from rim to rim, the loss of fear in the presence of lions or grizzlies.

I'm not sure about you, but I am entirely convinced that I, at least, am alive and conscious of the universe around me but once, and now is it. So if the generations before me, including my ancestors, have so remade this part of the world that my sensibilities cannot bear it, that full immersion into place-based nature simply is not possible here, then what? Of course, try to restore its power; restoration to make the continent whole again will be the great conservation theme of the twenty-first century, and it's a noble enterprise, worthy of a life. The problem is that creating a successful system of preserves and restoring nature in a place as damaged as the Llano Estacado is going to take more lifetimes than those of us alive now have to give.

My ancestors have been creatures of place in the Near Southwest for nearly three centuries, and there's nothing I respect more. But after 20 years, living on the Llano Estacado has made me a man of dreams. And maps.

6 Inventing the Southwest in Abiquiu

I have never experienced anything like New Mexico. . . .
the fierce, proud silence of the Rockies . . . the desert
sweeping grey-blue . . . the pine-dotted foot-hills. . . .
What splendour! . . . Never is the light more pure and
overweening than there. . . . In New Mexico the heart is
sacrificed to the sun and the human being is left stark,
heartless, but undauntedly religious.

D. H. LAWRENCE, 1926

. . . The desert . . . seems to be a painters country but God
knows nothing worth speaking of has come out of it yet—

GEORGIA O'KEEFFE, 1931

Historically, the seizure of the commons—east or west—by
either the central government or entrepreneurs from the
central economy has resulted in degradation of wild lands
and agricultural soils.

GARY SNYDER, 1991

[Opposite: The cliffs of Ghost Ranch, which Arthur Pack's misfortune made into
Georgia O'Keeffe's backyard in the 1930s.]

202 Driving north on U.S. Highway 84 up from Santa Fe, warily eyeing the traffic boiling around the string of new Pueblo casinos, I am having an argument in my head that I think, since I'm judging the thing, I ought to be winning.

Me: It won't do to dismiss climbing a mountain out of hand as an arrogant and peculiarly male desire to conquer nature. There is, after all, the question of knowledge. Was Petrarch committing a sacrilegious act against the Alps when he scaled Mont Ventoux in 1336, attempting to resolve his arcane little academic debate about the distant landmarks that could be seen from its peak? And what about aesthetic inspiration, the (very probably) genetic thing among us upright primates that altitude equals beatitude? What about mountains as ladders of transcendence to the spiritual, as in Paleolithic art, Taoism, Mount Rushmore, for chrissake? As for the implied link between testosterone and "topping out," what the hell about Elizabeth Bird, et al., and a third of the female population of Colorado?

The opposing voice doesn't win these arguments so consistently by sitting there sipping wine and looking bemused while I flounder. She's got plenty of arguments of her own—detailed cosmologies of goddess religions whose earthy priestesses sought out caves, not peaks, for instance. And today as I drive to Abiquiu, New Mexico, I'm recalling all of them in perfect clarity. In fact, this little cerebral joust I'm holding as I'm dodging the gamblers is actually a reprise of a sweet reunion with an old girlfriend the evening before, an old girlfriend who just happens to have lived for the past two years in the shadow of the mountain I innocently announced I was about to climb.

The mountain is the Chama River Valley's crowning pinnacle, the angled, mystical, and famous 9,000-foot-plus peak called the Pedernal. And cocktails in the Pink Adobe and the follow-up meal in a restaurant a little too proud of its cuisine and its clientele ("Look, Gene Hackman. No, don't *look*. Jeez! Kevin Costner was in here last week, you know") were devoted to trying to talk me out of climbing it. Kate's argument for appreciating the Pedernal from a distance but not profaning it by an actual ascent didn't rest on the Taoism the idea sounded like to me but on feminist principles. The woman has always been at her best at puncturing my illusions. Innocent drone, I thought I was about to climb the mountain *on* feminist principles. I want to do it because of Georgia O'Keeffe.

Summer storm cell echoes in inverted form the shape of the Pedernal, Chama Valley, New Mexico.

Now, playing the spirited exchange over in my head in that brilliant New Mexico light that exposes all, I was squirming a bit. Because of O'Keeffe, yes. But it's more personal than that. Georgia O'Keeffe is one of my heroes, and I'm too critical to have very many. I've studied her life on my adopted ground in Texas, where she fell in love with a country few others have loved. I've admired her penchant for living remote and for immersing herself in place. I've also been struck by our pure coincidence of shared topography. Not just canyonated and hot-colored Southwestern settings but actually living in the shadow of a slanted, flat-topped mountain, a powerful and simple earth anchor that forces you to pay attention. Turkey Mesa out my door is a miniature Pedernal that I've used as a base from which to understand the Southwest. I know she did the same, and for all those reasons (I keep arguing) the Pedernal has called to me for at least a decade.

The Pedernal is something else, too. O'Keeffe's Rancho de Los Burros was scenically sandwiched between this mountain and the soaring, striped cliffs rising from the grass 200 yards behind her home. She painted those cliffs and much else of the world here. But the Pedernal became something special, a mountain God might give her, she said, if she would just paint it enough. And as she did with so many of the landforms and life-forms and light forms around the little Hispanic village of Abiquiu, O'Keeffe made table-topped mesas like the Pedernal known worldwide as a defining icon of an emerging geographic place in American culture. More than John Wesley Powell or Mary Austin or John C. Van Dyke or the Taos Society—or Kenneth Hewlit or Mabel Dodge Luhan—more than anyone else, O'Keeffe used her art to draw in our heads a good part of the definition of our modern "Southwest." Here along the Chama River, where the waters that shape and define the Horizontal Yellow have melted down from the Continental Divide for 20 million years, an Irish-surnamed woman artist from Wisconsin created the Southwestern landscape in the world's mind.

Village limits of Abiquiu, a place even New Mexicans often can't locate or pronounce (in a country-western song it could rhyme with barbecue). I have my gear and am heading out into the nearby desert to make a base camp, but I stop at the Abiquiu Inn and ask to use the phone. Kate hasn't talked me out of the climb, but I'm unnerved enough that I've decided I need someone along. A woman, preferably. I call back to Texas.

When she answers, I explain that I thought I might tell from the view atop the Pedernal how close to the reality of this place O'Keeffe got. She agrees in the possibility.

Bode's Store, Abiquiu, on a thunderstormy morning in late June 1995, the lint from the big female cottonwoods lining the Chama swirling by the gas pumps on the wind, bound for the stratosphere. Camping by the river over where the Chama's multihued gorge breaks into the west side of this broad valley the Hispanic pioneers called *Piedra Lumbre* ("Fire Rock"), I've risen early and driven the 15 miles into Abiquiu for supplies. But despite the long-standing trading tradition in the Abiquiu country (the old *camino real* to California laid out by Dominguez and Escalante in 1776 brought horses, pelts, and Indian slaves into New Mexico through the Chama Valley; there were eight merchants here by 1830), today Bode's and Trujillo's just up the road about it. Obviously I've arrived too prematurely even to replenish my water or air up a low tire. Not only are Bode's doors double and triple bolted, but everything normally left lying around a service station—pails of water, paper towels, air and water hoses, even the trash cans—has been locked inside for the night.

At precisely five minutes of seven, pickup trucks of every creative hue and custom design come skidding into Bode's. Their occupants, mostly young men from the local villages, step out and wander about, exchanging greetings, eyeing the *estranjero* briefly. At exactly seven Bode's front door swings open.

Beneath a poster print of Maria Chabot's wonderful photo, "Women Who Rode Away," I pay for my supplies, pay for my gas (in advance, of course), stroll outside, and fill my tank. When I'm done, I put the Jeep in reverse and begin to back up to the air hose.

Suddenly there is a tremendous whack on the side of Jeep. I jam the brakes, cut the engine, and get out, and as I do, another startling slap—*whack!*—rocks the car, and a young man I'd noticed eyeing me inside the store emerges into view and jabs a skinny finger in my direction. Cottonwood lint corkscrews by in eddies.

"Hey, *chingaperro*, watch wha' the hell you doing!" I step away from the car, confused and trying not to get angry before I know what this is about. Clarification isn't long in coming; he gestures at a shiny blue '70s model pickup at least 50 feet away. "Back into my ride and you gonna remember this day." With that he spits, whacks the side of my Jeep once more with the flat of his hand, and turns to stalk away. Five steps into it he turns, lets out a shout, and makes a one-step lunge in my direction. I fail to respond to the feint. Seeing this, he laughs to himself and stalks away to his pickup without a backward glance.

It's only 10 minutes down the highway from Bode's to Ghost Ranch, and there are trails there I want to hike and scenes I want to photograph today. I load the big Pentax while I'm driving, all the while keeping a real careful lookout for any pickups I might accidentally bounce off of.

Estranjero literally translated means "stranger," naturally, but in the mountain villages of northern New Mexico the term in the vernacular really means "someone whose kin ties are unknown." In the Chama Valley, that would be me. In a weird way that the residents and I both sense, I am connected to them, yet detached by a gap that will never be bridged and not just in the way that a stranger can never grasp a local's sense of place. My roots, too, spring from a colonial Spanish adaptation, in my family's case the Bayou Pierre country of Louisiana, 800 miles to the east. But the men of my family for a very long time apparently have regarded themselves as cross-cultural ambassadors. And being less remote, Louisiana offered possibilities that New Mexico didn't. In the early nineteenth century my male ancestors began marrying into the local French families, and the pattern stuck. My great-grandfather married an Italian girl, my grandfather a good Dutch-Irish woman, and my father an English-Scots lass from Arkansas. The Spanish language and the Catholic religion disappeared in my family a century before I was born, washed from my family's palate by French names and Celtic sacraments. Looking at me, these Abiquiu Hispanos intuit that I am remote kin but that they were long ago lost to me. They eye me the way a pack of wolves looks at a collie.

I look on them with utter fascination and know that it is not mutual.

I come to this place—a basin of many names: Piedra Lumbre and Ghost Ranch and Lower Chama Valley and simply Abiquiu to most Southwesterners today—because of a kind of religious conviction. Not, for me, the Presbyterianism of the Ghost Ranch nor the faith of the urban-bound Penitente returning to a home *morada*. Nor as a member of Dar al Islam and the mosque up at Plaza Blanca on the north side of the valley or even a Benedictine acolyte at the Christ of the Desert monastery up in the Chama River Gorge. I represent a more secular congregation but a numerous one, the members of which feel a certain passion for the idea of the Southwest. Chipping away at the origins of that idea, we recognize—or based on that list I just compiled we ought to—that this out-of-the-way place up the Chama is actually a form of sacred space, a place at the core of the idea.

In any hard thinking about what the Southwest entire is or has come to mean, Abiquiu has to be placed alongside Taos, Santa Fe, and Tucson as natal center. The element that Abiquiu has contributed is the intertwining of a particular genre of *scenery*, actually found across much of the West, with the regional idea called *South*west. In Abiquiu's case, the interpretive lens was provided by an eccentric woman artist whose eye mostly ignored history and culture as interferences with her personal reaction to nature. For the idea of *the Southwest*, a region that is gradually replacing the more general *West* as dreamland in American culture, Abiquiu is where region became synonymous with topography.

Here at the turn of the century it still matters little that since the 1960s there has existed a competing vision of what Abiquiu and its surrounding region ought actually to mean to American culture. But it should, because as place visions go, this one has much in common with an Alamo or a Wounded Knee.

28 June 1995, 2:30 p.m., with a light rain falling outside the open window of my room at the Abiquiu Inn, to which I've retired for a shower and dry accommodations after a couple of nights under the stars and the thunderstorms. Among meteorologists the Chama River Valley is known for a higher frequency of summer storms than virtually any other part of the continent. While I know the surrounding mountains may get as much as 35 inches of precipitation in a good year, the canyonated Ghost Ranch country I've been hiking through only gets about nine. That's less than the average in the Chihuahuan Desert far to the south. Booming storms and downpours and the vicious little bastard gnats that swarm up out of the needle-and-thread grass like an army of nano–Tasmanian devils don't seem a chapter out of a desert. But I know they are.

I am fairly immersed in Georgia O'Keeffe. Dinner I took with my friend Rose Gutierres, desk manager of the Abiquiu Inn, who a couple of years ago gave me directions to the White Place and the Black Place and had offered tips on how best to climb the Pedernal. Rose is a Californio by birth, but around 1970 she and her husband bought 40 acres on an 8,000-foot mesa south of the Pedernal, and she's lived there ever since. A friend to Maria Chabot, the Oxford-educated Texan who was O'Keeffe's girl Friday during the 1940s and '50s, Rose reflexively refers to Georgia as "Miss O'Keeffe," and every time I'm with her I fall into the habit myself. I also find myself absorbing Rose's respect for Maria Chabot and sharing her astonishment that the Texan Chabot was actually elected the mayordomo of the Alcalde ditch—the only ditch *madre* she says she's ever heard of in Northern New Mexico. "She was herself one of those strong women," Rose tells me, "one of the women 'who rode away' and came out here."

Even my schedule this morning has been O'Keeffe-like. I woke at five and by daybreak was on the trail up to Chimney Rock, the sandstone spire soaring skyward northeast of O'Keeffe's Ghost Ranch house. As the sun rose into a flawless desert sky and the shadows retracted black claws across the country, I was skidding down a red-and-purple slope of shale and mudstone and ambled about a few hundred yards east of her house, in the Chinle badlands that O'Keeffe named the Red Hills. Collared lizards ran, iguanalike, across the granulated brick red earth humping and rolling beneath my feet. The Red Hills is an exceptionally erodible and riveted badlands, I'd noticed, and not so unvegetated as I would have thought from the paintings. From time to time I'd glanced up at the slanted blue profile of the presiding Pedernal and wondered if it really is a *cuesta*—a mesa with one end higher than the other—or if, like my own Turkey Mesa in the West Texas canyons, the intriguing effect is merely illusion. A topo map could answer that question; my plans are for a more intimate ciphering.

But not just yet. This June dawn I stood engulfed by a place whose essence O'Keeffe tried to grasp and in her grasping made into one of the most inspiring landscapes on the continent. The real-life scenes of her paintings were everywhere here—the desert varnish streaks of waterfalls, the horizontally striped rose, saffron, and buff cliffs—the "Cliffs Behind Abiquiu," from the painting of that name. They were all right out her door.

There are those—and it seems to me that all of O'Keeffe's biographers are guilty, perhaps especially Roxanna Robinson—who find this country bizarre, garishly colored, hard, difficult of "possession." It's a landscape, Robinson writes, that "ought in fact to be extravagantly tasteless, vulgar, and unbelievable." Spoken like an Easterner. John Van Ness and Paul Kutsche, who authored a sociological study on the local village of Cañones, have written that in the 1960s local schoolchildren here were using a geography text with a chapter called "Deserts" that relied on a photo much resembling the Piedra Lumbre landscape. The caption beneath: "The desert is a nice place to visit, but I wouldn't want to live there, would you?"

In fact, those kinds of reactions to the far edge of the Horizontal Yellow are the most common ones as far back as the nineteenth century, particularly by travelers whose previous nature experiences had been woodland or even prairie. The seared lower reaches of the mountains where the rivers drain eastward off the Southern Rockies were not quite so horrifying to pre-Mary Austin observers as the Chihuahuan Desert was. But particularly here in the northern Rio Grande drainage, where the 60-mile-long Chama cuts a gorge exposing the vitals of the Colorado

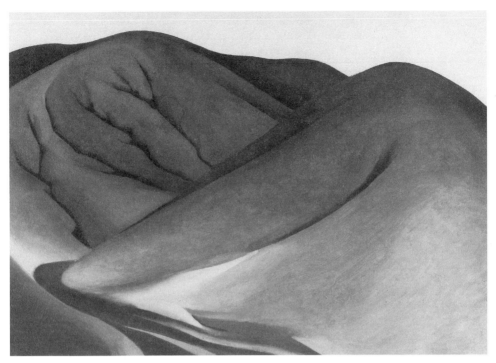

The spell of Abiquiu which magnified O'Keeffe's beloved Palo Duro Canyon.
Red Hills, Grey Sky Yellow *by Georgia O'Keeffe courtesy Anschutz Collection,*
Denver, Colorado.

Plateau, canyonation in sandstones and mudstones accentuates desert
qualities over mountain ones. Even O'Keeffe, as was her way, dissem-
bled when she told people about the Abiquiu country that she'd "not
seen anything like it before."

O'Keeffe's biographers may believe that. I don't.

With all respect to O'Keeffe's biographers and to those many afi-
cionados of her art who believe that she found here *a wholly unique
landscape* and that its presence defines *where* the Southwest is, actually
this Abiquiu country would not strike many Westerners as so unfamiliar.
And despite her own insistence that her "beautiful world" was singular,
in fact there is ample evidence in both her art and letters showing that
O'Keeffe understood well what Abiquiu *really* was: More than anything
else it was Texas's Palo Duro Canyon, the place of her original Western
infatuation, drawn on the larger scale of the Farther West.

The confluence between the Canyon, Texas, world of 1916–17 and the Abiquiu world after 1929 is so obvious to me, I think, because I share with O'Keeffe some deep experience of both. What she discovered in the canyons and badlands of the Texas plains during the Great War years, I discovered and went native to in the 1980s, building an adobe home in a pink-and-buff canyon with striped cliffs behind the house. O'Keeffe's fascination with high-powered Western light, her attraction to the simple curvilinear forms fashioned by erosion and aridity, and the soaring of her spirit at hot-colored soils all have their origins in her weekend trips into Palo Duro Canyon when she was in her late twenties. Some kind of conscious disconnect is required not to see the linkage between the New Mexico paintings and the early watercolors *Red Mesa* and *Canyon with Crows*. And now the newly discovered collection of 28 unknown Texas watercolors (published in Barbara Bloemink's *Georgia O'Keeffe: Canyon Suite* and on exhibit when the O'Keeffe Museum opened in Santa Fe)—pieces like *Abstraction, Green & Red, Canyon Landscape, Dark Mesa, Purple Mountain, Dusk in the Canyon,* and hoodoo dreamscapes called *Abstraction, Dark* and *Abstraction, Pink & Green*—make that connection all the more plain to see.

Photographing her Abiquiu country this morning, I realized how familiar it must have felt to her when she experienced it for the first time. "I am West again and it is as fine as I remembered it—maybe finer— There is nothing to say about it except the fact that for me it is the only place," she wrote in 1929. The bunchgrasses; the creamy miracle of flowering yuccas, prickly pears, and many-armed cholla cactus; the shrubby green junipers; the brick-and-buff coloring of the cliffs; undulating badlands, dusty dry underfoot; the wide and limpid sky with the promise (as, famously, in Texas) of seeing Venus before the sun dropped—the déjà vu pull of it must have been potent. But I also noticed other similarities. Canyon wren song would have been an auditory trigger that would certainly have called up Palo Duro and nowhere else in her prior experience. What Abiquiu would have *added* to her remembered natural history were big evergreens like piñons, ponderosas, and Doug firs (although it was junipers she continued to love most) and a replacement of the sand sagebrush of Texas with the pungent, big sagebrush of the Mountain West (which she embraced). Mesquite doesn't grow along the Chama, and that's a change in the coloring and look of the country from Texas. But it is all really very much the same in its effect on the senses.

Despite what O'Keeffe said publicly about Ghost Ranch's singularity,

Palo Duro Canyon in Texas, where O'Keeffe first fell for the Southwest.

there is in fact a tacit recognition of this connection in her own letters. She had seen New Mexico for the first time in August 1917, on a pilgrimage through the Mountain West that took her from Santa Fe to Silverton, Colorado, a line of travel that's hard to do without passing *somewhere* close to Abiquiu. Of this Farther West she wrote Paul Strand that "the nothingness is several times larger than in Texas." But these were the years when the pull to New York and Stieglitz was stronger, although as Stieglitz mentioned in 1925, O'Keeffe continued to have frequent dreams "of the plains—of real spaces."

O'Keeffe's discovery of Abiquiu is a story that I suspect one day will be mythic, a kind of "this is the place" fable of Western art and Southwestern self-identity. Her absence from the West had stretched to 12 years when she and Rebecca Strand finally visited Mabel Luhan in Taos in the early summer of 1929. O'Keeffe seems at once to have realized that while the Taos Valley was a different West and not quite *it* for her—"It's a different kind of color from any I'd ever seen—there's nothing like it in north Texas or even in Colorado"—she also knew she was close to her home source. She wrote to Paul Strand from Taos that May of 1929, "It seems queer to me now that I did not have to come sooner—" And to Mabel, off in New York for an operation, Georgia remarked that for her, the days in Taos "seem to be like the loud ring of a hammer striking something hard—" And finally to Ettie Stettheimer, while Georgia was en route back to New York that August, she confessed: "I feel so alive that I am apt to crack at any moment. . . . It is my old way of life. . . . I would just go dead if I couldn't have it. . . . Maybe painting will not come out of this—I dont know—but at any rate I feel alive—"

Writing to Beck Strand, who had gone east earlier, from the same train, O'Keeffe offered two hints about the topography that indicate to me that she was, perhaps unconsciously, building on her love affair with what she'd found in Texas. She had gone on an auto tour into Arizona to see the Grand Canyon, but the country that drew her most emotional response had not been the big canyon itself but the Triassic badlands of the Painted Desert: "incredible color—and what shapes!" Then in the tiny village of Alcalde, southwest of Taos, O'Keeffe had rented a cabin from another of the accomplished Eastern women who had found a new world in the West, Marie Garland. At Alcalde, Georgia was on the threshold: "We had one of the finest drives I had from Alcalde west—up toward Abiquiu—very beautiful. . . . I weigh 118. . . . I feel terribly alive—"

In 1931 Georgia went directly to Alcalde, an escape from Taos that has most often been interpreted as a flight from mercurial Mabel. Taos no doubt was too distracting for someone like O'Keeffe, but my sense from her letters is that what really motivated her was a search for the right topography. She found the New Mexico landscape tilting her westward from Taos as if she were being poured from a beaker. From Alcalde, she wrote to Vernon Hunter, she drove almost every day "toward a place called Abiquiu—painting and painting." She had "never loved the country more," she wrote, and felt as if she were approaching some true source.

Actually, O'Keeffe wasn't the first New Mexico painter to discover the Abiquiu area. As early as 1917 John Sloan had painted one of his most powerful New Mexico landscapes, *Chama Running Red,* from an over-look of the river just west of the village. But for O'Keeffe, with the flowing, sculpted earth of Palo Duro Canyon etched deeply onto her aesthetic template, the emotional undertow was different. "It was the shapes that fascinated me," she wrote of the Abiquiu area, "the shapes of the hills."

In 1934 she again returned to New Mexico in June and again resumed the search from Alcalde. Her technique was to rise before dawn and head out in her car into the countryside. At one point early that summer she came to an overlook, and with the sudden shock of seeing a dream image made corporeal, realized that below her in the distance was *it*. Truncated mesas, rimrocked cliffs, stripes of red, yellow. What she was seeing from an overlook was the Piedra Lumbre Valley, the sprawling basin below the Chama River Gorge, and what it had to have appeared more like than anything else in her experience was a Jupiter-sized Palo Duro. But she could not get down. Enlisting the assistance of her friend Charles Collier, she set out a couple of days later, but again they were unable to find a way off the rimrock, once more leaving her desert memory-dream just out of reach. But with the same determination she had called on in her pursuit of deepest Palo Duro, she returned within days, this time driving the dim two tracks along the Chama. And this time she found it.

Years later, after she had lived there and immersed herself in the Abiquiu country, O'Keeffe continued to think of her "beautiful Western world" as extending eastward to the Llano Estacado escarpment in Texas. "Crossing the Texas Panhandle is always a very special event for me," she wrote, and even from the air, "It is very handsome way off into the level distance, fantastically handsome . . . the evening star—the many lakes under the long hot sunset line." Palo Duro Canyon, she finally confessed self-knowingly in 1938, was her "spiritual home." Eastward from there the moister, monotone green closed in: "Ahead looks very hazy and grey as we go toward the low country. . . . I have left the good country."

Of course she hadn't, and now never will.

Walking the Red Hills and driving about the valley, I've reflected a bit more on the incident outside Bode's Store and now am wondering. I've had long hair and a ponytail for so long I never think about *hair* anymore, but there it is, and glancing down at my feet as I point the Jeep into those initial turreted cliffs and roadside lavender badlands in the Piedra Lumbre Valley, I notice that I've also got my moccasins on and at the same time realize there's a decade-old but still readable environmental sticker on my rear window.

God-damned hippie. For three decades now, ever since the Taos commune brought an influx of flower power—and competition for jobs with native New Mexicans, who further resented the hell out of the spectacle of America's privileged youth playing peasant, using food stamps, and openly sneering at the upward mobility Hispano villagers were just beginning to embrace—the locals have reserved a special venom for "hippies." Like most people who have spent any time in Northern New Mexico since the '6os, I've heard the stories: Unmarried hippie couple living together in Vadito finds the head of their pet dog nailed to the trailer door; Anglo construction workers framing up a convenience store in Mora enjoy the whine of .22 long rifles laconically tossed off at them from pickups cruising through town.

I look at myself in the rearview mirror. The sight's not encouraging. A hippie environmentalist? No wonder the guy at Bode's was such a jerk.

We ought to be agreed that the term *Southwest* is a very recent invention, situational in the sense that a region defined as a direction implies a *central locus somewhere else.* Southwest of what? Texas and New Mexico and all the country farther west was *El Norte,* the North, until the Mexican War transferred the region from Mexico to the United States. So recent is the term Southwest that the region is still in the process of defining itself and its boundaries. What, then, are its qualities? Is it *longue durée* history, the Southwest as the broad region consolidated under inhabitation by the Pueblo Indians, as some anthropologists have argued? Is it—as Georgia O'Keeffe apparently believed and as her landscape art and that of many other "Southwestern" artists has convinced us—in fact *landscape,* the part of the continent where sere cliffs, hotly colored bare earth, and cactus dominant?

Or should we be more truly historicist: As Reies Tijerina and a small but angry core of Hispanos have averred, is the "Southwest" actually the northern end of the Hispano homeland commons, where imperialist forces like the Santa Fe Ring, the U.S. Supreme Court, and the Forest Service a hundred years ago conspired to rob Northern New Mexican Hispanos of their birthright?

Where U.S. Highway 84 begins to curve northward around the Ghost Ranch cliffs, up the Colorado Plateau through thick piñons to Chama and the Continental Divide, more candy cane walls like those behind

O'Keeffe's house sculpt lovely sandstone overhangs. One of them, a high amphitheater with a vivid desert varnish swipe bisecting its face, is so close to the highway that after 84 was completed through here in the 1940s, Carson National Forest officials decided to develop it as a public roadside stop. A raven, slow and loitering about, looking at interesting things on the ground, would fly from here to Miss O'Keeffe's house in about five minutes. Tourists walk the trails today, wheezing at the slight incline, making Kodak and Fuji richer, never at a loss for inane things to say when they get into range of the cliff's echoing wall. But I stand here in the sagebrush in 1995 and I know that almost 30 years ago, in 1966, Echo Amphitheater bounced back angrier words, words that amounted to the across-the-bow shots in the *Norteño* campaign to take back the mountains.

The leader of this movement and architect of world-famous events over the next two years was not even a New Mexican. Reies Tijerina was a Tejano, born in the valley. But like so many of the New Mexicans in the country between Abiquiu, Chama, and Cuba, Tijerina was descended from a family whose land grant had been lost to the Anglo sharpsters who had finned about the Southwest like land sharks, grinning through bright teeth, in the last century. It's a sorrier Northern New Mexican story than John Nichols ever novelized, but with the cast of characters about the same. Tijerina, who studied land grant history in Mexico and Spain for three years before moving to New Mexico and founding Alianza in 1963, believed that of all the places where Hispanos had been deprived of their lands, this place—particularly the former Tierra Amarilla and San Joaquín del Rio Chama grants—was such a blatant landscape of wrongs that it could serve as rallying symbol.

Individual land grant history in the Southwest is a bottomless morass of origins, mostly because the Spanish system of awarding property did not feature survey but the more pragmatic (even ecological) method of setting boundaries based on natural landmarks. This tree. That boulder. Landmarks, unfortunately, that could disappear over time. But the general trajectory of land grant history is clear enough, and the short version goes something like this: Spain in its 223-year rule in New Mexico, and Mexico on a more grandiose scale in its 25-year rule, awarded most of the landscape of New Mexico, Colorado, and Texas to grant applicants in two forms, private grants and community grants. In the latter, individuals usually owned particular strips of ground along irrigable streams, but the

Desert varnish of Echo Amphitheater, Carson National Forest, New Mexico, where the Reies Tijerina–led land grantee revolt began in 1966.

larger mass of the grant consisted of *ejidos*, or commons, that swept up the mountainsides and were used by all the villagers for woodcutting, hunting, and plant gathering, more particularly for grazing the sheep and goats that were the mainstay of the subsistence mountain economy. In New Mexico, which includes 77.6 million acres, 67.6 million had been awarded as grants. Article Eight of the Treaty of Guadalupe-Hidalgo that ended the Mexican War had promised full protection for these grant lands. It said nothing, unfortunately, about that distinction between *private* and *community* grants.

Bad mistake. American law, with its elaborate development of private property rights, was little prepared to deal with community property rights. In the 1897 *Sandoval* decision, the Supreme Court decided that the *ejidos* had not in fact been deeded but like the American public domain had actually been retained during all those centuries of inhabitation as *tierras realengas*, crown lands. Thus at the end of the Mexican War the great *ejidos* of the Southwest had legally passed to the United States government and were proclaimed a part of the public domain. Indeed, Pecos Forest Reserve had already been created out of several Northern New Mexico land grants in 1891. Of that 67.6 million acres, the United States approved only 12.4 million acres of grant lands in New Mexico.

The modern denouement of land grant history is this: More than one professional historian has concluded with varying degrees of outrage that the United States either wantonly misinterpreted or was ignorant of Spanish law regarding the *ejidos*. Victor Westphall is convinced that "the U.S. Supreme Court surely violated international law when it held that the common lands of community grants passed to the United States after Mexican cession" and that at least 16 million acres out of 22.7 million granted in Northern New Mexico should have been patented to the descendants of the grantees. Malcolm Ebright's 1994 study of the question comes to the conclusion that the Sandoval decision "was based on scanty Spanish legal authorities." Ebright goes on: "The New Mexico community land grant itself owned the common lands."

His winters spent studying in Mexico and in the archives in Madrid had convinced Reies Tijerina, too. The seizure and occupation of Echo Amphitheater in October 1966 were designed as a signal to the world that most of what was Carson National Forest legally belonged to the heirs of the San Joaquin and Tierra Amarilla grants. This occupation, a full six years before AIM's occupation of Wounded Knee, was not a sweet civil disobedience action in the tradition of Thoreau. Alianza attempted citizen's arrests of rangers sent to remove them. There was violence, and Tijerina was arrested and charged with inciting the event. But the arrest did not prevent Alianza from proclaiming a Puebla Republica de San Joaquin—a free republic that sought independence from the United States—in early 1967.

Alianza's "mountain revolt" did not end there. Six months later, on June 5, 1967, two dozen local Hispanos from Tierra Amarilla, Canjilon, and Coyote exploded into the Rio Arriba County courthouse on a blustery and wet afternoon, looking for local district attorney Alfonso Sanchez, who had broken up an Alianza meeting in Coyote and who was not, it turned out, present that afternoon. Random shots wounded two officers, and then like *Norteño* Robin Hoods, the raiders dispersed on foot and horseback through their thickly wooded ancestral mountains. New Mexico Governor David Cargo felt obliged to call on the National Guard to help apprehend them.

Nothing about the incident seemed forgettable at the time. It was high drama, and it ought to have produced something more than it did. But it quickly became bad tabloid fare. When the raiders were captured, one of them turned out to be a young woman, Tijerina's 17-year-old daughter, Rose. Governor Cargo, a bachelor, promptly fell for her. (Even today the photos in the yellowing newspapers in the New Mexico archives in Santa Fe show why: She was a slender, flashing-eyed beauty, who went on to a minor career as a chanteuse and a film star in Mexico.) Just days before Tijerina's trial was to commence, one of the officers wounded in the Courthouse Raid was kidnapped from his driveway and brutally murdered as he was preparing his testimony. Never solved.

Tijerina ended up getting three years in jail—for inciting the confrontation at Echo Amphitheater. The whole episode briefly drew international attention even if some folks, forever confused about New Mexico anyway, had a bit of trouble grasping the essentials. The Brown University alumni magazine reported the story this way: A band of Indians rode their cars into the county seat to arrest the DA. The genesis was a problem with developers wanting to build ski resorts and homes. No one was hurt, but word went out that Commies were involved and so the National Guard was mobilized. As for historic wrongs or illegal land grant seizures by the United States, the Brown alumni magazine just

didn't seem to get it. Despite some significant Forest Service reforms in
response, neither have a lot of other people.

Standing here in the sagebrush and the wind on a summer day 30 years later, the irony of this Abiquiu place is almost too hard to bear. Two very different visions of it have been created and offered up to the world from points on the ground less than three miles apart. Both visions have seen this ground as the very embodiment of how the Southwest ought to be perceived by the observant and thinking world. What has that meant, if anything at all?

The Red Hills. The Black Place. The White Place. Hundreds of years of Indian and Hispano presence here had produced topographical names like Chama (from the Tewa, *Tzama*, "Here They Have Wrestled," the name of a pueblo on the river), Abiquiu (perhaps a corruption of the Tewa word *pay shoo boo-oo*, "timber end town"), Pedernal (Spanish: "Flint"), Piedra Lumbre ("Fire Rock"), Rancho de los Brujos ("Ghost Ranch"). But for the places that were most important to her here, the spots where the landscape energy welled up and infused her with an emotional charge, Georgia O'Keeffe had her own names. It was part of her artistic process of going native to her place.

O'Keeffe's life and career beg an old question: Does a person become a great artist just because she lives below a great mountain? The answer is still no, but for an artist who seeks to go native to the continent—and that really ought to be all of us, artists and natives all—an unobstructed access to the natural world is probably essential. O'Keeffe finally got that in 1935, when Arthur Pack had no place for her at his Ghost Ranch resort unless she wanted to stay over at his little abandoned adobe two miles west of the main house.

I have long wondered how it happened that O'Keeffe landed a seven-acre ranchette at the base of one of the most stunning cliff faces on the continent in the middle of a 30,000-acre ranch. It would be as if you were allowed to have the only house and property at the foot of the Grand Tetons or that fate decreed that you and no one else got to pass your days looking out the windows of your house on Artist's Point over the Grand Canyon. How did she get that lucky?

Sucked away from Taos by her probes at the edges of the Chama Valley in the early 1930s, O'Keeffe began her process of identification with "the country" before she had a proper base there. Her avenue to a base was through a New Jersey adventurer of a type we would now be tempted to call a trust funder, although that wouldn't do Arthur Newton Pack justice. Pack was the son of Charles Lathrop Pack, who'd made a nineteenth-century fortune logging his way across the continent and in the twentieth had become the president of the American Forestry Association. The son's responsibility, through outdoor writing and a magazine, *Nature*, that his father bankrolled for him, was to seek redemption for earlier sins through conservation work. While Pack was a useful environmental-minded citizen, one suspects that a certain amount of noblesse oblige colored his life. A proper grasp of his particular burden can be inferred from the title of one of his books: *The Challenge of Leisure*.

Pack had first seen the Chama Valley on a car-camping trip in a Pierce Arrow convertible in 1929. In 1933 his leisure challenged him to look for a dry climate Western ranch for his wife and daughters. After some looking in New Mexico they at length entered "a place where a half-remembered flat-topped mountain stood sentinel over a grassy basin rimmed with sheer sandstone cliffs of pink, purple and gold." Mr. Bode and Carol Stanley, who owned part of the valley, told them the cliffs were called "Rancho de los Brujos" because they were haunted by a variety of ghosts. "Earth babies" that slunk out of the ground and were furred over with red hair and a cow with wings competed against the most fearsome of all, a *vivaron*, or giant rattlesnake that frequented Mesa Huerfana and had the locals terrified. Earth babies and flying cows turned out to be fairly scarce, but the *vivaron* actually surfaced. It turned out to be a phytosaur, a Triassic age reptile fossilized in the cliff face.

Having already bought 390 acres from Stanley, in 1933 Pack talked Manuel Salazar, a local rancher from Cañones facing tough times in the Depression, out of 30,000 acres. Thus he had purchased for himself "the most beautiful and spectacular piece of privately owned real estate in the Southwest." Picking a site at the base of the great, imposing cliff on the ranch, he had a low adobe built around three sides of a patio that opened toward the Pedernal and in a play on names called the house "Rancho de los Burros," since the cliffs were lousy with feral burros.

In 1936, the second year O'Keeffe came out to use Ghost Ranch as a base, Pack was suffering through a personal crisis. Earlier that year he had come home to a note from his wife informing him that she was leaving him for the young archeologist (Frank Hibben) they had hired as a tutor for their children. Pack was traumatized. He was also unable thereafter to live at the little adobe and so transferred his belongings over to the ranch headquarters at Yeso Canyon, where soon thereafter he met a "girl whose background I knew" (she was Phoebe Finley), and they decided to continue the ranch's fortunes as—what else?—a dude ranch. When O'Keeffe arrived that summer, Pack asked if she wouldn't prefer living in the isolated little house over at the base of the cliffs. Thus did O'Keeffe fall into such a spectacular place to live and work. By 1940 she had talked Pack out of the house and a few acres—she wanted enough for a horse but always complained that Pack sold her only enough for a septic system—for a price Pack referred to as "virtually nothing" (actually it was about $6,000).

Rancho de los Burros won her absolute and undiluted love at first sight. She was smitten by the spot and the house, painting *My Backyard* and *The House I Live In* her first summer there. Now there was no longer a necessity to drive to paint; she could instead concentrate on the variety of stunning scenes stretching away from her windows—the red badlands, the multihued cliffs, stripes of desert varnish, and of course the Pedernal. As she wrote Arthur Dove,

> I wish you could see what I see out the window—the earth pink and
> yellow cliffs to the north—the full pale moon about to go down in an
> early morning lavender sky behind a very long beautiful tree covered
> mesa to the west—pink and purple hills in front and the scrubby fine
> dull green cedars—and a feeling of much space—It is a very
> beautiful world—I wish you could see it.

She took enormous pride in Rancho de los Burros, particularly when her visitors, awed by a moonrise or by the subtle shades that briefly envelop the Piedra Lumbre Valley at twilight, fell silent and got it. In 1940 she told Ettie Stettheimer with obvious pride in her circumstances that

> I am about 100 miles from the railroad—68 from Santa Fe—95 from
> Taos—40 miles from town—18 miles from a post office and it is
> good. . . . so far away that no one ever comes—I suppose I am odd
> but I do like the far away. . . . Colored earth—rattlesnakes . . . I have
> no radio—and no newspaper.

When I had started out walking the trails through her country, I was not certain why a woman born to the diffuse light of the Wisconsin farm country would react so emotionally to the hard-edged cliffs, the bad-lands, and the fathomless depths of sky blue that characterize so much of the Near Southwest. But picking my way through the low White Place cliffs in the flat ambience of noon, the reason came to me with a shock of recognition in the memory of a dream. One night years before I had dreamed that O'Keeffe and I were face-to-face. It was the dark-haired Georgia of the Texas years and she was boldly running her hands down her body, telling me what a small waist she had, "my best feature after my hands." In my dream she was looking at me with *the* look. You know what I mean. Not flirtatious. Direct. Frank sexual desire. Hell, we can all dream.

Think of Palo Duro, the Red Hills, the Black Place, the White Place. If you don't know them, look at the paintings. What every landscape that inspired Georgia O'Keeffe has in common is its direct, even overt, sex-uality of form. Most of us recognize, in spite of the artist's protests, that her fascination with floral sexual architecture is precisely the same sym-bolism that led Linnaeus to name an entire genus of plants *Clitoria*. Maybe this was subconscious. Given her husband's worship of female genitalia (he and Rodin swapped their intimate pictures of femalia with each other), it probably wasn't. Frankly, I've always been a little amazed that there wasn't as big a furor over the sexuality of the Red Hills, the Black Place, and the White Place paintings as over the notorious jacks-in-the-pulpit.

The White Place, now owned by the nearby Dar Al Islam Mosque and kept open to the public for purposes of inspiration, is an outcrop-ping of gleaming white Cretaceous sandstone capped by a black vol-canic rim fissured into shoebox-sized blocks. By car it is only 10 to 15 minutes from Abiquiu. It is tiny, no more than 10 acres at most, and the cliffs are not high. As a female friend who's hiked here with me has pointed out on more than one occasion (coyly, of course, like, "Wow! Look at *that* one! It's beautiful!"), O'Keeffe's White Place is a spot the Druids would have made a temple. It has some of the most graphically phallic columning anywhere in the Southwest. Those stone phalluses are there in most of the White Place paintings, *The White Place in Shadow*, for example, done in 1942, when O'Keeffe's immersion in her place was fully matured.

The Red Hills of the Chama River Valley, New Mexico.

The Red Hills outside O'Keeffe's door carry off their seething sexuality partly through tint, but here color is mere preface. The graceful and organic sweep of these badlands lines, the folds and the curvilinear overlappings struck O'Keeffe—as they did the Pueblo Indians, and as they certainly do me—as a profound manifestation of earth eroticism, close enough to the eroticism of the human form to be subtly arousing. O'Keeffe's Black Place, the stretch of mostly gray Triassic badlands (striped with black and copper and often a thin line of vermilion) scattered across northwestern New Mexico, has the same appeal.

O'Keeffe was not in the throes of a "psychological rejection of water" (Jeez, Ms. Robinson!) when she gravitated to these places. Rather, as her assistant and camping companion, Maria Chabot, has insisted, Georgia's healthy sexuality was bottled up in the years when she was going native to New Mexico; the early 1930s was when Stieglitz was having his affair with Dorothy Norman. Diverted, her sexuality emerged rousingly, as ever, in her art. Even O'Keeffe, who rarely admitted such, was aware that works like *Pedernal and Red Hills* (1936), *Red Hills and Bones* (1941), and *The Grey Hills* (1942) fairly pulsed with the erotic. The graceful, feminine sexuality of a "memory image" like *Black Place III* (1944) isn't so overt as something like Alexandre Hogue's *Mother Earth Laid Bare*, perhaps, where a voluptuous and fully realized female form is exposed by erosion. But even in their abstraction, it seems to me that O'Keeffe's New Mexico landscapes stand as a visual, feminine counterpart to what Henry Miller was trying to pull off in words in those years but couldn't.

Even with the head start she got in the Texas canyon country, from the time O'Keeffe discovered Abiquiu it took her a decade to perfect her capture of the feeling the Piedra Lumbre Valley gave her. In 1932 she had written to Beck Strand about her show that winter that "the landscapes and the bones were both in a very subjective stage of development . . . so that memory or dream thing I do that for me comes nearer reality than my objective kind of work—was quite lacking." But after she bought Rancho de los Burros, daily life surrounded by the monuments of her inspiration soon wafted her onto that dream-level plane.

I don't believe, as the art historians like to say, that O'Keeffe "created a world" with her art. The cliffs and colors, rocks and mounds, trees and sky and bones that she painted—the world we now call the Southwest—are tangible. They exist, and they had existed all along. What O'Keeffe did, merely by responding to the joy of looking, tasting, feeling, was to give this world an identity in human culture. By making the ordinary objects of nature around her into personal totems, she made space into place.

And my admiration? I think I've spent time enough in the worlds she fetishized to understand my attraction to her. I do not find O'Keeffe a personal hero because of what she "did for women," because she was "a desert recluse," or because she could be so nastily cantankerous and unsympathetic that she struck some as refreshingly natural and honest. What compels me about her is the way she searched for her place, found it, applied all her energy and creativity to going native to it. And I am intrigued by her refusal thereafter to paint other places that mightily impressed her (Yosemite, Peru) because she knew full well how long it had taken her to rise to that "dream thing" in the place she knew best. O'Keeffe was all about one world at a time. That I grasp.

Art, we are all convinced, is a subjective and individualistic creation. But history? Isn't history, at least professional social science history with all its methodologies and footnotes and objective stances, more detached? More reliably honest and accurate, if you will?

Depends, of course, and what it depends on is who you are and who wrote your history. More than anything else, history is the art of explanatory storytelling. And if you are a resident of Northern New Mexico who reads very many of the very variable stories about your history—Horgan's romance of the Great River, Swadesh's social science objectivity, Fray Chavez's pride in Spanish blood and near embarrassment over "genízaro excesses," Quintana's outrage over Anglo "pseudo-history of the Southwest," Kutsche and Van Ness's wanna-be sociology, and more recently the fine local history of the valley by Lesley Poling-Kempes, or the debate over Hispano environmental history between DuBuys, Rothman, McCameron, and Peña—you may conclude that the only things that are real in this world are the rocks and the sky and the certainty of entropy.

Perhaps the fellow at Bode's Store knew instinctively: "Aha, another goddamned storyteller."

From the earth I was made,
And the earth shall eat me,
The earth has sustained me,
And at last earth I shall be also.

Thus goes a verse from *Adiós, Acompañamiento*, a Penitente *alabado*. For the two centuries that the Penitentes have been singing it, one of the landscapes that has been regularly digesting them back into the earth is the Piedra Lumbre Valley. For so many of those aspects of history that seem peculiarly *Norteño* (or "Northern New Mexican" today), among them a toughness washed in the blood of Indian wars, a kind of village socialism resting on land grants and great mountain commons, the peculiar local mixture of Hispanicized indigenous Indian ancestry known as *genízaro*, and the secretive and uniquely New Mexican religious brotherhood of the Penitentes, this Chama River country seems essential heartland. Made into New Mexico's principal experimental *genízaro* settlement in the eighteenth century, Abiquiu is home to *Norteños* who still carry the blood of Comanches, Kiowas, Apaches, and Navajos and who still celebrate it. A Spanish *castizo* like Fray Angelico Chavez will insist that Chamaseños are associated with revolt and resistance, that it is their sort that makes up the ranks of the Penitentes, that "they are the ones who join the agrarian and urban Mexicans or Mexican-Americans in their social protests, and consequently like to be called 'Chicanos' along with them," and that none of this is reflective of the true *ánima hispánica* (the Spanish soul). Chavez would be right that one of the oldest surviving Penitente *moradas* in New Mexico, Morado del Alto, is in the Chama River Valley. But he misses the point. Across the great Horizontal Yellow of the Near Southwest, few modern peoples can claim a more intertwined immersion in place than these Chama River people. *Ánima hispánica* is all well and good. But what about *querencia*, love of place? Isn't *ánima indigenisma* what we ought really to be seeking nowadays?

One of the things about history as a form of storytelling is that stories about the past are most effective when they either have a moral or they connect us to the time string of the now and the beyond with a set of sharp insights that shift the field of thought. I can, for example, tell you place-centered stories about the Abiquiu country that carry morals about religion and intolerance, a sort of New Mexico version of *The Crucible*, wherein the Hispanic women in the Chama settlements reacted badly to the experiment to make Abiquiu a *genízaro* settlement, charging that the *genízaros* were performing the Turtle Dance, a winter solstice Pueblo ceremony featuring (so it was claimed) "the lasciviousness of Pueblo women who offered themselves freely to all the men." The denouement featured an epidemic of Chamaseños who claimed possession by demons and when exorcised demanded that all Pueblo shrines, petroglyph sites, and sacred caves in the region be destroyed—and many were.

So with much Abiquiu history, or any history of place. A rich record of settlement, Indian raids, and the use of the Chama corridor as a trade route westward is available in the archives in Santa Fe, and detailing it might point up a few fun things to know and tell—why, for example, Martinez and Serrano are such common names in the valley 275 years later. But from the enormous mass of information and stories available in a place inhabited by Hispanic New Mexicans for almost three centuries, the narrative arc that late twentieth century concerns call up for the Chama River country is a fairly singular one, and it's the one that speaks directly to Alianza's concerns. Did the Americans blatantly steal rightfully owned Hispano lands? Was *Norteño* village socialism, as Mary Austin championed and even John Wesley Powell believed, a model adaptation for the Southwest? As owners and users of those enormous granted *ejidos*, or commons, how successful as environmental stewards were the settlers of the Abiquiu country? And should the American people and the American government turn the Southwestern national forests over to them?

"I know *you* prefer living as if you're perpetually camping out, but I have no problem getting this at all." *This* was Georgia O'Keeffe's house in Abiquiu village, and my companion, arrived from Texas the evening before, wasn't bothering with my response. She'd already stepped through the doorway into the clean and dazzling light of O'Keeffe's interior patio, and the sight of sunlight haloing her fine hair against that impossibly blue sky swept whatever clever retort I'd had entirely out of my head.

"Well, I guess she eventually got tired of camping out over at the cliff. But at least she stayed committed to her spot." I do find it impressive that O'Keeffe's second home was only 15 miles from her first.

Remote ranches, however inspiringly situated, carry problems. How do you get in and out during winter snows and spring mud? By the late 1940s year-round living at O'Keeffe's Rancho de Los Burros seemed problematic for another reason, too: The setting was too hot and sterile for the garden she needed to eliminate regular commutes to town. In 1945, then (reportedly for the price of $10) she bought a crumbling adobe and three acres atop the mesa in Abiquiu and turned over to

Maria Chabot the four-year task of making a home out of the place. Rancho de Los Burros remained her love, but the Abiquiu house increasingly became O'Keeffe's home.

It had been almost a decade since O'Keeffe's death when we were taken through the Abiquiu house, but the artist's lingering presence was everywhere still tangible. It was there, the elegance of simplicity, in the rock collection on the windowsill, in the sagebrush she planted in that otherwise empty patio, in the plywood dining table that will shame every Yuppie who takes the tour, in the door that she "just had to have," in her good library with dozens of books (and magazines still marked to stories about her) with paper scrap bookmarks intact. There, too, is the friendly little chow dog padding about the house, and there most palpably of all in her tiny and simple bedroom, plastered the color of the Black Place and looking down on Highway 84 curving eastward past the view. O'Keeffe seemed most present in the garden, its pathways laid out with white gravel so she could see to walk when her eyes no longer registered that holy New Mexico light.

Driving through the valley bound for the Pedernal afterward and mentally trying to suppress the buildup of any anvil-headed thunderstorms that might abort our climb, we tried to use that felt presence to figure out what her life meant. For the West and the Southwest, we decided, O'Keeffe's vision and model seem to stand more transparently when they're held against those of the other expatriate artists and writers to northern New Mexico, who either by intent or default fashioned a response to place that exalted and ruined in the same motion.

Of all those others, the two whose Southwestern visions shape Rocky Mountain New Mexico most are, inescapably, Mabel Dodge Luhan and D. H. Lawrence. (Lawrence's bones up in his present redoubt at Kiowa Ranch might spin in anguish at yet another linkage to Mabel were it not that Frieda mortared them into the very concrete of his astonishing, flower-festooned mausoleum.)

Mabel Luhan's vision of the Southwest was a very different one from O'Keeffe's. In many respects it was a less common vision, one more associated with the Eastern class that produced so many reformers and intellectuals. Mabel's vision goes back to the first European who was beset with self-doubts about the colonizing enterprise. Something like it was there among those who deserted early European expeditions to join the Indians, among the Indian traders (like my great-great-great-great grandfather) who went native, among all the Euro-American children captured by Indians who found lifestyle more bonding than blood. It was an allure that faded some in the nineteenth century but has remained a core idea in an American counterculture repelled by materialist, industrial, urban modernity throughout the twentieth century. In the early century Mabel Luhan articulated this old idea more forcefully than almost anyone else. And Mabel was a force, the sort of individual who either transfixed you through a hypnotic fascination with her style or else made you writhe with the certain conviction that someone very smart and arrogant was manipulating you for the sheer pleasure of it. She must have been hard to feel warm about.

Mabel Dodge Sterne was the spoiled, precocious daughter of a wealthy American banker, a young woman whose attraction to ideas and romance and men who possessed both had led her to convoluted liaisons and experiences in European salons and the Greenwich Village of the pre-Great War years. Mabel collected and discarded ideas and lovers with a rapidity that would seem to make her life a case study in attention deficit disorder. Or alternatively, maybe she was what her biographer, Lois Rudnick, has called her, "The American Bitch Goddess" who more people imagined dead in a greater variety of ways than any American woman ever. If she *was* pretty, she fell far short of the slender 1920s ideal. But Mabel had real power beyond the sexual: money, right connections, and a mind that synthesized brilliantly. "Very clever for a female," D. H. Lawrence said, a compliment that carried with it all the latent misogyny that smoked from his soul when he was around her.

Reading her books today, especially *Edge of Taos Desert*, though, I conclude that her reaction to the New Mexico landscape was authentic. Mabel was 38 in 1917, the year she took a Santa Fe train to join her new (third) husband in the unimaginable Southwest. Eastern artists and writers, like the members of the Taos Society of Artists, had been falling in love with the landscape and cultures of Northern New Mexico since Ernest Blumenschein famously broke a wagon wheel outside Taos in 1898 and never left. The year before Mabel arrived, no less an American master than Robert Henri had painted in Santa Fe; John Sloan and Marsden Hartley were barely enough behind Mabel to be out of sight. But Mabel's reaction to New Mexico does seem to have been her own. On the train out she began to see "the loveliest light all over everything and . . . the bluest mountains I had ever seen." The Horizontal Yellow's indigenous smells—sagebrush on the night air, piñon and juniper bathing the streets with incense—sent her into a manic ecstasy. There was "a smile in the sunlight"—"From the very first day I found out that the sunshine in New Mexico could do almost anything with one"—and "the sky was a burning, deep blue over us." En route to Taos she traveled "over the strangest landscape I ever faced. . . . a passage through a pink and yellow dream . . . blue sky staring down and the bright air making everything seem to waver and vibrate around us." In "this shining ether" the very mountains seemed to exist in "the bliss of effortless being." Northern New Mexico was a sensuous feast for Mabel, and she never got over it. "Holy! Holy! Holy! Lord God Almighty," she wrote. I believe her.

Mabel was a searcher and a visionary, and Taos quickly came to seem not only the Holy Grail but, the more she thought about it, the American Redemption, too. Before she'd left New York, her husband had written her that she should come West to "save the Indian." Looking about her in 1917–18, it struck her that redemption might flow in the opposite direction. Despite the powerful pull of the landscape on her, Mabel wasn't much impressed with human culture in New Mexico. That "shining ether" also "made mankind appear dingy and alien to the environment," she wrote. Specifically, the Hispanos struck her as "pinched, discouraged, and baffled," a people who had been in place for centuries, yet "nothing much had happened to them." As for the few Anglos, she found Taos colored by "hateful thoughts and feelings." Despite the beauty of the country, "Everyone in the place seemed to have gone negative."

There was only one exception: the Indians. Taos Pueblo, which dominated the town in 1917, captivated Mabel in part because it seemed so elusive, so fully realized, and so resistant to possession. So naturally she had to possess it, just had to "be a part of this Indian thing" and discover the secret of that strange Indian self-awareness that led Pueblo men (as D. H. Lawrence would write of them) to stand round observing the strange Anglos "in white cotton sheets like Hamlet's father's ghost, with a lurking smile." But how?

Well, of course you *know* how. Tony Lujan was a looming presence at Taos Pueblo, a huge man whose face (as photographed by Ansel Adams) conveyed the sense of an ancient bodhisattva. Women were drawn to him. O'Keeffe called him "a force of nature," and Willa Cather is sup-

posed to have responded, when asked how Mabel could marry an Indian, "how could she help it?" When Mabel encountered him, he already had a wife, Candelaria, whose story does not appear in *Edge of
Taos Desert* but who ended up with a monthly stipend from Mabel and
continued conjugal visits from Tony. In her forties Mabel seems to have
lost some of her sexual drive; Tony didn't, and not only kept Candelaria
but a series of other lovers, too. But however difficult their relationship,
however far they evolved from those first erotic summer nights in Tony's
tipi in her yard, with Maurice seething at the windows in his night-
clothes, Mabel and Tony stayed together. As John Collier, Jr., has written, he was "the only man she could not send away."

What Mabel drew from this experience was her vision for a Future
Primitive America, and with it she tapped into a powerful wellspring
among the many who were finding (and still do) modernism's world a
deadening one. Among liberal and elite artists and intellectuals of the
era, the search led Gauguin to Tahiti, Picasso and Hemingway to Africa.
Independently of Mabel it had already produced the beginnings of the
Taos and Santa Fe art colonies, and it led Mabel and through her a flood
of others to New Mexico. Something like Mabel's vision continues to
lead many of us into sweat lodges and on vision quests three-quarters of a
century later.

Mabel looked at Taos Pueblo and imagined a national clone of it,
where community would replace individualism, a religion of nature
would replace a religion of money, the simple and the natural would
replace a thicket of technological artifice. Or alternatively she imagined
the town of Taos as a city on a hill, an Indian-inspired Plato's Republic of
philosopher-artist dropouts from the dominant paradigm—at least some
of whom would follow her into intermarriage with the Pueblo Indians.

It was a positive vision, and it did endorse regionalism. I'll give her
that. Beyond that it was a cultural vampirism of the sort that one is
tempted to predict would crop up among the imperial class as colo-
nialism triumphed. It failed to take into account the Pueblos' bitterly
learned lessons about religious privacy, or that their "secret" ("It's *life*,"
an exasperated Tony finally told her) lay in their own historical context,
something that can't be borrowed the way a shirt can be. It even ignored Pueblo sanctions against intermarriage with outsiders. Tony's own
strength, as he tried to tell Mabel, rested in peyotism; peyote made him

know "how good, how happy, the life is." But a psychotropic plant at the heart of her New World Renaissance? It threw Mabel into a panic, and she tried repeatedly to get him to give it up.

Back East being treated for the syphilis Tony had passed on to her, Mabel had a session with a woman who announced that there was an ancient "doctrine" representing the key to the earthly garden, that the Pueblos were now in possession of its secrets, and that she had been "chosen" to tell the world. From Los Gallos, her first Taos house, Mabel issued the call, and it seemed that a good part of the world—everyone from Carl Jung to Thomas Wolfe to Georgia O'Keeffe—responded. One of her most devout converts was John Collier, who knew next to nothing about Indians when he arrived in New Mexico but was so thrilled by the Pueblos that in 1922 he wrote a piece about them whose title ("Red Atlantis") prefigured his Indian New Deal a decade later.

But as Mabel worried with her vision, she became convinced that only one person had the power and grace of language to tell her story properly. She first wrote D. H. Lawrence the good news about Taos— "like the dawn of the world"—in 1921. The invitation to tell this new, unfolding story of America did intrigue Lawrence, and he replied on November 5, 1921: "I believe what you say. . . . Is Taos the place? . . . I think we will come to Taos." As he put it to Catherine Carswell shortly after he arrived in Taos in 1922: "Perhaps it is necessary for me to try these places, perhaps it is my destiny to know the world." But, he continued, "It only excites the outside of me. The inside it leaves more isolated and stoic than ever. That's how it is. It is all a form of running away from oneself and the great problems: all this wild west." That kind of angst made Lawrence's translation of Mabel's vision problematic.

If the start was shaky, it only went downhill from there. Lawrence brought his German wife, Frieda, with him, and she and Mabel were famously at each other's throats within days. Mabel's biographer, Lois Rudnick, believes that menopause was driving Mabel away from sexuality and toward spiritually in these years and that this explains her resentment toward erotically charged women like Frieda and O'Keeffe. She and Lawrence both accused each other of attempted seduction, but Mabel knew (and hated) that she could not compete sexually with Frieda, a "spiritually stupid" woman but the "mother of orgasm," as she called her. As for Lawrence, Mabel drove him crazy. Within days of arriving in Taos he was referring to her in his letters as "false," "La strega" (the witch), and "a serpent." And there is this rather more elaborate characterization of her, point by point:

> rich—only child—from Buffalo, on Lake Erie—bankers—42 years old—short, stout—looks young—has had three husbands . . . Has now an Indian, Tony, a fat fellow. Has lived much in Europe . . . little loved—very clever for a female . . . hates the white world, and loves the Indians out of hate—is very "noble," wants to be very "good," and is very wicked . . . woman power, you know—wanted to become a witch, and, at the same time, a Mary of Bethany at Jesus's feet—a stout white crow, a cooing raven of misfortune, a little buffalo.

But Lawrence, who had little use for disembodied bliss and loved the material world, was captivated by New Mexico's physical setting. In *Lady Chatterly's Lover* he had written that "a clear sky was almost the most important thing in life." He found that, and sacred sunlight, and the celestial shows of one of the great night skies in the world in New Mexico. But first he had to escape Mabel, which he did by moving out to her Del Monte Ranch between Taos and Questa. Here he wrote his friend Jan Juta:

> We have come to this wild ranch—only about 17 miles from Taos— live in an old 5-room log cabin, and chop down trees and ride away on horseback to the Rio Grande. Quite a good life, physically. It is a very splendid landscape—Rocky Mountains behind and a vast space of desert in front, with other mountains far west. Very fine indeed, the great space to live in. But humanly, nothing.

Lawrence never wrote the great Southwestern work Mabel called him out to write. His New World novel, *The Plumed Serpent* (1926), did deal with the theme of Indian-white marriage but was set in Mexico. But some of his stories and essays—"Spirit of Place" and "Pan in America" and "The Woman Who Rode Away"—make it clear that Lawrence did believe in some parts of Mabel's vision. While he could sneer at the mystical and thought Mabel's "great idea" was more about Mabel's egomania than about saving America, Lawrence was convinced that Puritanism had caused Americans to sublimate their sensuality and thus the chance for a primal connection to nature. Typically contradictory, he thus railed against the silly noble savagery he found in New Mexico while simultaneously implying that America's chance to go native to the continent might well lie in internalizing the Indian.

Three-quarters of a century later it is possible, I think, to give this Mabel/Lawrence vision its due. Hers and Mary Austin's and Collier's idea that "the *next* great and fructifying world culture" (as Austin called it in *Land of Journey's End*) would come out of the indigenous Southwestern models proved to be naive and untenable. It would have been quite a magic trick, after all, to persuade Americans that they should recast their civilization based on the model of the materially poorest among them. Ultimately what Mabel actually helped to create was a sense of place in Northern New Mexico as an escape and refuge from mainstream America, one based on landscape and cultural diversity and some incorporation of Indian ideas as Anglo culture came to dominate the area. By the time Mabel died in 1962 and it was Dennis Hopper's turn to take over her house and her niche, this was the role Northern New Mexico had begun to play for the Southwest and the country.

As wealthy Easterners and Californians have flocked in and indulged the American genius for commodifying even something as abstract as place distinctiveness, this role, unfortunately, has come close to ruining Northern New Mexico as a real place and threatened to make it, remarkably, a Disneyland of itself. Anglo newcomers who profess dismay at this interpretation might do well to peruse sometime the work of native Taoseño and UCLA anthropologist Sylvia Rodriguez. Rodriguez's work, admittedly, is not exactly user friendly, replete as it is with titles such as "The Tourist Gaze, Gentrification, and the Commodification of Subjectivity in Taos" and sentences that say things like, "The notion of the gaze as a cultural-ideological construct derives from poststructuralist and feminist analyses of systems of meaning implicit and embedded in paradigmatic structures of power." (This is how they teach you to write in graduate anthropology seminars.) Decipher Rodriguez's semantically challenged language, however, and interesting ideas settle out.

The Northern New Mexico that a century of art and railroad tourism and Mabel Luhan have bequeathed us, she asserts, is a classic reflection of capitalism's effect on a place once the money changers realized that places outside the American mainstream could be marketed to consumers as exotic, romantic, or picturesque. New Mexico's arid landscape, its adobe architecture, and especially the Indians, who Mabel saw as native apotheosis, thus have ended up as objects consumed by sight-seeing tourists, who travel not for enlightenment but to collect cheap knickknacks and visual mementos. And they unwittingly perpetuate the imperial-colonial relationship between themselves and the Indians even when, Tony Lujan–like, the natives are seduced by the romantic and mystical image they see reflected in the eyes of the sightseers. As for the Hispanos, they remain just as Mabel and the Taos painters saw them, occupying a less attractive and even menacing background but encouraged by the tourist economy, historian Hal K. Rothman's "devil's bargain," to remain unchanged lest the exotic and picturesque lose their luster.

The "amenity migrants" from California and elsewhere, the gentry who affect "pseudo-ethnic" wanna-be attire and whose goal seems to be to build houses in the very scenes that were painted by the landscape artists? Pathetic yearners and poseurs who apparently lack a culture of their own, or else hate it, or are shopping for a new one in the Great Mall of the Southwest, Rodriguez implies. Even Anglo support of some ethnic and environmental conservation in New Mexico ("museumization" in Rodriguez-speak) is suspected self-aggrandizement. Of course, this is all a bit heavy in victimology 101, as postmodern feminist deconstruction is inclined to be. But no one who spends a summer morning on the plaza in Taos or an evening at the Pink Adobe in Santa Fe can miss seeing all the disturbing emblems of the New Mexico that Mabel Luhan's vision bequeathed us.

Unlike Mabel's vision of Taos, I don't think O'Keeffe's message was, "Abiquiu holds the secret to a new American culture; come hither and buy, sell, and own it" (although some of Rio Arriba County's realtors seem to hope that's what she meant). O'Keeffe's message was a more fundamental one: Find your own place. Exult in the wonder of the sensual and elemental world around you. Learn its intricacies with passion and with all your senses. Respect the locals and their customs, but go native in your own way. Above all, find your *own* place. It's Thoreau's maxim, gone Western: Creating your own original relationship with the universe is the most important thing of all.

Or so we concluded after a morning in Georgia O'Keeffe's house.

This summer of my Abiquiu immersion is briefly wet, but in fact this is the third year in the mid-1990s that the shadow of a great drought has reached up out of the deserts of Mexico to drape its effects across the Southwest. When the rains have come, they have been blinding downpours, and everywhere in the valley the fierce runoff has left spray fans of rocks and soil across the roads and turned the Chama roiling red. Not an unusual circumstance in an erosional country, right?

So you would assume. But there have been times in the history of the surrounding country when erosion here has struck certain observers as environmentally excessive and economically destructive. In fact, they've called it by a different name—gullying—and have wondered at the causes of its ebb and flow. The explanations and arguments lie at the heart of Northern New Mexico's environmental history. To me, they also strike at the core of claims by Reies Tijerina's followers down through the years that most of the high mountains surrounding Abiquiu belong to them as heirs of the *ejido* grants of the eighteenth and nineteenth centuries.

The erosion that is laying these fans across the highways of the 1990s has twice in the last hundred years produced extraordinary episodes of gullying in this country, and the question is why. So for the moment set aside the assertions by scholars who have studied the land grants that history and law are on the side of the land grant heirs; set aside the calls for heroic solutions, for something like a Hispanic Claims Commission to do the work the Indian Claims Commission did in addressing Native American claims against the United States. Simply consider this: Few of us today would endorse returning the New Mexican land grants to people who have not historically been good stewards of their mountains. It's a classic instance where environmental history ought to help.

You do not look today at the Piedra Lumbre Valley and think, "Aha, agricultural mecca." But apparently, if you were a seventeenth-century Pueblo or Navajo, an eighteenth-century Hispano, or a nineteenth-century Texan, you would have looked at this valley and said, "Aha, a place designed by nature for *sheep* (or goats, or horses, or cattle); nature erred in not putting them here; I'll help out." You might have wondered at Providence's shortsightedness in not providing the valley with grazers in the first place, but probably not for long. In fact, while there are grasses (like blue grama) here that coevolved with bison, and while archeology does show that small herds of bison sometimes ranged into the valley, recall that this is a valley floor that averages only nine inches of precipitation a year. Except for bands of bighorn sheep, grazers were mostly absent in the Southern Rockies. The mountain grasses did not evolve with heavy cropping at all.

To human eyes, however, all of the Horizontal Yellow including the Piedra Lumbre Valley looked like pasturage ready to be stocked to the rafters with the Mediterranean species Hispano colonists patiently drove up from Mexico in the early 1600s. To a proud Spaniard like Fray Chavez, New Mexico was the North American equivalent of Palestine and the Spanish Extremadura—a natural stock range—and thus was granted by God to one of the world's great stock-raising peoples, and it was good. The local Indians saw some advantages, too. In fact, the first herding of exotic grazers in the Chama River Valley probably was done by Tewa Pueblos (or, Curtis Schaafsma has argued, Navajos) as early as 1640. In the 1970s an archeological dig near the Abiquiu Dam unearthed the remains of an Indian settlement occupied from 1640 to 1710 that featured corrals made of boulders and significant evidence of sheep and goats. The Chama Valley was also one of the places the Pueblos took Spanish stock after the 1680 Revolt, and it became the principal corridor of livestock diffusion into the West thereafter, a sort of topographical nozzle that spewed Spanish horses, goats, and sheep into Ute, Comanche, and Navajo hands.

The first Spanish land grants made up the Chama were made in 1724, northwest of present Abiquiu, and in 1734 south of the river. These grants were mostly individual grants, made to farmer/herders who created extended family settlements and also brought in a Mediterranean complex of floristic exotics—wheat, pinto beans, peppers, and vegetables, along with a flotilla of garden and medicinal herbs—to the valley. Sixty-six scattered families were there by 1744, among them José de Reaño, whose ranch facing Pedernal Peak ran 2,300 sheep and more than 400 cattle. Atypical, maybe, since most families had fewer than a hundred head, but Reaño's operation alone argues for some thousands of stock in the vicinity of the Piedra Lumbre Valley by the mid-eighteenth century. In the Old World they called what sheep and goats can do to an arid country "Mediterraneanization." It was a process that had already devastated parts of Mexico like the Valle de Mezquital, and by 1750 it had already been going on for a century here.

When the descendants of the Chama pioneers think on their history today, they recall it as hard. On August 1, 1747, a combined party of Comanches and Utes enjoying the new freedom of horses between their

Reconstructed house—portholes only, no windows—from the time when Hispanic settlers on the margins of New Mexico dealt almost yearly with Indian altercations. Sacramento Mountains.

knees carried off 23 women and children from the Chama settlements. It was a pattern repeated too many times to relate, only the actors chang- ing, Navajos replacing Comanches, and every generation of Hispanos adding a new adaptive wrinkle to survivability. They built adobe struc- tures with windows only to the inside patio or castlelike rock dwellings, and they lived ever more scattered because they lost fewer animals (and children) to the Indians that way. As humans kept humble by large forces often do, they became fatalists.

They were also becoming more numerous. In the wake of the arrival of Hispano settlers, the Pueblo Indians had seen their population plum- met from over 80,000 to an eighth of that, where it leveled off. But there were almost 8,000 Spaniards and Castas in New Mexico by 1760, more than 20,000 by 1805, and 30,000 in 1822. Abiquiu's population was 1,152 in 1789, spread across nine plazas. By 1827 the population had grown to 3,557 in the Abiquiu district, and by that time, too, the great community grants like San Joaquin (1806), which draped for half a million acres across the canyon of the Chama, and Tierra Amarilla (1832) north of there were in place. Utilized mostly as sheep ranges, these featured the enormous mountain *ejidos* whose use for pasturage, wood, hunting, and so forth was a common right of grantees. Those rights continued to be exercised even after the Honorable Thomas B. Catron (one of the most vilified gringos in a state with an unsurprisingly long list) managed to fleece the grantees out of both the Tierra Amarilla and Piedra Lumbre grants in the 1880s.

Garrett Hardin, whose "Tragedy of the Commons" essay famously made the case that environmental exploitation is inevitable in any re- source owned in common (and hence that private ownership equals environmental health), may be the only thinker on the subject of com- mons who never read John Wesley Powell. Powell's experiences among nineteenth-century Westerners who had already worked out bioregional adaptations to local places—Mormons, especially, but Powell did speak of the New Mexican Hispanos—made him an advocate of local com- mons as opposed to full privatization. One of the reasons was that unlike Hardin, Powell understood that commons of the Mormon type or the Hispano *ejidos* were, in fact, managed. And so as the West approaches the twenty-first century, there are those like Colorado academic Devon Peña and Montana statesman Dan Kemmis who are resurrecting Powell and arguing for a federal surrender of the mountains and a re-creation of something like the old New Mexican "homeland commons." This, the argument goes, is the only way for us Westerners to become true bioregionalists. We have to have full control of our surrounding lands.

What I want to know first is how the original "homeland commons" functioned ecologically, and the Chama River country seems the perfect place to pose the question. Here localism was almost complete. Kin groups, the Penitentes, and the community ditch association determined power, and there was enormous *campanilismo*, or loyalty to one's village. Sociologists who have studied valley settlements like Cañones insist that long tenure on their grants gave settlers a deep attachment to their land, which they did actually call *madre*. They had priests bless their fields, ditches, and gates. The Mormons did something similar.

Something can be said about stewardship from this and from the existence (according to Devon Peña) of more than 40 folktales having to do with the Hispano relationship with the land and water. But the *ejidos*, which usually extended from irrigable stream up to the crest of the surrounding mountains and constituted a hydrographic basin, seem to me to be the litmus test. They weren't "wilderness," of course, although some of the highest zones went almost unvisited. Unlike the house plots and the irrigable plots of individual settlers within a community grant, the *ejido* could not be privatized, although a family could sell out its plots and a new buyer got the rights to the *ejido*, too.

In Europe and apparently in New Mexico, what governed the commons were rules like levancy and couchancy, which meant that on the commons you could only run the stock that you had sleeping and standing in your quarters, and you couldn't bring in extra animals in the summer. Chama Valley households generally owned 50 to 100 animals each, sheep and goats outnumbering cattle and horses by 20 to 1. Stock didn't increase indefinitely because there was insufficient time for the men to work large numbers of animals. These Old World usufruct strategies also ousted anyone who tried to hog land or water or who caused critical damage to riparian areas. The key to it was this simple: Until well after the arrival of the market and the cash economy, Hispanos in the Chama Valley did not grow crops or raise stock or cut timber for the market. Firewood cutting, plant gathering, and hunting all were essentially unregulated in the New Mexico *ejidos*, but so long as populations remained low and trespassers were held at bay, it seemed to work. Theoretically, outsiders weren't allowed in except with special permissions.

But I have to make the observation: If there was an Achilles' heel in commons management, it was the local villages' inability to deal with powerful interlopers. The near eradication of beaver on the streams of the New Mexican *ejidos* by mountain men trespassers in the 1820s was one threatening portent.

Like Mary Austin, most modern writers on the mountain villages of New Mexico have been rapt admirers. Comparing their adaptation to that of free-enterprise Anglo ranchers, John Van Ness goes so far as to assert in his careful academic language that "from an ecological perspective . . . the Hispanic mixed subsistence economy of northern New Mexico and southern Colorado was much better suited to effectively exploit the varied local environments and to sustain a modest population at an adequate level without causing permanent damage." That's not a troublesome statement to me; I've argued the same about the Mormon adaptation.

On the other hand, that comparison doesn't exactly address the questions we ought to be interested in from the contemporary perspective. Two centuries of occupation in place constitute pretty good evidence that the mountain villages were capable of sustaining *themselves.* The real question is, how good were these Hispano villager strategies at maintaining the ecological health and diversity of the *mountains? Ejidos* established in northern Mexico as a result of the land reforms of the twentieth century have compiled a notoriously poor record so far as nature is concerned. So how does New Mexican *ejido* management compare, not to the market-profit style of the private ranchers but to the Forest Service that replaced them as managers when the Carson and Santa Fe National Forests were created out of the old *ejido* lands in 1905?

These fans of mud and rocks across the roads of the Chama Valley in 1995 serve as an entrée to the answer. Beginning in the 1840s on the Rio Puerco, which drains the west Jemez slopes just over the ridgeline from Chama waters, travelers were taken aback by the 30-foot gully that the stream had begun to cut as it swept down the mountains. Continuous and lengthening gullies began to ramify like latticework up the slopes at the end of the nineteenth century. The Puerco had sliced a gouge 41 feet below its banks by 1927 and 55 feet deep by 1964, at which time the river's headwater streams had eaten angry red furrows into the mountains all the way up to ridgeline.

Although nineteenth-century Southwestern gullying began on the

Puerco, the phenomenon did not remain localized. Soon Tesuque Wash, and Galisteo Creek, and the Chaco drainage were carving raw slashes into New Mexico. The Department of Agriculture reported in 1937 that 75 percent of the upper Rio Grande drainage in the state was experiencing accelerated erosion and that every small valley in the watershed was rapidly gullying to bedrock. In the 1930s West Texas suffered gullying, and the problem was so severe in Arizona that it led to the famous draconian livestock reductions among the Navajos to prevent Hoover Dam from silting up. Flooding and gullying were so dramatic in Utah during the early twentieth century that several Mormon communities were abandoned and the La Sal/Manti National Forest closed.

What on earth? Well, to observers across the region, it was the cow, the sheep, and the goat on the Southwestern earth that was the problem. One of the first to advance this theory was Aldo Leopold, who in an article called "Pioneers and Gullies," written in 1924, insisted that the "virgin Southwest" had been despoiled by "the devegetation of the range through overgrazing by domestic livestock." But Leopold was even more specific. His investigation of the Santa Fe Trail, still visible as "an old earth scar" in the vicinity of Mount Taylor, not only found impassable gullies in the bottom of every arroyo the trail crossed, but according to him the tree-growth rings of adjacent junipers indicated 1850 as the date when the erosion commenced. To Leopold the lesson was clear: The Southwest had been a virgin paradise, with all the characteristics of an untouched garden, until the Forty-niners started traveling the Santa Fe Trail and introduced their domestic cattle to the Southwest.

Aldo Leopold usually was a pretty good historian, but here he erred badly, because of course it wasn't the Forty-niners who had introduced domestic stock to the Southwest but the Hispanic colonists 250 years earlier. Was it, then, Hispanic Mediterraneanization finally taking its toll on that "natural grazing paradise" that produced the gullying phenomenon?

A pair of famous geographers, William Denevan and Yi-Fu Tuan, took separate stabs at this problem half a century after the experts had concluded that grazing was the culprit. Tuan, struck by geological discoveries of an even earlier episode of gullying some 400 years before Spanish stock had arrived, thought another explanation had to be found. In a more direct test of the linkage between livestock and gullies, Denevan reconstructed the grazing history of New Mexico and concluded that stocking rates were extremely heavy in the Spanish-Mexican pe-

riods—as many as 3 million sheep, many concentrated by Indian depre-
dations in places like the Piedra Lumbre Valley—yet without gullying!
Perhaps, Denevan speculated, the villager check dams and irrigation
systems acted like giant beaver earthworks and offset overgrazing. Or
maybe the 5 million sheep and million-plus cattle reported in New
Mexico by 1880, after the railroads had arrived and Texas grazers fleeing
the depleted plains flooded into the territory, ate enough additional
forage that the watersheds were pushed over the edge in a kind of chaos
theory shift.

Or maybe, just possibly, the causes that brought the Southern Rockies to the point of unraveling weren't quite so linear and simple as
Leopold and the government bureaucrats believed. For instance, what
about *climate?* Specifically, what about the effects of rainfall during
droughts, when vegetation is beaten back by dry? Tuan's research into
Southwestern gullying in the twelfth and thirteenth centuries found that
while tree rings indicated a severe drought then, pollen analysis didn't.
The only possible explanation for that pattern is winter drought coupled
with episodes of heavy summer rainfall. It makes me think of those
intense summer thunderstorm cells building over the Pedernal and the
conclusion that the period from 1880 to 1950 may be very similar to
the thirteenth century, only magnified at the turn of the twentieth century by an additional factor: all those millions of idiotic sheep, eating
drought-weakened vegetation to the bare ground.

Three centuries after Pueblo (or Navajo) herders first brought Old
World animals to the valley where Abiquiu would one day perch on its
mesa, an American congress almost absentmindedly passed the Forest
Reserve Act of 1891, paving the way for the replacement of the bioregional adaptations local folks had made across the West. What replaced
them was a national plan that was a victory of elites, of urban people in
faraway cities, of scientific ideas about nature over local, rural, folk customs of living on the land. It was precisely this legacy of conquest that
ties the Old West to the new one.

It was a time of major loss for Northern New Mexicans. Their *ejidos*
had been declared inoperative by the court of private claims and the
Sandoval decision, and now rangers for the Santa Fe and Carson National Forests were asking fees for the rights that had been theirs by
birthright for centuries. You'd have to think that the final insult came

when forest officials concluded that the old Hispanic communal practices were largely responsible for the sad shape of the Sangre and Jemez ranges. Elk had disappeared from the mountains by 1888, sheep by 1903; only eight deer were killed in the entire Carson National Forest in 1915. Villagers were now traveling 15 to 20 miles to find sources of firewood. The mountains were so gullied that flooding became a perennial menace. The Rio Grande was now so silted up that after a major flood in 1884, it flooded in rapid succession in 1904–5, in 1912, in 1920, in 1929, and in 1941 and 1942. The Chama, which normally carries 357,000 acre-feet of water, poured 660,000 down its channel in 1941. Because its gullied watershed was fingered as a major source of siltation for the region, the Chama eventually got targeted for a dam by the Flood Control Act of 1948. The Abiquiu Dam was finished in 1963, burying 14,000 acres of this most beautiful valley under water and sediment in an effort to tame mountain runoff.

The Piedra Lumbre Valley wasn't just singled out for a dam. In the 1930s the Soil Conservation Service attempted a grasslands revegetation project on the valley floor, and it was clear about the major obstacle: the feral horses and burros that swarmed the surrounding cliffs, which were entirely removed. In fact, they were shot. Even so, revegetation proved tough.

And then there was the Forest Service, the direct representative of the new order. From the very first it seemed to have particular difficulties in the Chama country, where the villagers did not surrender their ancestral land rights meekly. The problems began with violence in Cuba in 1909, when herders were told they now had to pay grazing fees. Relations spiraled into open resentment and secret resistance in the '30s and '40s when government agronomists proclaimed grazing the cause for the ravaged condition of the Carson and Santa Fe forests.

The writers who have looked closely at this experience, like Bill deBuys and Paul Kutsche, insist that Forest Service officials did not purposefully set out to destroy the Hispanic villages, that their charge was to restore the health of the mountains and they believed the conclusions of their science as to how to do it. Quite a number of them *were* contemptuous of villager grazing traditions ("ridiculous" Kutsche quotes a forester asked about Hispano conservation practices), and when the inevitable reductions of stock permits came, the *Floresta* appeared obliv-

ious that the reductions hit these small operators so hard, then baffled by
the villager reaction. First goats, mainstays of the old pastoral bioregional economy, were banned from the forests. Then the number of
permittees, 2,200 individuals in the 1940s, was scaled back to a goal of
1,000 by 1970. By the 1960s there were permits for 21,637 cattle and 32,203
sheep in the two national forests of Northern New Mexico; carry capacity studies showed this stocking level was still almost 30 percent too high
and that even with the best possible management cattle would still have
to be reduced by 12 percent, sheep by 20 percent. The result at places
like Canjilon, near Abiquiu, was the announcement of a 75 *percent*
reduction in animal units.

These were the conditions that produced the Hispano uprising in
1966–67, and to say the least they got the Forest Service's attention. In
1968 then District Supervisor Jean Hassell authored a report, "The People of Northern New Mexico and the National Forests," that (in the form
of a working document called "The Hassell Report and Follow-up") has
been in effect since, causing national forests in Northern New Mexico to
be managed differently from those everywhere else. In addition to a host
of small changes that made the local Forest Service bureaucracy more
user-friendly and more inclined to seek local input in decision making,
the philosophy in the "Hassell Report" was almost revolutionary. It began by recognizing that the local Hispanos loved the region, lived close
to the land, and they intended to stay. And that since 22 percent of the
Carson and Santa Fe National Forests was formerly granted lands, this
was a crisis unlike anything the Forest Service had faced anywhere else.
The end result? To perpetuate itself in the region, for the first time ever
the Forest Service had to recognize the legacy, uniqueness, and value of
a preexisting local culture and to commit itself to cultural as well as
environmental preservation.

The peace since has been an uneasy one, but it is still in place.
Sufficient grazing lands remains a tremendous problem in Northern
New Mexico, firewood cutting has famously run afoul of the Southern
spotted owl and the Endangered Species Act, and the "Floresta" remains
an alien interloper to many. But local Hispanos have responded with a
new sense of themselves and with cooperative projects like Ganados
del Valle/Tierra Wools, with its promotion of local artisans and churro
sheep. And not only has Ghost Ranch, now owned by the Presbyterian

Church, opened the lands of the former Piedra Lumbre Grant to local grazers, in 1975 it even traded some of its land for National Forest parcels that were turned over to local Hispanos.

Tijerina himself, now more than 70 and still living in Cuba, is convinced that "the land has been freed," that the issue will be resolved in his lifetime. He has plenty of followers who think he's gotten soft and don't agree at all, as signs along Highway 84 through Tierra Amarilla still demonstrate. Moises Morales, a former member of Alianza, told an interviewer in 1992:

> We're still prisoners in our own land. First, the Forest Service took our winter pastures, then they took our mile cow permits and our saddle horse permits. They're manipulating us whichever way they want, and we're left with nothing. It's a disgrace what the United States did to our people. All they care about today is tourism.

The actions continue, too. In July 1979 heirs of the San Joaquin Grant set up a roadblock to stop logging trucks from hauling timber out of Santa Fe National Forest. Then in 1988 49-year-old Amador Flores was jailed for contempt of court in a dispute with a developer over a 500-acre parcel in the old Tierra Amarilla *ejido*. "Vista del Brazo" eventually settled, giving Flores $117,250 and 18 acres of land and turning over another 200 acres to El Consejo de la Tierra Amarilla, a group of descendants of the grantees. In an artful touch Flores's compatriot, Pedro Archuleta, fired three pistol shots in the air as Flores was released.

For a time in the early 1990s El Consejo was running a summer camp for young revolutionaries of color from around the country out of Tierra Amarilla and preaching the doctrine of a common oppressor. "Who's the enemy?" an Albuquerque reporter asked in 1991. "White people" came the reply in unison. Then sophistication set in. "Europeans" a young man corrected. "Upper-class Europeans" offered another.

Not a conversation, you have to guess, the real estate trainees are busy memorizing to regale their California customers.

It must have been especially galling to *Norteño* villagers. Imagine listening to rapt newcomer admiration for the respect your Pueblo and Navajo neighbors have for the land while singling out your own practices as the particular cause of local environmental degradation. Insisting to the

Sign on Highway 87 outside Tierra Amarilla, New Mexico, May 1996.

Forest Service that "we are natives" and that they understood how to use their country, the villagers didn't buy it. They still don't.

Devon Peña insists that we ought to celebrate *Norteño* land use management, that it is another example of a locally based bioregional society with benign ecological effects. "Our communities," he's said, "created ecologically balanced lifeways well before 'conservation' entered vernacular speech. Our land-based origin cultures did not need Leopold, Muir, or Thoreau to develop environmental ethics." Maybe. Over 150 years the Chama Valley Hispanos *had* become natives; they *did* know their country well; the feedback loops were short. And while their animals changed the sierra, there was no wholesale remaking, no campaigns of execution against predators, for instance. *Fatalismo* offered a pragmatic argument against wasting effort trying to control the uncontrollable. Besides, the goal was subsistence, not profit.

Peña doesn't deny that the Southern Rockies were falling apart at the beginning of the twentieth century. But he argues that it wasn't until "imperialist" forces arrived in the form of the railroad and Anglo stockmen that the mountains began to unravel. In this claim there is a chorus.

Frances Quintana blames the environmental degradation exclusively on the Americans and traces erosion and gullying in the Chama watershed to Thomas Catron's lumber railroad and its clear-cutting of Chama River ponderosa groves after his acquisition of the Tierra Amarilla Grant. Other writers, Westphall and Van Ness particularly, think that overgrazing didn't commence until Texans and other herders glommed onto New Mexico in the 1880s. And now the geographers have questioned grazing itself as the principal cause of Southern Rockies deterioration.

So are Peña and all those grantee descendants who insist that the land grants be returned right? What about people like Dan Kemmis, with their arguments for new bioregional societies and homeland commons to replace the West's centralized and federal system? Were John Wesley Powell and Mary Austin correct to hold the *Norteño* villages up as models for a future West?

I think they were, and while classic *ejido* management strikes me as more concerned with human needs than nature's health, modern proposals (like one in Colorado's San Luis Valley) for homeland commons make me think that Hispano environmentalism has come a long way. On the other hand, a sense of Chama Valley history leads me to suspect that low human population, kept that way largely by the Indian threat but unleashed after U.S. acquisition (New Mexico's population skyrocketed from 61,500 in 1850 to 93,500 in 1860), was central to both the health and decline of the mountains. So while I am persuaded that the *ejidos* were proclaimed U.S. public domain illegally and that the *Norteño* bioregional societies were not the ultimate cause of environmental degradation in northern New Mexico, I also am unwilling to promote the wholesale turning over of the *ejido* portions of the national forests to the local villages.

Why? It's a question of power, and what history says about it. Even if the Hispano mountain villagers recognized their own culpability as nineteenth-century gullying erupted (I've seen no evidence that they ever admitted as much), New Mexico environmental history seems to show that the granted villages lacked the power to keep trespassers from the world of markets and profits at bay. Again and again their *ejidos* were overrun by trappers, roving sheepmen, outlaw loggers, cattlemen who talked them into leases and quickly depleted their grass. That has been the case many times in history when locals with coveted resources came up against big economics; I fear it would be the case now. For a host of very compelling reasons, the descendants of the grantees should be compensated by a Hispanic Claims Commission for their wrongful losses. They should be given special rights on the national forests and an important role in comanaging their old homeland commons in some form of new, experimental, community-based conservation initiative with the Forest Service.

I am a believer in the public lands, though, and beyond those changes I would have to say that however satisfying a turnover would be to grantee descendants, the greater good is served by the national system.

It is almost noon when my companion and I sling cameras and canteens across our backs and finally set out up the back side of the Pedernal. There are no friendly Forest Service trails up the Pedernal, and on a mountain this steep the boulder field cascading from the south rim is too loose and fresh for us to follow a single line of ascent without someone getting tattooed by bouncing rock. We split up and climb. Nothing technical about it; it's just advance, slide, suck in air as the altitude increases, reposition, push on. And dart glances at the sky as the late morning clouds gather. Can we crest out before the convection currents build a whorly afternoon storm cell over the Pedernal? It's a bit of a race.

Nothing technical, but when we get to the base of the rimrock, I'm wishing I'd brought a rope. The Pedernal's rim is a 35-foot vertical face, broken enough with cracks to climb up okay. Coming back down would be a lot easier rappel than a climb. But we have no rope; we'll worry about getting down later.

It takes a few minutes and a few muscles. And then we're on top, and of course it is perfectly level, not slanted as it appears from below. Just as I'd thought. And what an apt name Pedernal is! Standing on the crest is to balance on the blade of a knife, its razor edge in rest now from what would seem a stab skyward up through the bowels of the earth. A mere 20 steps through scattered piñons takes you from one edge to the other.

From the north edge there it is, the entire middle Chama Valley spread out below, a panorama in earth Technicolor, speckled with cloud shadows to the far edge of the encircling Horizontal Yellow. To the west is the Chama, exiting its 33-mile gorge after tumbling down through old Tierra Amarilla lands from its sources in Colorado. The reservoir, mirroring the blue that will always dome this world, glitters like an irregular turquoise stone in the red desert below. From this view, the geology rimming the Piedra Lumbre Valley is laid out as if in a computer simulation: The brick red Permian shales of the river gorge on the bottom, the maroon-red Chinle mudstones (the "Red Hills") above that, providing a Triassic age base for those buff-and-yellow Jurassic sandstones—the Entrada formation—that fashions the cliffs and turrets that drew O'Keeffe here. From this eagle's vantage view we can see that the white Todilito band capping the cliffs runs the circumference of the whole valley, like a rim decorating a pot. Atop it sit the younger sediments of the Colorado Plateau—another badlands slice (the Morrison) and finally up to the level of the Pedernal beneath our feet, flints and sandstone blocks from the heyday of the dinosaurs.

My companion points. There, exactly north, are the cliffs of Ghost Ranch, and at their feet O'Keeffe's Rancho de Los Burros. It's the mountain's view of the artist, and we realize that we're standing at the other end of the most famous visual dialogue in Southwestern history.

O'Keeffe liked to climb, but none of the locals is sure whether she ever climbed the Pedernal—Rose Gutierres thinks she did—or if she was merely content to look on it until it became too dim for her failing sight to see. Regardless, she's here. When she died and finally merged with that fathomless blue, Juan Hamilton brought her ashes up here and scattered them across the valley from this mountain. But she was a climber, and in honor of that I've hauled to the top of her mountain a copy of a letter she wrote to Cady Wells in the early 1940s, and as we sit in the dirt and look at the view I take it from my pocket, unfold it, and read some of it aloud. These lines particularly:

> Tonight—at sunset I walked alone out through the red hills. . . . I walked some distance—then climbed quite high—a place swept clean where the wind blows between two hills too high to climb unless you want to work very hard—I didn't want to climb so high—it was too late—but from where I stood it seemed I could see all over this world—When the sun is just gone the color is so fine—and I like the feel of wind against me when I get up high—My world here is almost untouched by man—

Just so. Enthralled by her vision, that's the image of Abiquiu and the Southwest the world has inferred from her art—"almost untouched by man." The Southwest defined as landscape.

Behind me there's an ominous rumble from some faraway/nearby point in the sky. Time to go before the lightning bolts come to play in the peaks. But I walk to the eastern point of the blade for one last look, just to satisfy myself. You have to look hard to see them in the vast space below, but sure enough, there are Abiquiu, and Canjilon, and the roads past the view go to equally old places: Cañones, Tierra Amarilla, Coyote, and Cuba.

With all respect, your world was not just landscape after all, Miss O'Keeffe. It was a world of history, of people, and of pathos. All along.

7 Wolf Song Redux

He calls himself part wolf, part man. . . .
With the "man" he packs in everything spiritual and
sublimated or even cultivated to be found in himself, and
with the wolf all that is instinctive, savage and chaotic.
HERMANN HESSE, *Steppenwolf*

Dreams and beasts are two keys by which we are to find
out the secrets of our nature.
RALPH WALDO EMERSON

Before wolves, coyotes were the big dogs on the block. Now
wolves are the big dogs. And they're swaggering through
the Lamar Valley and putting the fear of God in these
coyotes.
DOUG SMITH, YELLOWSTONE BIOLOGIST, 1997

[Opposite: Petroglyph, eastern New Mexico. (Photo by Kate Dowdy.)]

Long ago, it is said, in the time of the First People, who existed before humans and who made the universe as we know it, Wolf was walking down the road, thinking big thoughts. Now, Wolf was what you might call a visionary or a mystic. He had some power to see what was going to happen in the future, and he knew human beings were coming.

"These will be interesting neighbors to have," Wolf said to no one in particular. He was just chewing the fat, you know, thinking aloud. "I think I should be their friend and help fashion a world that's perfect for them in every way." Pleased with this idea, Wolf kept on walking, talking to himself about how he could make the world the kind of place humans would really enjoy.

Up ahead, near a fork in the road, there was a big mesquite tree giving off a little skimpy shade, and sprawled underneath it, panting in the heat, was Wolf's brother, Old Man Coyote. But Wolf was so completely absorbed in his reverie of the future he was going to create that he failed to notice Coyote and walked right on by, muttering things to himself that Old Man Coyote, slyly perking his ears, overheard.

"And I'll hunt rabbits and deer with them," Wolf was saying, "and show them how to stampede buffalo off the cliffs, and I'll catch all the sick and injured and stupid animals so the ones they catch will be healthy and fat." Old Man Coyote arched an eyebrow at this, but he remained silent and immobile as Wolf padded by and continued on down one of the forks in the road. The last thing he heard was Wolf's voice, growing ever fainter and muttering things like, " . . . and teach them what a good thing fire is, and all the best places to live, and so they aren't lonely at night I'll sing for them, and maybe I should take a bone and show . . . " And Wolf's voice faded away.

Old Man Coyote crawled from beneath the mesquite, stretched and scratched, and watched Wolf disappearing off to the west, talking to himself and switching his tail from side to side with pleasure. As he prepared to piss on a prickly pear, a grin started at the corners of Old Man Coyote's mouth and then deepened into a jolly smirk that spread across his whole face as he thought of a grand and glorious joke.

The insights of evolutionary psychology and the pursuit of religious spirituality, everyone will agree, are separate spotlights playing across the human condition. But one of the points where evolutionary psychology and religion seem to converge is that however disposed we are toward the pull of our genes or our longing for external meaning, one of the secrets of a happy life is learning to let go of what cannot be. Life is change, and change is passings. Experiences, relationships, youth—life—now savored inevitably dwindle in the wake of time's arrow. Best to experience the world rapturously, use it sparingly, and be Zen about change and the atrophy principle.

Sound wisdom, maybe. But when it comes to the devastation of the natural world and the loss of biological diversity that has so skewed sense of place in the modern world, Zen acceptance is just not an easy thing. The Hispanic cultures of the Southwest possibly excepted, we Euro-Americans arrived in the Americas at a time when all the forces of history were urging individuals on in their freedom to tear the place to bits. This is a declensionist take on the process, I'll admit, but our Old Worlder ancestors who seized the continent from the native peoples by no stretch accepted the world they took as it was. And they quite literally applauded it as a positive good, for humanity and progress, when the native animals were erased . . . especially when those animals were wolves.

We contemporary enviro-romantics who want the wolf back haven't been very Zen about the animal's passing, either. We've argued, loudly, on grounds of scientific ecology and predator-prey balance that wolves and mountain lions are necessary to natural design. You want elk, deer? Then you have to have wolves. And we insist on biocentric grounds and rather more softly that every species after all has an innate right to exist. Given the power of our surroundings to shape our values, among ourselves many of us suspect that five centuries after we've arrived on the continent, going truly native to America may not be possible on a continent without wolves. The conclusion (which won't surprise anyone who's attended a wolf reintroduction hearing) is that the whole American West, including the Near Southwest, at the turn of the twenty-first century is not a psychologically well-adjusted place. And that wolves have something deeply fundamental to do with that.

Except for the occasional strays that continued to drift up from Mexico as late as the 1960s, the Horizontal Yellow has been No Wolf's Land for the entirety of the last three-quarters of the twentieth century. Yet here it is the 1990s in West Texas, and I am riveted by the presence of a wolf staring directly at me through the mesquite from a distance of no more than 50 feet.

She is ebony black, and at this distance I can see that she is a muscular and reflexive miracle in the prime of robust ability. She looks huge, although I know that the thick wool beneath her four-inch growth of guard hairs is one of the things that gives her size, that she probably weighs under 80 pounds. Her legs are long, brindle colored, tapering down to delicate ankles where bone and sinew execute a 90-degree flare into padded feet the size of a woman's hand. Gliding away through the mesquite and cactus, she moves on those feet like black water pouring, her fox bush of a tail carried low, her hindquarters slightly lower than her withers as she trots, rendering her movements vaguely hyenalike. But it is when she stops to stare back at me over that sharp, refined muzzle that I most feel the power she represents. Her eyes are yellow amber, and they do not break contact furtively as do those of a dog but emit intelligence—presence is the best word—unwaveringly into mine. There is explication in that look. It makes you understand, somehow, why this animal above all the other natives engenders both fierce hatred and consuming love. The look in those yellow wolf eyes speaks to the heart of the dilemma—of the untamable wildness that frightened Europeans into an orgy of wilderness destruction but also the spirit of a continent that has to be embraced if we are ever going to be Americans.

The possessor of that look has a name: Ysa, short for Ysambanbi, which in the Comanche language means "Handsome Wolf" and was the name of a prominent Comanche *nomnekaht*, or war leader, who 200 years ago often camped in the High Plains canyon where I'm now watching her. The name is apt, for at three years old she is truly a beautiful animal. Ysa and her mate, Wily—a strapping, cream-colored cross from Arctic tundra wolf and McKenzie River husky parentage—are "my" wolves, or wolf hybrids, as they both have some small percentage of domestic canine ancestry, although short of a genetic analysis of their DNA, I don't think anyone could say how much "dog" and how much "wolf" is there. As with most of these feared and much maligned animals ("Worse Than Pitbulls" was the title of a piece airing on national television at the time), it doesn't take much wolf ancestry to color behavior sharply, and Ysa and Wily act like dogs about the same way buffalo act like cows. Not very, in other words.

Isa, my female wolf hybrid.

Wolf hybrids are something of a phenomenon in the United States these days, one about as welcome to many Americans as the phenomenon of armed middle-aged rednecks nursing black helicopter and New World Order fantasies. As Susan Stewart of Knight-Ridder news service put it in a review of a documentary on the return of the wolf, "What is wolf behavior? Basically, wolves kill little animals." Wolf fascination "may succeed with those viewers who have not lately been reading *Little Red Riding Hood,*" she wrote. As for her, "Mary, her little lamb and the Christmas season are too potent as symbols to leave any room for wolf sympathy." In sum, in America any animal that's regarded as a threat to little girls, cuddly lambs, and Santa Claus has a definite spin problem.

I can't say why most people who do something as impractical as acquiring wolf hybrids do so, and I confess I am as leery as the next person of someone like the truck driver from Pampa, Texas, who called me wanting to know where he could get a wolf hybrid to train as a guard-attack animal and who hung up on me when I told him that animals that were high-percentage wolf were far too shy around people to work as guard dogs. I think that what I can say, though, is that my own experience with wolf hybrids is grounded in a kind of quest for native authenticity in a landscape—the Southern High Plains—that had every last buffalo stripped from it by 1878, every last wolf by 1924, and almost every last blade of grass in my own time. My concession (and confession) is that I think I have been driven a little crazy by this, and in the longing to repossess the essence of the banished, I ended up committing sins I never intended to commit.

The cuddly lamb types (and the ranchers) are right: I suspect that owning wolf hybrids is a symptom of a disturbed personality. What sort of illumination this casts on the wolf in American sense of place could be peripheral, but probably isn't.

One thing we know for certain from evolution is that with the single exception of other primates, wild canids have been intimately associated with humans longer than any other animal on the planet. One of the best biological clues for the temporal depth and intimacy of human relationships with other animals is shared diseases. We humans share 50 diseases with cattle (including one of the deadliest killers of humanity, smallpox, evolved from cowpox), 46 with sheep, 42 with swine. But we share the most diseases of all, 65, with canines. The relationship is so old, it probably predated our manipulation of fire as a tool. In fact, in his 1920 *The Origin of Man*, one of the first books to advance a Darwinian explanation for human evolution, psychologist Caveath Read argued that early proto-human hunters may well have modeled their social and cooperative life after that of the canid packs in their midst. The evolving human mind was "a sort of chimpanzee mind adapted to the wolfish conditions of the hunting pack," Read thought, and he believed that when the fossils of humanity's earliest ancestors were found, they should be named *Lycopithecus*—"wolf-ape."

Like humans (and few other species), wolves are so ecologically flexible that in the last several million years they have become cosmopolitan, spreading across the globe. Native virtually to the entire planet, like humans, wolves proceeded to evolve into many different regional types, genetically related pools of animals specific to particular geographic settings, that acquired in the minds of early recorders of wolf information in the West something like the status of regional Indian tribes. I notice, looking over at my Hall and Kelson *Mammals of North America*, that wolf taxonomists have designated 24 North American subspecies of

Canis lupus and another three of *Canis niger*, the red wolf. Too much taxonomic splitting there, certainly. But it still says something about what regionalists wolves are.

If the old Hall and Kelson taxonomic exercise really does represent reality in the West of a century ago, then there were some wolf tribes worthy of recognition. And in the Southwest, of most interest to those of us who've dreamed the dream of the wolf's return is a handful of subspecies of *Canis lupus*—not all of which, it is feared, left their genes to the future. One is *C. l. baileyi*, the Mexican wolf, whose original range extended across Chihuahua and Sonora to southern New Mexico and Arizona and Trans-Pecos Texas. In a kind of regional wolf maelstrom centering on the White Sands dunes country, the Mexican wolf's range there met the range of *C. l. mogollonensis* (the Mogollon wolf), of the upper desert Southwest, *C. l. monstrabilis* (the Texas gray wolf), and *C. l. youngi*, whose range covered the Colorado Plateau and Great Basin. *Canis l. nubilus*, the Plains buffalo wolf, roamed originally from the Texas Panhandle to Saskatchewan. The range of the Rocky Mountain wolf, *C. l. irremotus*, centered around the Northern Rockies of Wyoming, Idaho, Montana, and Alberta but extended down the Rockies into northern New Mexico. Way north, in Alaska and the Yukon, were three subspecies, *C. l. alces* of the Kenai Peninsula, *C. l. pambasileus* of the interior, and *C. l. tundrarum* (the tundra wolf) of the northern coastline.

Other than some celebratory records of their trapping and annihilation and Ernest Thompson Seton's stories of a few particularly charismatic wolves—canine Crazy Horses or Sitting Bulls—who were able to put up an effective resistance for a time against their extermination, no American naturalist or conservationist ever made an effort to study these Western wolf subspecies when they were all extant. Of the brawny plains lobos, or buffalo wolves, we can today find out little other than what their executioners preserved, for this is an animal whose pure genetic makeup has been literally erased.

Sitting beside the clean yellow flame of a piñon fire in the canyon country of the Llano Estacado, as I write this I am surrounded by buffalo wolf country, buffalo wolf denning sites, buffalo wolf folklore: all the wolves in one of the river valleys of the Red River poisoned out in a season by a Comanche market hunter; cowboys pulling wolves apart with ropes from horseback; professional wolfers like Allen Stagg and

Jack Abernethy poisoning 200 to 300 wolves a year on the XIT Ranch in the 1890s; accounts of a mass wolf self-exodus westward into New Mexico, like Mormons or Jews searching for a refuge; people in the Trans-Pecos using newly installed phone lines to put gunmen onto wolves; an account of the last wolf in the Texas Panhandle, gutshot with a .22 and run down with a Model-T. But there are no buffalo wolves. One of our close relatives, one of the animals that defined the very nature of this country for 10,000 years, whose adaptive strategies set a pattern for mammalian life here, has been wiped clean from the topography. Look to the wolf for an inspiration for how to go native here, and you look into a black hole where things disappear and never return. Or so the modern world seems to think.

I mark it a measure of the madness of the world I have been born to that I made it to my forties and had to drive 3,000 miles northward from the Near Southwest before I saw my first wolf in the wild.

It was the summer of 1990. Jerry Griffin and I were in British Columbia, closing in on Stone Mountain and a campsite for the night, driving the Alcan Highway in a kind of tribute to the last great American wilderness, when suddenly in the mundane world of blaring twentieth-century music and whining rubber on asphalt, a dream loped up out of my subconscious and across the road. Enclosed in our technological shell, hurtling across the continent at a hundred kilometers an hour, we were still looking at the vastness around us as scenery. But British Columbia is not like the Llano Estacado. British Columbia is alive, and it is one of the places that has simply been too vast, cold, and remote for humans to have killed everything.

I was driving and was rounding a curve with the low Northland sun in my eyes when I saw the motion of her, a rocking-chair rhythm coming up the highway embankment 50 yards ahead. By the time she was halfway across the road and had turned her head to fix me with her eyes, I knew exactly who she was. Perhaps dredging up from some eons-old genetic memory I knew the lope and I knew the look, and I knew she wasn't a coyote or a dog.

You will think me a strange, sheepish, romantic idiot, perhaps (and if you're a Western rancher you may want to direct a sidelong spit at my guts from that reservoir between cheek and gum), but I have already admitted that my mental health is not good—or at least it is not Zen—

when it comes to wolves. So I have to write that the sight of this beautiful young female wolf, alive and unafraid in her home country, still makes me shiver a little when I conjure it.

When I drove back from Alaska several weeks later, Wily, a year-old male wolf cross who'd been abandoned in an Anchorage kennel, rode in the back of the Jeep, a late-twentieth-century White Fang bound for warmer climes.

Old Man Coyote was talking, and Bear and Roadrunner and Rattlesnake were listening.

"So you see what a great joke it is," Coyote was saying. "I've fixed it so that every single thing that Wolf plans to do to help out these human beings is going to work in reverse. They're going misinterpret all of Wolf's intentions. They'll claim credit for fire, cooperation, even the notion of pair-bonding! They'll think Wolf is cruel and—get this— 'inhuman' when he tries to make the herds healthy for them. They'll think his culling steals animals from them, and they'll use his serenading of them to hunt him down. And hoo, boy! Wait'll you see what they're gonna end up doing with that bone/tool trick Wolf plans to show them." Old Man Coyote doubled over with laughter. "Hoo, boy!" He danced hyperactively around a cholla.

Roadrunner and Rattlesnake shot worried glances at each other, wondering how a world with so much misunderstanding in it was going to work. But it was Bear, whose posture, diet, and general demeanor were something of a pattern for the way humans were going to be, who spoke.

"So this is going to be one of your big cosmic jokes, huh, like that idea of yours that everybody's got to die?" Bear fixed Old Man Coyote with a reproachful look. "That one kind of backfired on you, didn't it, Coyote?" Rattlesnake, who had been responsible for biting Old Man Coyote's child and first bringing death into the world, slithered out his tongue but kept his thoughts to himself.

"Well?" asked Roadrunner, tapping Coyote with her stiletto beak. "What's your guarantee that if we go along with this foolishness it's not going to backfire? Against Wolf, against all of us. The humans might not even find this joke funny. What if it turns on you, Coyote?"

At this Old Man Coyote stopped dancing. "Turns on me?" he repeated, thinking. "Nah, no way. And if it does, I'll think of something.

Besides, Wolf can take care of himself. I know he'll think this is the funniest spin I've put on the world yet."

And Coyote cackled so hard he sat down, thump, in the dust. He cackled so hard he had to stick his nose straight up in the air to gasp for breath. Gasping and laughing and interjecting an occasional "Hoo, boy," Coyote sounded like this:

"Hoo, boy, hoo, hooooooo, yurooooooo, hoo-yip-yike-yik-yip-yip-yip-yurooooooooo, hoo, boy."

I am crouching, on hands and knees in an exposed spot, and if you're into self-revelation, you just can't get more exposed anywhere on the planet than on the Llano Estacado of West Texas. Except for shorts and a pair of moccasins, I am naked in the baking sun and the powder dust, nothing but a flimsy arrangement of yuccas to protect me. Eyeing me with alarm, dung beetles waddle away into the short grass, performing their handstand technique to roll away their delicacies, a strategy enabling them to keep a complicated array of beady eyes on me all the while. Evidently they don't think much of my chances, either.

Fifty yards away I can see two pairs of sharp ears emerging out of another big clump of soapweed. Something about their intensity signals to me that another rush is coming, but before I can figure out how I know that, there is a perceptible gathering, and then two very large forms explode out of the yuccas, bound directly for me. The forms approach so rapidly and directly and with such lack of wasted motion that I should be able to register knife-edge detail, but it's a bit like trying to pick out the stitches on a Nolan Ryan fastball. Instead there is a slur of cubist images—red, open mouths, a tongue streaming saliva, yellow eyes gyring in on my movements—carried by a thumping rhythm that reminds me of something primal and ancient that I am too mesmerized to fix.

The 50 yards takes less than three seconds. Twenty feet from where I crouch, dripping sweat into the dirt, the careening forms part. One—the bigger, cream-colored one—low-hurdles me without missing a stride. It makes no attempt either to bite or slash. The black one is smaller and quicker and waits until I am distracted by the hurdler before whirling behind me, exposed fangs gleaming curved and white in the sun, and snapping the end of my ponytail. Gotcha!

Wily trots up to give me a quick kiss and then jaw-wrestles with Ysa while I regain my composure after their charge. It is the fall of 1991, almost 18 months after I'd brought Wily back to Texas. Through one of those complicated sequences of events that karma or the gods or pre-science (or owning land in the country) seems to set me up for, I've been bequeathed another wolf. Ysa, now an eight-month-old female pup who's supposed to be 90 percent eastern timber wolf is the result.

Getting rushed by a couple of wolf hybrids is obviously not quite the same thing as witnessing life from the perspective of a wolf's prey—but then that's been a harder one for humans to experience than you might think. Fact is, except where rabid animals are concerned, wolves simply do not prey on people. Some predator biologists argue that wolf pups, which have to learn almost everything about how to survive from in-struction, are given certain prey templates to look for. Humans don't seem to be one. Supposedly there have been only three attacks on humans by wild wolves in the twentieth century. The most famous wolf attacks in history occurred in Languedoc, in France, in 1767, when wolves were supposed to have killed and feasted on more than a hundred people, mostly children. The story is hard to document, and wolf lovers claim the guilty animals were actually—naturally enough—wolf hybrids. My favorite part of this story has always been the practical and entirely modern solution proposed by the Languedoc politicians, though. Sup-posedly they recommended that the French government round up all the wolves in the province and then relocate them (properly rehabili-tated, wouldn't you think) among the peasants of England.

All the wolves we have left in North America seem to have come from a common ancestor, the Dire wolf, a massive predator the size of a Shet-land pony that pursued and pulled down camels, sloths, giant long-horned bison, and perhaps mammoth calves during the late Pleisto-cene of 10,000 years ago. That world, a world of science fiction giants that hardly seems real to us a hundred centuries later, nonetheless be-queathed to the Dire wolf's descendants their proper place in the scheme of North American ecology. So you vegans who make up the Fund for Animals, all you "wolf adopters" who send your money to Wolf Haven, all you consumers of cutesy wolf mugs and medallions and wolf-adorned electric toothbrushes—best you look wolves in the eye and envision a wolf life for what it is.

Because what wolves do is hunt, kill, and eat other animals. Not nearly so omnivorous as coyotes or bears, wolves like mammal flesh, and they prefer it freshly killed. As "in" as the charismatic wolf has become for a certain environmentalist element in the late twentieth century, we ought to be agreed that since Dire wolf days, the wolf has been the most efficient killer of large mammals, especially big ungulates, of any American predator. Big 700-pound grizzly bears like to eat army cutworm moths and grass and marmots, things that die, to be sure, but not quite so dramatically as the way an elk or a bison dies. Wolves, while they *will* pursue mice and rabbits and other small stuff, prefer caribou, deer, elk, buffalo, moose. Wolf kills are marvels of athleticism, speed, endurance, and teamwork on the part of the wolves. For their prey a fatal encounter is marked by terrified flight, resistance, and the horrible capitulation of a crippled and overwhelmed animal. It is nature. It has little to say to human morality or aesthetics or ethics, whose nuances spring from culture.

We are never going to know well how the ecology of pre-European North America worked. Indian oral traditions can give us some inkling, but not much. Modern wolf recovery studies are probably the closest we can get, and these show that when wolves are reintroduced, they produce a staggering effect on wolfless ecologies, a kind of top-down reshuffling of populations and relationships among dozens of species from prey to competing predators (like coyotes!) to ravens, magpies, and eagles. Even beetles! But how can we grasp the full dimensions of Plains buffalo wolf impacts on bison, for example, without either free-roaming buffalo herds or a genetic population of buffalo wolves to study? Moreover, like most science, the results of contemporary predator-prey studies are soaked in political debate. Every side, wolf advocates, sports hunters, ranchers, has a favorite one.

It has been fashionable in recent years to argue against predation as a factor in controlling prey populations. But this idea is ecological revisionism. Beginning in the 1920s, when ecologists began to probe the possible beneficial effects predators might have on nature, the classic view was that the predator-prey relationship worked mechanically, that predators were the key to holding prey populations under some carrying capacity fixed by nature, and that the relationship worked as a rhythmic oscillation around a steady line. As rabbit or deer populations increased, in other words, the number of bobcats or wolves also increased until a point was reached where predation dampened prey population growth. Declining numbers of prey in turn suppressed predator population growth until the scenario commenced once again. This concept, which was given a name—the Lotka-Volterra equation—furnished evidence from predation that ecosystems worked in simple, linear, mechanical fashion. For much of the twentieth century the Kaibab disaster, when all the big predators had been eliminated from Arizona's Kaibab Plateau and the mule deer population went through an efflorescence, destroyed its browse, and then crashed spectacularly, was used to demonstrate the role of predation.

In the 1940s, though, an ecologist named Charles Elton discovered that the records of the Hudson's Bay Company, whose trappers had been harvesting furbearing animals from the boreal forest of Canada for almost two centuries, indicated something otherwise. While the HBC trapping records did show regular cycles in the populations of snowshoe hares and lynx, the cycles didn't match the assumed equation. Hares seemed to have four-year cycles, while lynx populations revolved around a 10-year cycle. A subsequent and more critical look at the HBC records indicated that in fact, the hares and lynx had been trapped in different areas, so any attempt to combine the data painted a false picture. But Elton had set predator rethinking in motion.

Similarly, at midcentury Durwood Allen's work on moose and wolf interactions in Isle Royale National Park in Minnesota showed what seemed to be wild swings in the populations of both species. It also showed the precarious nature of predation: Wolves commonly "tested" more than a dozen moose before they were successful in bringing one down. By now predation revision was in full swing, and in 1973 a New Zealand ecologist, Graeme Caughley, published a soon famous paper asserting that predators played little or no role in controlling populations of many prey animals and that for some ungulates an autogenic (internal) mechanism slowed or stopped population growth when it approached carrying capacity. Furthermore, Caughley argued, for a variety of reasons the whole Kaibab episode probably didn't mean what ecologists thought and likely was a hoax, anyway.

Here at the turn of the twenty-first century predator revisionism seems to be in retreat. Studies from the western Canadian provinces, from Alaska, and from Minnesota, where wolf populations are still healthy, all seem to demonstrate a significant role for wolves in establishing the dynamic equilibrium of nature. In southeastern Alaska wolf predation is said to have exerted strong evolutionary pressure on the behavior and habitat selection of mountain goats. In Alaska and the Yukon wolf harvest has been assessed along with factors like nutrition, snow depth, and disease, and in one controversial study wolves and bears were labeled the chief influence on moose and Nechina caribou demographics, taking over 30 percent of the moose population annually. Wolves are also known to play a central role in bison populations in Wood Buffalo National Park in Canada. And in Minnesota, in a particularly compelling study done by well-known biologist and wolf advocate David Mech, wolves were assessed as a key cause (among several interacting ones) responsible for an almost complete deer herd collapse in the Superior National Forest in the 1970s.

So if I try to reconstruct in my mind's eye how the Great Plains bison-wolf interaction worked out on the Horizontal Yellow, you must forgive the thinness of my sketch and the transliteration required. I have no choice.

In modern chaos theory, natural systems like the bison-wolf ecology of the ancient Great Plains are characterized by considerable variation within a normal equilibrium. Disruptions or disturbances are inevitable, and if they are of sufficient magnitude, they can cause the whole system to shift suddenly to a new equilibrium. The Pleistocene extinctions were one such disturbance, a massive shift that struck the West roughly 10,000 years ago. Unlike many native genera, wolves and bison both survived, although the new species that evolved from the process represented a dwarfing within each genus. As the dwarfed modern bison proliferated by about 5,000 years ago to fill all the grazing niches left vacant, Plains buffalo wolves, too, must have enjoyed a heyday. The new equilibrium, so far as I can tell, lasted right down to about 100 years ago.

When early Euro-American diarists like Meriwether Lewis and Audubon and Frémont first observed wolves on the Great Plains, they called them the "shepherds" of the buffalo herds. Although connections between particular bison herds and particular wolf packs have been observed at Wood Buffalo National Park, the analogy probably didn't work that way on the open plains. Individual wolf packs probably did not follow the herds as they shifted north and south, summer and winter. Under normal conditions wolves are territorial. A wolf pack, which com-

George Catlin left this time machine imagery, which no one in twentieth-century America got to see until wolves were reintroduced to Yellowstone Park in 1995. (Courtesy National Museum of American Art, Smithsonian Institution.)

monly consists of the alpha breeding pair and from one to two litters of its pups, establishes a home range that, to be sure, may encompass several hundred square miles. But it has boundaries, the center of which is usually the denning site. Areas adjacent to the denning sites get hunted harder. Periphery areas where pack boundaries overlap are commonly avoided by wolves, creating a phenomenon that both biologists and anthropologists have noticed in North American ecology. Periphery zones occurred where Indian tribal boundaries met as well and served the same function: They allowed the buildup of relatively unmolested herds of animals. Canine and human hunters alike must have possessed a mental map of the continent as a vast network of overlapping, concentric rings of wildlife populations.

Individuality is marked in wolves, and it must have meant that the packs had many different strategies for hunting bison. George Catlin preserved for us a marvelous pair of watercolors showing a wolf pack attacking a grown, but ailing, bison bull. Particularly in deep snows that inhibit their movements, adult ungulates do attract wolf attacks, although Catlin's paintings—showing lobos getting tossed like bowling pins—underlines the risk to wolf life and limb. Some wolf packs may also have learned how to stampede bison off cliffs, feasting on the mangled and injured animals. Some anthropologists believe Indian hunters learned the technique of the bison jump from wolves.

But by far the most common wolf strategy for buffalo hunting was described by William Clark, on April 22, 1805, when the Lewis and Clark expedition was ascending the Missouri River through what is now North Dakota. As Lewis recorded it, "Capt. Clark informed me that he saw a large drove of buffaloe pursued by wolves today, that they at length caught a calf which was unable to keep up with the herd. The cows only defend their young so long as they are able to keep up." What William Clark had noticed was a phenomenon Plains Indians had long observed as well. For every 10 of those cuddly little yellow-red buffalo calves dropped, the Pawnees said, wolves usually ran down and devoured about four. (That may be a little high: Environmental history indicates wolves probably took about 30 percent of the natural bison increase every year.)

"See those circles in the grass?" travelers on the overland trails would say, pointing to revegetating buffalo wallows. "They're wore down by mother buffalos trying to protect their calves from the wolves."

This time it was Bear who was talking. And this time Buffalo was there. So were Rattlesnake, and Roadrunner, and Magpie. Old Man Coyote was there, too. In fact, he was standing in a circle made by the rest, and he wasn't looking so hot.

"So what do you think now, Coyote?" Bear was saying. "Your trick didn't fool all the humans but it fooled a whole lot of them. Look what they're doing to Wolf! They don't understand how the world works!" He looked accusingly at the Old Trickster. "Dying is one thing, and I think we're all agreed that your dying idea hasn't been bad. It has made living well more important, and that's good. But murdering? Killing not for food but out of jealousy and spite and misunderstanding, the way those humans are doing?"

"It makes the world too absurd," Rattlesnake said quietly.

Old Man Coyote was pretty glum, but he was irrepressible, and he couldn't help himself. "It hasn't been such a bad deal for my kind," Coyote offered.

"Weak," Rattlesnake hissssed. "Pretty friggin' weak."

The wolves Euro-Americans encountered in the West beginning in the sixteenth century had been behaviorially conditioned by long centuries of peaceful relations with the native peoples not to fear human beings. It's not that they were aggressive—Europeans consistently expressed scorn at what "cowards" wolves in the West were—but that they were so tame. Catlin, the German nobleman Prince Maximilian of Wied, farther south people like Washington Irving and Josiah Gregg—virtually every diarist of the nineteenth century West speaks of how trusting wolves were, trotting in front of their horses like dogs or sitting curiously on a sandbar as their flatboats passed within feet. William Clark finally yielded to some irrepressible urge and actually killed one with a bayonet, just because he could.

So you get the impression that the wolves were completely unprepared for what happened when the great shift came in the 1870s and 1880s. For almost 10,000 years they had lived and died and taken their (roughly speaking) allotted third of the natural increase of the teeming wildlife of the West. Now things began to change. At first they were better. In the years when the Plains Indians were getting caught up in the market hunting of buffalo, after about 1820, the wolves must have done very well on the offal resulting from a mounting human harvest. The return and spread of horses across the West during the sixteenth through nineteenth centuries was also a boon, although maybe more to mountain lions than wolves. But the wolf bonanza of all time clearly was the white slaughter of the remaining few million buffalo for their hides and tongues from 1872 to 1884.

It was likewise the biggest setup. Like coyotes, wolves have some autogenic mechanism that enables them, within limits, to match the size of their litters to environmental potential for wolves. When the old bison-wolf-Indian equilibrium flew apart, the Indians taken out of the equation, the bison virtually canceled as an effect—wolf populations across the West were, briefly, at a high-water mark. The new equilibrium was slow to form, but it involved the replacement animals, domesticated stock like cattle and sheep, raised by ranchers who would brook no losses to predators. To the wolves, sheep and cattle must have seemed critters that *needed* killing—all of them helpless, infirm, and lame witted. To the ranchers, to the professional wolfers, to the governments that backed their actions, wolves were a visible and hateful symbol of the wilderness that civilization was on a mission to suppress. By 1880 the great Western wolf war was joined.

I realize there are people who yet take satisfaction in this cleansing, this final solution, because I have met some of them. But the details of the wolf war make up about as sorry a story as you'll find in Western history, and that's saying some given what happened to ethnic minorities and nature in general in the winning of the West.

Wolves were shot, roped, gassed, stomped, strangled. They were trapped with the new steel leghold trap invented by Sewell Newhouse (to replace the wild with "the wheatfield, the library, and the piano," Newhouse said). They were hung from trees as if they were human outlaws. Germ warfare was tried: In Montana a 1905 state law required veterinarians to infect captured wolves with sarcoptic mange and release them to spread the disease. But mostly they were poisoned, and by the thousands. Everyone in the West for three decades or so seemed to regard it as a patriotic duty to carry a vial of strychnine around to lace every carcass with poison. It was civilization's revenge on the animal that more than any other has reminded the civilized how brief is their separation from the animal.

Between 1901, when the professional wolfer Ben Corbin published *The Wolf Hunter's Guide* explaining the wolf war in terms of Christianity, democracy, and the depravity of wolves and enlisting converts to the crusade, and 1924, when the Predator and Rodent Control (PARC) section of the federal Bureau of Biological Survey was distributing 3.5 million strychnine baits annually, the West was cleared of all but a few pockets of wolves. Montana alone executed over 80,000 by 1918. As someone has put it (or should have), it was not that the wolf killed the sheep. In reality, sheep killed the wolf. Wolves were gone from Yellowstone and Glacier Parks by the early 1930s. The last buffalo wolf killed in the Texas Panhandle was miserably gutshot by picnickers in 1924; by midcentury both Texas grays and buffalo wolves had been rendered extinct genetic types. Mexican wolves were essentially cleared from the Southwest by 1926. Loners that drifted up from Mexico's Sierra Madre and tried to reestablish a foothold in the Southwest were hunted down like escaped convicts. Arizona bagged its last wolf in 1960, Trans-Pecos Texas its last one in 1970. Only in the far north of the continent, in Alaska, Alberta, and British Columbia, were there still healthy populations of wolves. Even there 17,000 wolves were poisoned across western Canada to protect the caribou herds in the 1950s, and a rabies eradication program reduced Alberta's wolf population from 5,000 to fewer than 1,000 by 1960.

But at least *some* wolves were still there. Except in those remote, northwestern wildlands, wolves, wolf predation, wolf song had been entirely erased from the interior American West. Coyotes, flexible, adaptable, capable of living in civilization's shadow, reaped the benefit, assuming most of the wolf's former range across the continent.

The age of the wheat fields, the libraries, the pianos—and the pathological—was upon us.

Everyone knows by now that there is such a thing among wolves as an alpha pair, the dominant male and female of a pack that make most of the decisions and do all the breeding. What those of you who haven't spent time around canines of wolf ancestry may not know is that the alpha animal doesn't necessarily have to be a wolf.

Female wolves come into heat once a year, usually in midwinter, so their pups (born 63 days later) have the advantage of nature's lush time. A female wolf becomes sexually mature in the winter before her second birthday. For Ysa that time arrived in the winter of 1991–92. The problem was that it was me she had the hots for.

By this time Wily was well over a hundred pounds of muscle and gristle. He could shear through a pound of rock-hard, frozen hamburger with a single, lazy crunch. Like most wolves and high-percentage wolf hybrids raised by humans, Wily and Ysa were not domesticated animals, but they were socialized, which means in effect that they accepted me and a very small handful of other humans (mostly women, interestingly) as fellow wolves with whom they interacted lovingly and playfully. Most other humans they regarded with abject horror, and they hid and fled from them. Me they assumed to be a member—the alpha male—of their pack.

So in the gray of a plains winter in late 1991, when Ysa began to evince signs of the onset of estrus and began to flirt with me unashamedly, eventually presenting herself to me every time I got in their acre enclosure, Wily dutifully assumed the role of the beta male and stood guard for our lovemaking. Of course there was a bit of a problem here. Ysa, it was true, had matured from awkward adolescence into a slender, lovely thing, with golden eyes and fine, jet-black hair. She was quite the kisser, too. But in fact I was already involved. She was attractive, but I found myself having to decline her advances.

She was insistent, but so was Wily, every time I left their pen. When I returned from a Christmas trip taken during the height of her estrus, I immediately noticed a newfound intimacy between them. Ysa still flirted, and Wily still yielded to me—but he also mounted her now with a kind of public recklessness, my "wolf live-sex act," as a friend called it. And I noticed that after I left their pen, often as not he would chase her down and roll her in the dirt for her indiscretions with me. For this she would pop her jaws at him—*whack, whack, whack*—with a sound that echoed off the canyon walls. But I also got the impression she approved of his possessiveness.

On a snowy day in January, I felt her belly and could tell she was pregnant.

Nature abhors a vacuum. A couple of years ago a friend who happens to be a wildlife biologist in Texas explained to me the economics of coyote control. He and his graduate students had decided to poison, trap, and helicopter-gun every last coyote off a large West Texas ranch just to see how long population recovery would take. In under a year, through migration and expanded litter sizes of other coyotes in the region, the coyote population on the ranch was up to 80 percent of what it had been when the scorched earth policy was implemented. "What'd the rancher say?" I asked. "Hell," my friend laughed, "he read our report, spat in the dirt, and opted for coyote control anyway." The wolf vacuum in the American West may have lasted a little longer than the coyote vacuum on that Texas ranch, but not by much.

Something fundamental in the American perception of nature seems to be changing at the turn of the twenty-first century. It may not be the paradigm shift the New Agers talk about. Maybe it's only the noblesse oblige of a society that thinks it has nature on the run and can afford to be a little generous. Environmentalist values, biocentric thinking, urban crackpotedness, the looniness of youthful idealism (Pete Story, Montana rancher, to Renee Askins of the Wolf Fund: "Dear, when you're my age you'll look back on this as one of the goofy things you were into")— whatever the root cause, the wolf has become a beneficiary. Remember the loonies of the Nixon years? Bless 'em, one of the things they bequeathed us was the Endangered Species Act of 1973. And one of the things that act brought us was federally mandated *recovery* of endangered species like wolves.

Like those West Texas coyotes, of course, just how much help the wolf actually needed is open to question. In the 1980s Alberta's wolf population rebounded to some 4,200, and it was only a matter of time before all those elk and moose and deer in places like Glacier National Park in northwestern Montana attracted wolf attention. While biologists for the U.S. Fish and Wildlife Service were working on wolf recovery plans— one for reintroducing the Mexican wolf into the Southwest was completed in 1982, and the Northern Rocky Mountain Wolf Recovery Plan was released five years later—wolves were eyeing the vacuum in the American West and making their own plans.

Once I helped a friend band hawks. The first one we caught was a big, mature redtail, and after Eric clipped on the band and made his notes, I held the big raptor's wings with one hand and its scaly, powerful legs with the other and tossed it into the air. But I must have done it unevenly, because there was a fraction of an instant between the lift of its wings and the return of its legs to freedom when it seemed . . . to carry me up. For about a thousandth of a second of my life, I flew.

The pups were born during a cold, rainy night, and maybe it was the rain—maybe it was her inexperience—that decided Ysa not to have them in one of the pair of mine shaft/railroad tunnel–size dens she'd excavated. Instead they were born on the flat, open ground, and since she couldn't keep them in a warm pile of pups without a depression, she lost five of them. That left two males and two females, which she moved into one of the dens once it stopped raining. For months she and Wily had been howling—the first wolf howls heard in this country for decades— and hearing only coyotes and their own echoes in that West Texas wolf vacuum. Maybe that's why she had that whopping litter.

I wish I could say that I assumed the role of the beta male and helped them raise their litter, but I can't. It's not that Ysa wasn't willing or that Wily resented his former rival. It was the pups. I did not, as some people advised me, take Ysa's pups away and raise them in the house to socialize them. From the time I first pulled them out of the den when they were three weeks old—little walruses with ears already erect and muzzles already elongating, already growling at one another—I handled them almost daily. But I wanted to watch Ysa and Wily raise them and teach them, with minimal interference. What I failed to anticipate was that they would raise wild animals.

Neotony, or the biological tendency of offspring to spend a significant percentage of their lives in the company of their parents, "is a characteristic of all species that have not inherited a fixed repertory of behavior, but must learn how to survive," according to Hope Ryden. So I got to see some remarkable things close-up that spring of 1992. I saw the vocalizations and expressions the pups resorted to in order to prompt their parents to regurgitate meals for them. I witnessed their instruction in how to avoid a rattlesnake and was rapt at Ysa's catlike (read repeated) demonstrations of how to pounce on hapless Plains wood rats that idiotically kept blundering into their pen. I dreamed about their wild circuits around their enclosure, tails under and rollicking along in a long lope that looked from a distance like gray waves surging above a green surf. One dusk a pair of coyotes took possession of the low hills across the road and started to yip and yodel. The wolves froze, peered for a moment at the coyotes . . . and then threw back their heads and joined in, the pups' adolescent howls breaking into yips and barks that were indistinguishable from the high-pitched yodeling of the coyotes.

They were all individuals. One, a little female that was a clone of her dad, was curious and happy and with lots of attention finally got friendly. A male I called Big Boy was James Dean sullen, but I could eventually handle him, too. But my favorites, the male and female that were near twins, with beautiful wolf markings and gray pelage, began scampering away from me by the time they were four weeks old. The female—Wolf Girl is what I called her—was oh, so beautiful, never more so than when I would reach out to her. But she steadily grew wilder the older she got. By the time they were two months old, I had found good homes for the other three. But Wolf Girl—yellow eyed, achingly beautiful in her nervous alertness, by now uncatchable and undoctorable—had become a big problem.

Whether creatures as intelligent as wolves can reason is as much a philosophical as a scientific question, in that the answer has significant implications for both. The creamy white female wolf that made conti-

nental history in the late 1980s could well have been engaged in de-
duction. But for some reason, where others had hesitated, she denned—
the first time close enough to the U.S. border that in November 1985
her litter, known as the Magic Pack, entered Glacier National Park
and became overnight celebrities. The white wolf's second litter was
whelped on Montana's Flathead River in 1986. It was probably the first
litter of wolves born in the American West in 50 years. Most of the wolves
that have since spread southward down the wild stringers of mountain
wilderness that make up so much of western Montana are the white
wolf's spawn. She was given a blue-collar name, Phyllis, so fittingly her
descendants are strapping big examples of *Canis lupus irremotus*, or the
Rocky Mountain wolf. A male radio-collared on the Sun River in 1993
weighed over 120 pounds.

Phyllis might have been famous in the United States, but in Canada
she was just a wolf. In December 1992 a Canadian hunter shot her. She
was running with dogs, he said, and dogs learning to go feral are of
course hated by everyone, ranchers and environmentalists alike. Univer-
sally we seem to think on *ferus* as a state of betrayal not much different
than that of a white renegade gone native with the Indians.

The wolves are on their way back, but as I write this, where they
are back in the flesh, it is as much through their designs as ours. The
Northern Rockies recovery approach has tried to take cognizance of the
Rocky Mountain wolf's plans and has proposed "natural recovery" in the
Northern Continental Divide Ecosystem in Montana, supplemented
with the 1994–95 human-assisted restorations in Yellowstone National
Park and (simultaneously) the Greater Selway/Bitterroot wilderness
areas in Idaho-Montana. The Northern Rockies wolf population will be
recovered, the plan says, when there are 10 packs of breeding wolves in
each of these regions. Meanwhile all the Rocky Mountain wolves are
considered an "experimental" population, a highly controversial environmentalist concession to ranchers with implications for more "flexible" management (livestock-killing wolves would be in the crosshairs,
in other words). How has it worked? Despite incidents of various kinds,
from shot and car-hit wolves and wolves falling into mud pots to the odd
few wolves that developed a fascination with the way sheep stand there
and let themselves be disemboweled, it has put wolf howls and the long
lope of a wolf through sagebrush back in the Northern Rocky Mountains
in our time.

As for the Southwest, the 1982 recovery plan for the Mexican wolf (reestablishing 100 wild wolves across a 5,000-square-mile area in the subspecies former range) was given a shot in the arm by these successful Rocky Mountain wolf programs and a kick in the butt by a lawsuit from wolf advocates in 1993. Over more than a decade before that, during which Mexican wolves may have become extinct in Mexico and thus in the wild, wolf recovery in the Southwest got no farther than a captive breeding program initiated from a single pregnant matriarch wolf captured in Mexico in 1980. During that interval wolf biologists were reworking Hall and Kelson's 24 subspecies, reducing the number of subspecies continentwide to five, the Mexican wolf among them. The sticking point was which of the abandoned subspecies were to be considered synonymous with the Mexican wolf. Although the most recent taxonomist to study the question argues that the wolves of the upper Southwest and Texas were more likely identical to the buffalo wolf (*C. nubilus*), the Mexican Wolf Recovery Team followed a study that considers the Mogollon and Texas gray wolves to have really been Mexican wolves all along. Arcane, perhaps, but all this has made a difference in where Mexican wolves eventually will be released.

The preferred alternative in the final environmental impact statement on Mexican wolf recovery (1996) borrows pretty heavily from the Northern Rockies experience. According to its summary, "Commencing in 1997, or as soon thereafter as practical, the Fish and Wildlife Service will gradually release up to 15 pairs or family groups" of wolves into the Southwest as a "nonessential experimental" population. And who of us in the Southwest gets to have wolves? Well, release sites were studied in Trans-Pecos Texas (the Big Bend area, essentially), southern New Mexico, and eastern Arizona just beyond the Continental Divide. And the winner? Texas, perhaps? Texas's response to bringing back wolves was to strengthen its stock raiser's law *prohibiting* predator introductions in the state. New Mexico, unfortunately, could do no better than the spot where the atomic bomb was tested—White Sands Missile Range with its herds of oryx and African exotics, calculated to confuse any sensible wolf. White Sands comes in for an honorable mention in the preferred alternative as a "backup" site for the possible release of five pairs or family groups. The winner was Arizona's Blue Mountains. And despite a New Mexico Farm Bureau lawsuit to reverse recovery, 11 Mexican wolves were released in the Blue Mountains in the spring of 1998.

OK, the Blues *are* probably the best site, and they're easy wolf travel from the Gilas and the Continental Divide. Through natural recoloniz- ation out of the Blues, the Near Southwest probably will have wolves in its mountains and canyons again one of these days. And of course the wolves could care less. They're on a mission from the gods, repopulating the earth after the devastation of a great war. It's we humans who, planted in particular places with the knowledge that wolves either are in the hills or aren't, have to deal with the great cosmic joke of wiping out a species we've coexisted with for a million years and half losing our sanity in the process. Interestingly, everywhere in the West that this wolf song redux is now a fact of life (Montana, for example), well over half of the citizenry approves. Ranchers and wolf haters are still capable of getting 40,000 signatures on an antiwolf petition, but Arlene Hanson of the No Wolf Option Committee is representing the last gasp of the vanished frontier holocaust, and nothing more, when she says, "The notion people have of hearing wolves howl and putting the ecosystem back together is just a bunch of malarkey."

For the growing army of us romantico-enviro-bioregional-primitive-earthists in the West, the possibility of a wolf howl is a possibility for peace of mind and the sanity of feeling a connection to place, to authenticity. There are those socialized beyond understanding such things, but this is a very real connection. And for some of us, when wild wolves are howling in the mountains again, wolf hybrids in the backyard are a crutch that can be put away.

There's one other oddity here that deserves mention. All over the West in the last few years, including famous instances in Yellowstone since 1992—and even near El Paso in 1995—there have been rampant stories of wolflike animals showing up in unexpected places, often in the company of coyotes.

Wolf sat well apart from Old Man Coyote as the two of them peered off the rim of the plunge at the world below. Who could tell anyway what Coyote was going to pull next?

"Are you ever going to learn, Brother?" Wolf asked. Wolf was not a vengeful sort, not the kind to hold a grudge. But his patience had limits, and most of Coyote's jokes seemed to turn out like this.

Old Man Coyote sighed. "Okay," he conceded, "that one did make for some weirdness." He took a couple of steps that brought him literally

The irrepressible God-dog.

to the edge of the precipice and looked off. "But we've been holding on to all of it down there for you. You know?"

Wolf didn't respond. He was gauging the distance, and contemplating a really funny idea.

Late August, 1992. I am standing in the wind on the edge of a red-and-green Technicolor world that stretches away 25 miles and more, beyond the curve of the earth. It's one of two or three of the wildest places still remaining on the Southern High Plains, and in this rainy summer it is flush with life. Springs are running, the grama grasses are green, and quail and pheasants with miniature coveys trailing them scurry underfoot everywhere.

Downslope an animal, a quadruped, has just disappeared behind a blocky sandstone boulder 200 yards away, and I am waiting for her to emerge. It has been many minutes now since a graceful bound carried her over the rim, and I have seen her only once—when she turned her face upslope, yellow eyes flashing a lock onto me across the distance. I could not read that look. It did not seem to be one of recognition, certainly not one of sentiment. Wolf Girl has never been mine.

The minutes stretch out to meet the dusk. She doesn't emerge. But from across the canyon a lone coyote raises its voice. It's a signal. Before the first one quits, there are coyotes singing in every direction, a symphony of coyotes fading into a kind of aural red shift that to my ears converts the cacophony into wolf song off in the direction of Montana. Where I'm bound.

I listen until dark without hearing her, and then I say a few words to the wind and the country and drive away.

Epilogue

I tell you this: No eternal reward will forgive us now for wasting the dawn.
JIM MORRISON

[Turkey Mesa, the cuesta (slant-topped mesa) out my door.]

Is it to be assumed that everyone in the world is born by accident or fate to exactly the right place for them? Since so many of us Americans relocate so often, the answer on the face of it would seem to be no. Some of us may have inherited traits of physiology or disposition that make sunny places better for us than cloudy ones, places with more (or less) sensory stimulation more (or less) satisfying. And everything we take in, from subtle socialization to outright manipulation and all between, gives us learned preferences in everything, and that includes landscapes and places.

Your affinity for place and mine are therefore different, and my experiences are thus only example. Born to the Louisiana edge of the Near Southwest, living at various times in the oak savannahs and the Hill Country of Texas and the Sangre de Cristo foothills of New Mexico, as an adult I discovered the Llano Estacado 500 miles around the swell of the earth from my nativity and proceeded to burrow in. But I went native less to the particularized culture of the place than to a topography—the arid, blue-domed, juniper-sunned-to-fragrance, vertical red slash in the Horizontal Yellow kind of country that (I realize) Georgia O'Keeffe has caused so many of us to see as the iconic Southwestern landscape. Culturally is a different matter. Culturally West Texas doesn't often get a fair look from people raised to other settings. But that can be a good thing, for in 20 years there I've not ever gotten over a sense of myself as a genetic, cultural, and certainly historical native of a larger Southwest than exists in the malls of Lubbock or Amarillo.

But big oil, agrochemicals, right-wingery, the Church of Christ, blue-haired ladies in Cadillacs, and bubba and bowhead couture are not why I left the Southwest for Montana. Those aspects of West Texas may strike many Southwesterners from more sophisticated places as "ghastly" (as a bookstore owner in Santa Fe sniffingly once said to me), but to me they've only been annoyances. I was not able to stay as a year-round resident because of the dissonance in my head between the ecologically rich world I know once existed here and the skinned and impoverished part of the Near Southwest I inhabited. I wanted a more entire heaven and earth.

The moon still rises over Turkey Mesa in Yellow House Canyon, of course, and such is my ancestral passion for that world that I still own my little ranch in the canyon. But except for a few weeks every year I do not reside full-time in my Llano Estacado canyons now, nor in Natchitoches or Austin or Santa Fe or Terlingua or anywhere else in the Near Southwest. I had other options, and so fennel green foothills smelling of sagebrush and encircled by the snowcapped peaks of the Northern Rocky Mountains is where I make my home for most of the year these days. There are wolves in the mountains round about, and grizzlies still, and wild horses in the red deserts not far distant. Public lands and big wilderness. A place where the natural world can be a large part of existence if you choose to make it so. Having exactly those things is why I live in Montana.

So it came to this. I left a Near Southwest with 90 times the population it had as an Indian-fashioned wilderness (and expectations of doubling that over the next half century) for a Northern Rockies where the population is only 10 times what it was five centuries ago. And did so very deliberately. As the grandchildren of Dust Bowlers return to Oklahoma, as New Mexico continues drawing immigrants to its sunshine and culture and hip image, as Texas nurtures an unquestioning vision of itself as a Third Coast, the Near Southwest seems to be replicating the destinies of California and the Far Southwest. With only one life to live, I don't think I want to be a part of that. But who knows? As Hemingway said, you can always go back.

Like Aldo Leopold pining away for New Mexico from green, distant Wisconsin, though, when I am away, I continue to think of the Southwest. The smells, first. Piñon logs burning sweetly in a fireplace. The perfume of a juniper thicket on a hot summer day. The smell of the Chihuahuan Desert in the first minutes after a thunderstorm has rumbled across to the next basin. The swirl of scents from a flower-spangled High Plains prairie in springtime. Then I think of the stories, and the places they evoke, and that light that will break your heart.

I suspect I'll always be a native.

Bibliography

Chapter 1

Abbey, Edward. *Confessions of a Barbarian: Selections from the Journals of Edward Abbey, 1951–1989.* Edited by David Petersen. Boston: Little, Brown and Co., 1994.

——. "Freedom and Wilderness, Wilderness and Freedom." In *The Journey Home: Some Words in Defense of the American West.* New York: E. P. Dutton, 1977.

——. "Thus I Reply to René Dubos." In *Down the River.* New York: E. P. Dutton, 1991.

Anderson, Gary. *Indian Ethnogenesis on the Southern Plains.* Norman: University of Oklahoma Press, 1999.

Botkin, Daniel. *Discordant Harmonies: A New Ecology for the Twenty-First Century.* New York: Oxford University Press, 1990.

Bowden, Martyn. "The Invention of American Tradition." *Journal of Historical Geography* 18 (January 1992): 3–26.

Breedan, James, ed. *A Long Ride in Texas: The Explorations of John Leonard Riddell.* College Station: Texas A&M University Press, 1994.

Cabeza de Vaca, Álvar Nuñez. "Relation that Álvar Nuñez Cabeca de Vaca gave of what befell the armament in the Indies whither Panfilo de Narvaez went for Governor from the year 1527 to the year 1536 [1537] when with three comrades he returned and came to Sevilla." In *Spanish Explorers in the Southern United States, 1528–1543,* edited by Frederick Webb Hodge. Reproduction of the 1555 edition, Austin: Texas State Historical Association, 1982.

Crosby, Alfred, Jr. *Ecological Imperialism: The Biological Expansion of Europe, 900–1900.* New York: Cambridge University Press, 1986.

Cronon, William. "Revisiting the Vanishing Frontier: The Legacy of Frederick Jackson Turner." *Western Historical Quarterly* 18 (April 1987): 157–76.

——, ed. *Uncommon Ground: Toward Reinventing Nature.* New York: W. W. Norton, 1995.

Denevan, William. "The Pristine Myth: The Landscapes of the Americas in 1492." *Annals of the Association of American Geographers* 82 (September 1992): 369–85.

Dixon, Olive. *Life and Adventures of "Billy" Dixon of Adobe Walls, Texas Panhandle.* Guthrie, Okla.: Cooperative Publishing Co., 1914.

Dobyns, Henry. "Estimating Aboriginal American Population: An Appraisal of Techniques with a New Hemispheric Estimate." *Current Anthropology* 7 (1966): 395–416.

286   ——. *Native American Historical Demography.* Bloomington: Indiana University Press, 1976.

Dubos, René. *The Wooing of Earth.* New York: Charles Scribner's Sons, 1980.

Emerson, Ralph Waldo. "The Method of Nature." In *Nature: Addresses and Lectures.* Boston and New York: Houghton, Mifflin and Co., 1905.

Graber, Linda. *Wilderness as Sacred Space.* Madison: University of Wisconsin Press, 1976.

Gutierrez, Ramón. *When Jesus Came, the Corn Mothers Went Away: Marriage, Sexuality, and Power in New Mexico.* San Francisco: Stanford University Press, 1991.

Jackson, Robert. *Indian Population Decline: The Missions of Northwestern New Spain, 1687–1840.* Albuquerque: University of New Mexico Press, 1994.

Jacobs, Wilbur. "The Tip of an Iceberg: Pre-Columbian Indian Demography and Some Implications for Revisionism." In *The Fatal Confrontation: Historical Studies of American Indians, Environment, and Historians.* Albuquerque: University of New Mexico Press, 1996, 77–89.

Leopold, Aldo. "Wilderness as a Form of Land Use"; "Pioneers and Gullies"; "The Virgin Southwest." All in *The River of the Mother of God and Other Essays by Aldo Leopold*, edited by Susan Flader and J. Baird Callicott. Madison: University of Wisconsin Press, 1991, 134–42, 106–13, 173–80.

Lincecum, Jerry Bryan, and Edward Phillips, eds. *Adventures of a Frontier Naturalist: The Life and Times of Dr. Gideon Lincecum*, with an introduction by Jerry Bryan Lincecum and foreword by A. C. Greene. College Station: Texas A&M University Press, 1994.

McNeley, James, *Holy Wind in Navajo Philosophy.* Tucson: University of Arizona Press, 1981.

Nash, Roderick. *Wilderness and the American Mind.* 3d ed. New Haven: Yale University Press, 1982.

Rostlund, Erhard. "The Geographical Range of the Historic Bison in the Southeast." *Annals of the Association of American Geographers* 50 (December 1970): 395–407.

Rudler, Gustave, and Norman Anderson, comps. *Putnam's Contemporary French Dictionary.* New York: G. P. Putnam's Sons, 1972.

Schambach, Frank, and Frank Rackerby. *Contributions to the Archeology of the Big Bend Region of the Arkansas River.* Fayetteville: Arkansas Archeological Survey Research Series 22, 1982.

Sessions, George, ed. *Deep Ecology for the 21st Century: Readings on the Philosophy and Practice of the New Environmentalism.* Boston and London: Shambhala, 1995.

Smeins, Fred, Sam Fuhlendorf, and Charles Taylor, Jr. "Environmental and Land Use Changes [in Texas]: A Long-Term Perspective." Paper presented at the Juniper Symposium, Texas A&M University, 1997.

Smith, Henry Nash. *Virgin Land: The American West in Symbol and Myth.* Cambridge: Harvard University Press, 1978.

Soulé, Michael, and Gary Lease, eds. *Reinventing Nature? Responses to Postmodern Deconstruction.* Washington: Island Press, 1995.

Worster, Donald. "The Wilderness Ideal in Canada and the United States," audiocassette presentation. In *Nature and Culture in the Northern West: A Symposium.* Missoula: Center for the Rocky Mountain West, 1994.

My account of the Freeman and Custis exploration of the sources of the Red River in this chapter is fictional, but the detail in Custis's letters to the Jefferson administration is as ecologically and historically accurate as I can make it. All the characters, save the Comanche shaman and Trujillo, the literate Comanchero, are real figures from history, consistent with their time and place, although Custis's She-day-ah would have been the mother of the woman of the same name whose portrait George Catlin painted in 1834. My Captain Viana is another exception. The real Viana would never have agreed to the kind of arrangement that in my time line allows Jefferson's explorers to continue upriver.

The events of the journey are real ones, assembled from an array of literature from the Horizontal Yellow. Briefly, Custis's description of the Blackland and Grand Prairies and the Wichita Indians (including Awahakei and Tatesuck) comes from Anthony Glass's 1808 journal and peripherally from Washington Irving's *Journeys in the Prairie*. The account of the Ouachita Mountains at the head of the Kiamichi River (which Custis calls the "Kiomitchie") is from botanist Thomas Nuttall's exploration in the area in 1819, and Custis's description of the Cross Timbers is from Josiah Gregg's *Commerce of the Prairies*. For the Rolling Plains country, the Wichita Mountains, and Tule Canyon I relied for a period reaction on Randolph Marcy's *Exploration of the Red-River, in Louisiana,* and for botanical discoveries on the borders of the Llano Estacado on botanist Edwin James's account of the Long Expedition down the Canadian in 1820. Custis's reaction to Palo Duro Canyon and the upper draws of the Red is similar to the reactions of the Texan–Santa Fe Expedition of 1841 and Ernest Ruffner's exploration in 1877. His response to the Llano Estacado is close to that of poet Albert Pike, who crossed the Llano and was stunned by it in the early 1830s. Cordero's aid and friendship of Americans is based on the Comanche leader's discussions with Dr. Sibley in Natchitoches in 1807 and his rescue of American trader Thomas James in this country in 1821. Custis's Comanche description follows Sibley's in an 1808 essay, "The Character of the Hietan Indians." Heinrich Mollhausen in 1853 witnessed a prairie aurora just north of where Custis saw his. The encounter at the pictograph site (today called Rocky Dell, near Adrian, Texas) is from Lieutenant James Abert's visit to the spot in 1846. And Custis's Wichita Mountains mustang country account is largely from George Catlin's experiences there in 1834. The mysterious dead buffalo scene comes from Charles Goodnight's puzzled description of a die-up (perhaps from anthrax) on the Concho River in 1867. She-day-ah's gift to Jefferson is the very prize the mustanger Philip Nolan (see chapter 3) was taking to Jefferson in the summer of 1800 but apparently sold (money before sentiment again!) in Kentucky.

I've added particulars of scenery and ecology in the region from some of my own explorations of the upper Red River country, beginning about 1968 and sporadically since then. The style and ideas about nature in these letters are Peter Custis's own, though, or at least I think they are if my grasp on what he actually wrote about the lower Red is secure. His ultimate impression of the kernel of the Horizontal Yellow is very close to Stephen Long's "Great American Desert" impression of 1820. No American who saw that country during this period could possibly have reacted much differently.

As for fictionalizing a continuation of Jefferson's Southwestern exploration, I ought to confess that I am not the first to find this irresistible. In 1983, in his novel *Valley Men*, the late Donald Jackson gave Freeman and Custis a chance to explore the Arkansas River the year after they were turned back on the Red. His narrator, like mine, was Custis but renamed "Dr. Raphael Bailey."

Allen, John. "Geographical Knowledge and American Images of the Louisiana Territory." *Western Historical Quarterly* 1 (April 1971): 151–70.

Amangual, Francisco. "Diary of Francisco Amangual from San Antonio to Santa Fe, March 30–May [June] 19, 1808." In *Pedro Vial and the Roads to Santa Fe*, edited by Noel Loomis and Abraham Nasatir. Norman: University of Oklahoma Press, 1967. Includes the journals of Pedro Vial, Jose Mares, and Francisco Fragoso.

Annals of Congress. 8th Cong., 1st sess., 1805, and 2d sess., 1805.

Barton Collection, Library of the American Philosophical Society, Philadelphia, which houses Custis's letters to his mentor from the Red River country, and later.

Bexar Archives. Barker Texas History Center, University of Texas–Austin, harbors the correspondence between Spanish officials relevant to stopping Jefferson's expedition.

Carlson, Gustav, and Volney Jones. "Some Notes on the Uses of Plants by the Comanche Indians." *Papers of the Michigan Academy of Sciences, Arts and Letters* 25 (1940): 517–42.

Carroll, H. Bailey. *The Texan–Santa Fe Trail.* Canyon, Tex.: Panhandle-Plains Historical Society, 1951.

Craven County Marriage Bonds, North Carolina State Archives, Raleigh, N.C.: Peter Custis application to marry Catherine Carthy on January 16, 1818.

Custis, Peter. Manuscript reports on the Red River Expedition. War Department, Letters Received, Main Series, National Archives Record Group 165, Washington, D.C.

———. "Observations relative to the Geography, Natural History, & etc., of the Country along the Red-River, in Louisiana." Pt. 2. *The Philadelphia Medical and Physical Journal* 2 (1806): 43–50.

———. Will and Testament. Craven County Original Wills, North Carolina State Archives, Raleigh, N.C., June 13, 1840.

Drinnon, Richard. *Facing Westward: The Metaphysics of Indian-Hating and Empire-Building.* Minneapolis: University of Minnesota Press, 1980.

Flores, Dan, ed. *Jefferson & Southwestern Exploration: The Freeman & Custis Accounts of the Red Expedition of 1806.* Norman: University of Oklahoma Press, 1984.

———, ed. *Journal of an Indian Trader: Anthony Glass & the Texas Trading Frontier, 1790–1810.* College Station: Texas A&M University Press, 1985.

Furtwangler, Albert. *Acts of Discovery: Visions of America in the Lewis and Clark Journals.* Urbana and Chicago: University of Illinois Press, 1993.

Goodman, George, and Cheryl Lawson. *Retracing Major Stephen H. Long's 1820 Expedition: The Itinerary and Botany.* Norman: University of Oklahoma Press, 1995.

Gould, Stephen Jay. *Wonderful Life.* New York: Pantheon, 1991.

Hollon, Eugene. *Beyond the Cross Timbers: Travels of Randolph Marcy, 1812–1887.*
Norman: University of Oklahoma Press, 1955.

Hunter, Clark, ed. *The Life and Letters of Alexander Wilson.* Philadelphia: American Philosophical Society, 1983.

Jackson, Donald. *Thomas Jefferson & the Stony Mountains: Exploring the West from Monticello.* Norman: University of Oklahoma Press, 1993.

——. *Valley Men: A Speculative Account of the Arkansas River Expedition of 1807.* New York: Ticknor and Fields, 1983.

——, ed. *Letters of the Lewis and Clark Expedition, with Related Documents, 1783–1854.* Urbana: University of Illinois Press, 1962.

Jefferson, Thomas. Papers. Library of Congress, Washington, D.C.

Kendall, George. *Narrative of the Texan–Santa Fe Expedition.* 2 vols. Austin: Steck Co., 1935.

Marcy, Randolph. *A Report on the Exploration of the Red River, in Louisiana.* Washington: Government Printing Office, 1854.

McKee, John. Papers. Library of Congress, Washington, D.C.

Miller, Stephen. Memoir on Physicians in Early North Carolina. Collection no. 371, East Carolina Manuscript Collection. J. Y. Joyner Library, East Carolina University, Greenville, N.C.

Nacogdoches Garrison Militia Muster, 1805–6, Bexar Archives.

Nuttall, Thomas. *A Journal of Travels into the Arkansas Territory During the Year 1819,* edited by Savoie Lottinville. Norman: University of Oklahoma Press, 1980.

Puellas, Fray José Maria de Jésus. *Mapa Geographica de las Provincias Septentrionales de esta Nueva España (año de 1807).* Map Collection, Barker Texas History Center, University of Texas–Austin.

Records of the Adjutant General's Office, 1780s–1917. National Archives Record Group 94, Washington, D.C., from which I assembled the muster rolls for troops assigned to the Red River expedition.

Robertson, James, ed. *Louisiana Under the Rule of Spain, France, and the United States, 1785–1807.* 2 vols. Cleveland: Arthur H. Clark Co., 1911.

Rowland, Eron Dunbar, ed. *Life, Letters, and Papers of William Dunbar.* Jackson, Miss.: Historical Society of Mississippi, 1930.

Ruffner, Ernest. "Survey of the Headwaters of the Red River, 1876." In *Report of the Secretary of War,* 45th Cong., 2d sess. U.S. Congress House Exec. doc I, vol. 2, pt. 2. Washington, D.C.: Government Printing Office, 1877.

Slotkin, Richard. *Regeneration Through Violence: The Mythology of the American Frontier, 1600–1860.* Middleton, Conn.: Wesleyan University Press, 1973.

Spanish Archives of New Mexico, New Mexico State Archives and Records Center, Santa Fe.

Wheat, Carl, comp. *1540–1861: Mapping the Transmississippi West.* 5 vols. San Francisco: The Institute of Historical Cartography, 1957–63.

Chapter 3

Abbey, Edward. "Wild Horses." In *One Life at a Time, Please.* New York: Henry Holt, 1989, 45–48.

Audubon, John James. *Ornithological Biography* . . . Vol. III. Edinburgh: Adam & Charles Black, 1835.

Bama, Lynn. "Wild Horses: Do They Belong in the West?" *High Country News* (Paonia, Colo.), 2 March 1998, pp. 1, 8–12.

Bandelier National Monument and Southwest Regional Office. *Amended Environmental Assessment, Feral Burro Management, Bandelier National Monument, New Mexico.* Albuquerque: National Park Service, 1979.

Benson, Nettie. "Bishop Marin de Porras and Texas." *Southwestern Historical Quarterly* 51 (1947): 16–40.

Becknell, William. "Journal." *Missouri Historical Society Collections* 2 (July 1906): 56–67.

Joel Berger. *Wild Horses of the Great Basin: Social Competition and Population Size.* Chicago: University of Chicago Press, 1986.

Berlandier, Jean Louis. *Journey to Mexico During the Years 1826 to 1834.* Translated by Sheila Ohlendorf, Josette Bigelow, and Mary Standifer. 2 vols. Austin: Texas State Historical Association, 1980.

"Birth Control for Nevada Horses?" *High Country News* (Paonia, Colo.), 8 March 1993.

Bollaert, William. *William Bollaert's Texas.* Edited by Eugene Hollon. Norman: University of Oklahoma Press, 1987.

Bolton, Herbert Eugene. Papers, pt. 1. Bancroft Library, University of California–Berkeley.

Bunderson, W. T. "Primary Production and Energetic Relationships of Wild and Domestic Ungulate Communities in African Ecosystems." In *Rangelands: A Resource Under Siege,* edited by P. J. Joss. Cambridge: Proceedings of the 2nd International Rangeland Conference, 1986, 397–401.

Burkhardt, J. Wayne. "Herbivory in the Intermountain West." In *Herbivory in the Intermountain West: An Overview of Evolutionary History, Historic Cultural Impacts and Lessons from the Past,* edited by Burkhardt et al. Walla Walla, Wis.: Interior Columbia Basin Ecosystem Management Project, 1994.

Burnet, David. "The Comanches." Pt. I of *Information Respecting the History, Conditions, and Prospects of the Indian Tribes of the United States,* edited by Henry Rowe Schoolcraft. Philadelphia: American Bureau of Indian Affairs, 1853.

California Manuscripts, Provisional Records, Letters Registers, 1794–1823. Bancroft Library, University of California–Berkeley.

Castaneda, Carlos. *Our Catholic Heritage in Texas, 1519–1936.* Vol. V. Austin: Von Boeckmann-Jones Co., 1958.

Catlin, George. *Letters and Notes on the Manners, Customs, and Conditions of the North American Indians.* 2 vols. New York: Dover Press, 1973.

Cobo, Father Bernabe. "History of the New World." 1891, typescript translation, Lawrence Kinnaird Papers. Bancroft Library, University of California–Berkeley.

Dawson, W. M. "Growth of Horses Under Western Range Conditions." *Journal of Animal Science* 4 (1945).

Dobie, J. Frank. "The Comanches and Their Horses." *Southwest Review* 36 (spring 1951): 99–103.

——. *The Mustangs.* New York: Bramhall House, 1934.

——. Papers, Items 16771–16776 (includes Bartlett, Collinson, Dwyer, Duval accounts). Ransom Humanities Research Center, University of Texas–Austin.

Dobyns, Henry. *From Fire to Flood: Human Historic Destruction of Sonoran Desert Riverine Oases.* Socorro: Ballena Press, 1981.

Foster, Morris. *Being Comanche: A Social History of an American Indian Community.* Tucson: University of Arizona Press, 1991.

Gelo, Dan. "Comanche Belief and Ritual." Ph.D. dissertation, Rutgers University, 1986.

——. "Comanche Horse Culture." Thundering Hooves Exhibit planning sessions, Witte Museum, December 1990.

Hackett, Charles Wilson, ed. and trans. *Pichardo's Treatise on the Limits of Louisiana and Texas.* 4 vols. Austin: University of Texas Press, 1931–46.

Hansen, R. M., et al. "Foods of Wild Horses, Deer, Cattle in the Douglas Mountain Area, Colorado." *Journal of Range Management* 30 (March 1977): 116.

Hulbert, Richard, Jr. "The Ancestry of the Horse." In *Horses Through Time*, edited by Sandra Olsen. Boulder: Roberts Rinehart Publishers for the Carnegie Museum of Natural History, 1997, 13–34.

Jackson, Jack. *Los Mestenos: Spanish Ranching in Texas, 1721–1821.* College Station: Texas A&M University Press, 1986.

James, Thomas. *Three Years Among the Indians and Mexicans.* Edited by Walter Douglas. St. Louis: Missouri Historical Society, 1916.

Jordan, Terry. *Environment and Environmental Perceptions in Texas.* Boston: American Press, 1981.

——. *North American Livestock Ranching Frontiers.* Lincoln: University of Nebraska Press, 1993.

Kust, Matthew. *Man and Horse in History.* Alexandria, Va.: Plutarch Press, 1983.

La Vere, David, and Kaita Campbell, eds. "An Expedition to the Kichai: The Journal of François Grappe, September 24, 1783." *Southwestern Historical Quarterly* 98 (July 1994): 59–78.

Laycock, W. A. "Stable States and Thresholds of Range Condition on North American Rangelands: A Viewpoint." *Journal of Range Management* 44 (1991): 427–33.

Linton, Ralph. "The Comanches." In *The Psychological Frontiers of Society.* Edited by Abram Kardiner et al. New York: Columbia, 1945, 47–80.

MacFadden, Bruce. *Fossil Horses: Systematics, Paleobiology, and Evolution of the Family Equidae.* New York: Cambridge University Press, 1992.

Neighbors, Robert. "The Nauni or Comanches of Texas." In *Information Respecting the History, Conditions, and Prospects of the Indian Tribes of the United States*, edited by Henry Rowe Schoolcraft. Pt. II. Philadelphia: American Bureau of Indian Affairs, 1853, 125–34.

Olsen, Sandra. "Horse Hunters of the Ice Age," in *Horses Through Time*, edited by Sandra Olsen. Boulder: Roberts Rinehart Publishers for the Carnegie Museum of Natural History, 1997, pp. 37–56.

Owen-Smith, N. "Pleistocene Extinctions: The Pivotal Role of Megaherbivores." *Paleobiology* 13 (1987): 351–62.

Peden, D. G., et al. "The Trophic Ecology of *Bison bison* L. on Shortgrass Plains." *Journal of Applied Ecology* 11 (August 1974): 493–95.

Pike, Zebulon Montgomery. *The Journals of Zebulon Montgomery Pike*, edited by Donald Jackson. 2 vols. Norman: University of Oklahoma Press, 1966.

Porter, Clyde, and Mae Porter. *Ruxton of the Rockies: Autobiographical Writings . . . ,* edited by Roy Hafen. Norman: University of Oklahoma Press, 1950.

Rendon, Gabino. *Hand on my Shoulder.* Rev. ed. New York: National Board of Missions, 1963.

Roe, Frank. *The Indian and the Horse.* Norman: University of Oklahoma Press, 1955.

Salter, R. E., and R. J. Hudson. "Feeding Ecology of Feral Horses in Western Alberta." *Journal of Range Management* 32 (May 1979): 221.

——. "Range Relationships of Feral Horses with Wild Ungulates and Cattle in Western Alberta." *Journal of Range Management* 33 (July 1980): 266.

Schultz, James Willard. *Apauk: Caller of Buffalo.* Boston: Houghton, Mifflin and Co., 1916.

Sherow, Jim. "Workings of the Geodialectic: High Plains Indians and Their Horses in the Arkansas River Valley, 1800–1870." *Environmental Review* (Summer 1992): 61–84.

Sieur de Cadillac to Pontchartrain, October 26, 1713. In *Mapping Texas and the Gulf Coast,* edited by Jack Jackson, et al. College Station: Texas A&M University Press, 1990, 5.

Simpson, Gaylord. *Horses: The Story of the Horse Family in the Modern World and Through Sixty Million Years of History.* New York: Oxford University Press, 1951.

Thomas, Heather Smith. *The Wild Horse Controversy.* South Brunswick and New York: A. S. Barnes and Co., 1979.

Vestal, Paul, and Richard Schultes. *The Economic Botany of the Kiowa Indians.* Cambridge: Botanical Museum of Harvard University, 1939.

White, Richard. "Animals and Enterprise." In *The Oxford History of the American West,* edited by Clyde Milner et al. (New York: Oxford University Press, 1994): 237–73.

Wolfe, Michael. "The Wild Horse and Burro Issue." *Environmental Review* 7 (summer 1983): 179–92.

Worcester, Donald. "The Spread of Spanish Horses in the Southwest." *New Mexico Historical Review* (July 1944, January 1945).

Chapter 4

Abbey, Edward. "Big Bend." In *One Life at a Time, Please.* New York: Henry Holt, 1989, 127–41.

——. *Confessions of a Barbarian: Selections from the Journals of Edward Abbey, 1951–1989,* edited by David Petersen. Boston: Little, Brown and Co., 1994.

——. Foreword to *The Deserts of the Southwest,* by Peggy Larson. San Francisco: Sierra Club Books, 1977.

Bailey, Vernon. *Biological Survey of Texas.* Washington: Government Printing Office, 1905.

Bedichek, Roy. *Adventures with a Texas Naturalist.* Austin: University of Texas Press, 1961.

Brown, David. "Chihuahuan Desertscrub." In *Biotic Communities: Southwestern*

United States and Northwestern Mexico, edited by David Brown. Salt Lake City: University of Utah Press, 1994, 169–79.

Bryant, Vaughn, Jr. "Late Quaternary Pollen Records from the East-Central Periphery of the Chihuahuan Desert." In *Transactions of the Symposium on the Biological Resources of the Chihuahuan Desert Region*, edited by Roland Wauer and David Riskind. Washington: U.S. Dept. of Interior, Transactions and Proceedings Series #3, 1977, 3–21.

Carraro, Francine. *Jerry Bywaters: A Life in Art*. Austin: University of Texas Press, 1994.

Chamberlain, Samuel. *My Confession*. New York: Harper & Bros., 1854.

Dallas Morning News. 1990–91 *Texas Almanac*. Austin: Texas Monthly Press, 1991.

Dobie, J. Frank. "My Friend, Roy Bedichek." In *Three Men in Texas: Bedichek, Webb, and Dobie*, edited by Ronnie Dugger. Austin: University of Texas Press, 1967, 1–12.

——. "A Texan Part of Texas." *Nature* (December 1930): 343–46.

Doughty, Robin, and Barbara Parmenter. *Endangered Species: Disappearing Animals and Plants in the Lone Star State*. Austin: Texas Monthly Press, 1989.

Douglas, William O. *Farewell to Texas: A Vanishing Wilderness*. New York: McGraw-Hill, 1967.

Editorial, *Texas Observer*, 17 September 1967, p. 2.

Fabry, Judith. "Guadalupe Mountains National Park: An Administrative History." National Park Service, 1988.

Findley, James, and William Caire. "The Status of Mammals in the Northern Region of the Chihuahuan Desert." In *Symposium on . . . the Chihuahuan Desert Region*, 127–39.

Furman, Necah. *Walter Prescott Webb: His Life and Impact*. Albuquerque: University of New Mexico Press, 1976.

Gehlbach, Frederick. "Biomes of the Guadalupe Escarpment: Vegetation, Lizards, and Human Impact." In *Biological Investigations in the Guadalupe Mountains National Park, Texas*, edited by Hugh Genoways and Robert Baker. Washington: National Park Service, Proceedings and Transactions Series no. 4, 1979.

——. *Mountains Islands and Desert Seas: A Natural History of the U. S.–Mexican Borderlands*. College Station: Texas A&M Press, 1981.

Gomez, Arthur. *A Most Singular Country: A History of Occupation in the Big Bend*. Provo: Brigham Young University Press, 1990.

Genoways, Hugh, et al. "Mammals of the Guadalupe Mountains National Park, Texas." In *Biological Investigations in the Guadalupe Mountains National Park, Texas*, 271–332.

Hailey, Tommy. "Past, Present, and Future Status of the Desert Bighorn in the Chihuahuan Desert Region." In *Symposium on . . . the Chihuahuan Desert Region*, 217–20.

Harris, A. H. "Wisconsin Age Environments in the Northern Chihuahuan Desert: Evidence from the Higher Vertebrates." In *Symposium on . . . the Chihuahuan Desert Region*, 23–52.

Henrickson, James, and Marshall Johnston. "Vegetation and Community Types of the Chihuahuan Desert." In *Second Symposium on the Resources of the Chihuahuan Desert Region*, edited by Jon Barlow et al. Alpine, Tex.: Chihuahuan Desert Research Institute, 1986, 20–39.

Hill, Robert T. "Running the Cañons of the Rio Grande: A Chapter of Recent Exploration." *The Century Magazine* 61 (January 1901): 371–87.

Jameson, John. "The Quest for a National Park in Texas." *West Texas Historical Association Year Book* 50 (1974): 47–60.

———. *The Story of Big Bend National Park.* Austin: University of Texas Press, 1996.

Johnston, Marshall. "Brief Resume of Botanical, Including Vegetational, Features of the Chihuahuan Desert Region with Special Emphasis on Their Uniqueness." In *Symposium on . . . the Chihuahuan Desert Region,* 335–59.

———. "The Guadalupe Mountains—A Chink in the Mosaic of the Chihuahuan Desert?" In *Biological Investigations in the Guadalupe Mountains National Park, Texas,* 45–61.

Kidd, Rodney. "Our Out-of-doors Hotel." In *Three Men in Texas,* 27–30.

Limerick, Patricia Nelson. *Desert Passages: Encounters with the American Deserts.* Albuquerque: University of New Mexico Press, 1985.

Miles, Elton. *Tales of the Big Bend.* College Station: Texas A&M University Press, 1976.

Miller, Thomas. *The Public Lands of Texas, 1519–1970.* Norman: University of Oklahoma Press, 1972.

Monroe, Monte. "Glenn Biggs and the Crusade for a Guadalupe Mountains National Park." Master's thesis, Texas Tech University, 1991.

———. "Ralph Yarborough: Legislator for the Texas Environment." Paper presented at the Texas State Historical Association Meeting, Austin, March 1995.

North, Gerald, et al. "The Changing Climate of Texas." In *The Impact of Global Warming on Texas,* edited by Gerald North, Jurgen Schmandt, and Judith Clarkson. Austin: University of Texas Press, 1995, 24–49.

Office of the Governor. *Texas 2000 Commission Report and Recommendations.* Austin: 1982.

Ramirez, Bernardo. "Major Game Mammals and Their Habitats in the Chihuahuan Desert Region." In *Symposium on . . . the Chihuahuan Desert Region,* 155–61.

Rangel, Emilio, and Eglantina Canales. "Habitat Preservation and Wildlife Management in Northern Mexico." *Third Symposium on Resources of the Chihuahuan Desert Region,* edited by A. Michael Powell et al. Alpine: Chihuahuan Desert Research Institute, 1989, 19–21.

Sansom, Andrew. *Texas Lost: Vanishing Heritage.* Austin: Parks and Wildlife Foundation of Texas, 1995.

Schmidt, Robert. "The Mega-Chihuahuan Desert." In *Third Symposium on Resources of the Chihuahuan Desert Region,* 105–15.

Schneider-Hector, Dietmar. *White Sands: The History of a National Monument.* Albuquerque: University of New Mexico Press, 1993.

Shreve, Forrest. "Desert Vegetation of North America." *Botanical Review* 8 (1942): 195–246.

Simonian, Lane. *Defending the Land of the Jaguar: A History of Conservation in Mexico.* Austin: University of Texas Press, 1995.

Texas Parks and Wildlife. *Big Bend Ranch State Natural Area Management Plan.* Austin: 1994.

———. *Texans' Opinions on Parks and Recreation Issues in 1982.* Austin: 1983.

Tolson, Hillory, Milo Christianson, et al. "Investigative Report on Proposed Palo Duro National Monument, Texas." Washington, D.C.: National Park Service Report, 1939.

Toney, Sharon. "The Texas State Parks System: An Administrative History, 1923–1984." Ph.D. diss., Texas Tech University, 1995.

Tweit, Susan. *Barren, Wild, and Worthless: Living in the Chihuahuan Desert.* Albuquerque: University of New Mexico Press, 1995.

Tyler, Ron. *The Big Bend: A History of the Last Texas Frontier.* College Station: Texas A&M University Press, 1996.

——. *Pecos to Rio Grande: Interpretations of Far West Texas by Eighteen Artists.* College Station: Texas A&M University Press, 1983.

Udall, Stewart. Interview by author. Missoula, Montana, April 1996.

Van Devender, Thomas. "Pleistocene Climates and Endemism in the Chihuahuan Desert Flora." In *Second Symposium on the Resources of the Chihuahuan Desert Region*, 1–19.

——, et al. "Late Pleistocene Plant Communities in the Guadalupe Mountains, Culberson County, Texas," in *Biological Investigations in the Guadalupe Mountains National Park, Texas*, 13–30.

Wauer, Roland. *Naturalist's Big Bend.* College Station: Texas A&M University Press, 1973.

Wells, Philip. "Post-Glacial Origin of the Present Chihuahuan Desert Less Than 11,500 Years Ago." In *Symposium on . . . the Chihuahuan Desert Region*, 67–83.

Wetmore, A., and H. Friedman. "The California Condor in Texas." *Condor* 35 (1933): 37–38.

Chapter 5

Ackerman, Diane. *A Natural History of the Senses.* New York: Random House, 1990.

Andruss, Van, et al., eds. *Home: A Bioregional Reader.* Santa Cruz, Calif.: New Society Publishers, 1990.

Bailey, Robert. *Ecoregions of the United States.* Washington: Department of Agriculture, U.S. Forest Service, 1976.

Berg, Peter, and Raymond Dasmann. "Reinhabiting California." *The Ecologist* 7 (December 1977): 399–401.

Berry, Wendell. *Sex, Economy, Freedom, & Community.* New York: Pantheon, 1993.

Biggers, Don. *Buffalo Guns and Barbed Wire: Two Frontier Accounts by Don Hampton Biggers.* With an introduction by A. C. Greene and a biography by Seymour Conner. Lubbock: Texas Tech University Press, 1991.

Butzer, Karl. "Environment, Culture, and Human Evolution." *American Scientist* 65 (1977): 572–84.

Dawkins, Richard. *The Selfish Gene.* New York: Oxford University Press, 1976.

Devall, Bill, and George Sessions. *Deep Ecology: Living As If Nature Mattered.* Boston: Shambhala, 1988.

Diamond, Jared. *The Third Chimpanzee: The Evolution and Future of the Human Animal.* New York: HarperCollins, 1992.

Flores, Dan. "Place: An Argument for Bioregional History." *Environmental History Review* 18 (winter 1994): 1–18.

Foreman, Dave. *Confessions of an Eco-Warrior.* New York: Harmony Books, 1991.

Gallagher, Winnifred. *The Power of Place: How Our Surroundings Shape Our Thoughts, Emotions, and Actions.* New York: Poseidon, 1993.

Ingerson, Alice. "Tracking and Testing the Nature-Culture Dichotomy." In *Historical Ecology: Cultural Knowledge and Changing Landscapes,* edited by Carole Crumley. Santa Fe: School of American Research Press, 1994, 43–66.

Kingston, Mike, ed. *The Texas Almanac, 1994–5.* Dallas: Dallas Morning News, 1994.

Lahar, Stephanie. "Roots: Rejoining Natural and Social History." In *Ecofeminism: Women, Animals, Nature,* edited by Greta Gaard. Philadelphia: Temple University Press, 1993, 91–117.

Manning, Thomas. *Government in Science: The U.S. Geological Survey, 1867–1894.* Lexington: University of Kentucky Press, 1967.

Mills, Stephanie. "Bioregionalism." Lecture at the University of Montana, Missoula, November 16, 1993.

Noss, Reed. "A Regional Landscape Approach to Maintain Diversity." *BioScience* 33 (December 1983): 700–6.

Parsons, James. "On 'Bioregionalism' and 'Watershed Consciousness.'" *The Professional Geographer* 37 (February 1985): 1–5.

Powell, John Wesley. "Arid Region of the United States, Showing Drainage Districts." In U.S. Geological Survey, *Eleventh Annual Report, 1889–90. Irrigation Survey, pt. II.* Washington: Government Printing Office, 1891.

Sale, Kirkpatrick. *Dwellers in the Land: The Bioregional Vision.* San Francisco: Sierra Club, 1985.

Samson, Fred, and Fritz Knopf. "Prairie Conservation in North America." *BioScience* 44 (1994): 418–21.

Sanders, Scott Russell. *Staying Put: Making a Home in a Restless World.* Boston: Beacon Press, 1993.

Shepard, Jerry. "Singing Out of Tune: Historical Perceptions and National Parks on the Great Plains." Ph.D. diss., Texas Tech University, Lubbock, 1995.

Shepard, Paul. "A Post-Historic Primitivism." In *The Wilderness Condition: Essays on Environment and Civilization,* edited by Max Oelschlaeger. Washington: Island Press, 1992, 40–89.

Snyder, Gary. "The Place, The Region, The Commons." In *The Practice of the Wild,* edited by Gary Snyder. San Francisco: North Point Press, 1990, 25–47.

Thomas, Ronny. *Geomorphic Evolution of the Pecos River System.* Waco, Tex.: Baylor Geologic Studies Bulletin 22, 1972.

Tuan, Yi-Fu. *Space and Place: The Perspective of Experience.* Minneapolis: University of Minnesota Press, 1977.

———. *Topophilia: A Study of Environmental Perception, Attitudes, and Values.* Englewood Cliffs, N.J.: Prentice-Hall, 1974.

Urban, Lloyd. "Texas High Plains." In *Groundwater Exploitation in the High Plains,* edited by David Kromm and Stephen White. Lawrence: University of Kansas Press, 1992.

Uvardy, Miklos. "World Biogeographical Provinces." 1975. Reprinted as frontispiece

in *The Next Whole Earth Catalog: Access to Tools*, edited by Steward Brand. New
York: Point/Random House, 1980.

Webb, Walter Prescott. *The Great Plains: A Study in Institutions and Environment.*
Boston: Ginn and Co., 1931.

Wilkinson, Charles. "Toward an Ethic of Place." In *The Eagle Bird: Mapping a New
West.* New York: Pantheon, 1992, 132–61.

Williams, Dennis. "Proposed Palo Duro Ecosystem National Park." Study conducted
at Texas Tech University, 1991.

Worster, Donald. "History as Natural History." In *The Wealth of Nature: Environmental History and the Ecological Imagination.* New York: Oxford University Press,
1993, 30–44.

———. *An Unsettled Country: Changing Landscapes of the American West.* Albuquerque: University of New Mexico Press, 1994.

Chapter 6

Atencio, Tomás. "The Human Dimensions in Land Use and Land Displacement in
Northern New Mexican Villages." In *Indian and Spanish American Adjustments
to Arid and Semiarid Environments,* edited by Clark Knowlton. Lubbock: Texas
Technological College, 1964, 45–46.

Bailey, Douglas, Abiquiu Dam Reservoir Manager. Interview by author. Abiquiu,
New Mexico, 29 June 1995.

Bloemink, Barbara. *Georgia O'Keeffe: Canyon Suite.* New York: George Braziller,
1995.

Bryan, Kirk. "Historic Evidence on Changes in the Channel of Rio Puerco, a Tributary of the Rio Grande in New Mexico." *Journal of Geology* 36 (1928): 265–82.

Chavez, Chris, Land Surveyor, Santa Fe National Forest. Interview by author. Santa
Fe, New Mexico, January 1998.

Chavez, Fray Angelico. *My Penitente Land: Reflections on Spanish New Mexico.*
1974. Reprint, Santa Fe: Museum of New Mexico Press, 1993.

Cordova, Gilberto Benito. *Abiquiu and Don Cacahuate: A Folk History of a New
Mexican Village.* Los Cerillos: San Marcos Press, 1973.

Cowart, Jack, Juan Hamilton, and Sarah Greenough. *Georgia O'Keeffe: Art and
Letters.* Washington: National Gallery of Art, 1987.

deBuys, William. *Enchantment and Exploitation: The Life and Hard Times of a New
Mexico Mountain Range.* Albuquerque: University of New Mexico Press, 1985.

Del Balso, Eric. "Paradigm of the Homeland Commons: Local Ecosystem Stewardship in the Upper Rio Grande." In *Social Justice and the Environment,* edited by
Richard Hofrichter et al. Washington: Island Press, 1995.

D'Emilio, Sandra, and Sharyn Udall. "Inner Voices, Outward Forms: Women Painters in New Mexico." In *Independent Spirits: Women Painters of the American West,
1890–1945,* edited by Patricia Trenton. Berkeley: University of California Press,
1995, 153–82.

Denevan, William. "Livestock Numbers in Nineteenth-Century New Mexico, and
the Problem of Gullying in the Southwest." *Annals of the Association of American
Geographers* 57 (December 1967): 691–703.

Doerry, Karl. "The American West: Conventions and Inventions in Art and Literature." In *Essays on the Changing Images of the Southwest*, edited by Richard Francaviglia and David Narrett. College Station: Texas A&M University Press, 1994, 127–53.

Earls, Amy, Christopher Lintz, and W. N. Trierweiler. *Analysis of Three Cobble Ring Sites at Abiquiu Reservoir, Rio Arriba County, New Mexico*. Albuquerque: U.S. Army Corps of Engineers, 1989.

Ebright, Malcolm. *Land Grants and Lawsuits in Northern New Mexico*. Albuquerque: University of New Mexico Press, 1994; especially chapter 5, "The San Joaquin Grant: Who Owned the Common Lands?"

Eldredge, Charles, Julie Schimmel, and William Truetner. *Art in New Mexico, 1900–1945: Paths to Taos and Santa Fe*. Washington: National Museum of American Art, 1989.

Flores, Dan. "Zion in Eden: Phases of the Environmental History of Utah." In *A World We Thought We Knew: Readings in Utah History*, edited by John McCormick and John Sillito. Salt Lake: University of Utah Press, 1995, 422–40.

Francaviglia, Richard. "Elusive Land: Changing Geographic Images of the Southwest." In *Essays on the Changing Images of the Southwest*, 8–39.

Hamilton, Juan. "In O'Keeffe's World," in *Georgia O'Keeffe: Art and Letters*, 7–12.

History File #129—Land Grants, Joseph Halpin Records Center and Archives, Santa Fe. Includes several articles from the *Albuquerque Journal* on the original Courthouse Raid (1967), Amador Flores (1989–1991), and the twenty-fifth anniversary of the raid (1992) featuring interviews with Tijerina and other members of Alianza.

Hassell, Jean. "The People of Northern New Mexico and the National Forests." Albuquerque: U.S. Forest Service, Southwest Office, 1968.

Kutsch, Paul, and John Van Ness. *Canones: Values, Crisis, and Survival in a Northern New Mexico Village*. Albuquerque: University of New Mexico Press, 1981.

LaChapelle, Dolores. *D. H. Lawrence: Future Primitive*. Denton: University of North Texas, 1996.

Lawrence, D. H. *The Letters of D. H. Lawrence*. James Boulton, gen. editor. 4 vols. Cambridge: Cambridge University Press, 1913–1987. Letters quoted are from vol. 4.

——. "New Mexico" and "Pan in America." *Phoenix: The Posthumous Papers of D. H. Lawrence*, edited by Edward MacDonald. New York: Viking, 1968, 141–50, 22–31.

——. "Spirit of Place." In *Studies in Classic American Literature*. 1916. New York: Viking, 1961: 8–9.

Loengard, John. *Georgia O'Keeffe at Ghost Ranch: A Photo-Essay*. New York: Stewart, Tabori & Chang, 1995.

Leopold, Aldo. *Aldo Leopold's Southwest*. Edited by David Brown and Neil Carmony. New York: Stackpole Books, 1990.

——. "Pioneers and Gullies." In *The River of the Mother of God and Other Essays by Aldo Leopold*, edited by Susan Flader and J. Baird Callicott. 1924. Madison: University of Wisconsin, 1991, 106–13.

Leopold, Luna. "Vegetation of Southwestern Watersheds in the Nineteenth Century." *The Geographical Review* 41 (April 1951): 295–316.

Luhan, Mabel Dodge. *Edge of Taos Desert: An Escape to Reality*. 1937. Introduction by Lois Rudnick. Albuquerque: University of New Mexico Press, 1987.

MacCameron, Robert. "Environmental Change in Colonial New Mexico." *Environmental History Review* 18 (Summer 1994): 17–39.

Martinez, Ruben. "Social Action Research, Bioregionalism, and the Upper Rio Grande." In *Subversive Kin*, edited by Devon Peña. Tucson: University of Arizona Press, in press.

Melville, Elinor. *A Plague of Sheep: Environmental Consequences of the Conquest of Mexico*. New York: Cambridge University Press, 1994.

Nostrand, Richard. *The Hispano Homeland*. Norman: University of Oklahoma Press, 1992.

Pack, Arthur Newton. *We Called It . . . Ghost Ranch*. 1966. Abiquiu: Ghost Ranch Conference Center, 1979.

Peña, Devon. "Introduction" and "A Gold Mine, An Orchard, and an Eleventh Commandment." In *Subversive Kin: Chicana/o Studies and Ecology*, edited by Devon Peña. Tucson: University of Arizona Press, in press.

———. "Spanish-Mexican Land Grants in Environmental History." Paper presented at the Western History Association annual meeting, Albuquerque, October 1994.

Perez Cebada, Juan Diego. Interview by author. Missoula, Montana, 10 April 1997.

Poling-Kempes, Lesley. *Valley of Shining Stone: The Story of Abiquiu*. Tucson: University of Arizona Press, 1997.

Powell, John Wesley. "Institutions for the Aridlands." *Century Magazine* 40 (May–October 1890): 111–16.

Quintana, Frances Leon. *Pobladores: Hispanic Americans of the Ute Frontier*. Aztec, N.Mex.: Published by Frances Quintana; original edition published by the University of Notre Dame Press, South Bend, Ind., 1974.

Rangel, Emilio, and Eglantina Canales. "Habitat Preservation and Wildlife Management in Northern Mexico." In *Third Symposium on Resources of the Chihuahuan Desert Region*, 19–21.

Robinson, Roxanna. *Georgia O'Keeffe: A Life*. New York: Harper & Row, 1989.

Rodriguez, Sylvia. "Land, Water, and Ethnic Identity in Taos." In *Land, Water, and Culture: New Perspectives on Hispanic Land Grants*, edited by Charles Briggs and John Van Ness. Albuquerque: University of New Mexico Press, 1987, 313–403.

———. "The Tourist Gaze, Gentrification, and the Commodification of Subjectivity in Taos." In *Essays on the Changing Images of the Southwest*, 105–126.

Rothman, Hal K. *Devil's Bargains: Tourism in the Twentieth-Century American West*. Lawrence: University Press of Kansas, 1998.

———. *On Rims and Ridges: A History of the Los Alamos Area Since 1880*. Lincoln: University of Nebraska Press, 1992.

Rudnick, Lois. *Mabel Dodge Luhan: New Woman, New Worlds*. Albuquerque: University of New Mexico Press, 1984.

———. "Renaming the Land: Anglo Expatriate Women in the Southwest." In *The Desert Is No Lady: Southwestern Landscapes in Women's Writing and Art*, edited by Vera Norwood and Janice Monk. New Haven: Yale University Press, 1986, 10–26.

———. *Utopian Visions: The Mabel Dodge Luhan House and the American Counterculture*. Albuquerque: University of New Mexico Press, 1996.

Schaasfsma, Curtis. *The Cerrito Site (Ar–4): A Piedra Lumbre Phase Settlement at Abiquiu Reservoir*. Albuquerque: U.S. Army Corps of Engineers, 1979.

Scurlock, Dan. "The Pinyon-Juniper in Southwestern History: An Overview of Eco-Cultural Use," *Human Ecology: Crossing Boundaries*, edited by Scott Wright et al. Fort Collins: Society for Human Ecology, 1993, 272–86.

Simonian, Lane. *Defending the Land of the Jaguar: A History of Conservation in Mexico*. Austin: University of Texas Press, 1995.

Spanish Archives of New Mexico, Joseph Halpin Records Center and Archives, Santa Fe, N.Mex. Here are the basic documents for the history of the Chama Valley through 1821.

Taylor, Virginia. *The Spanish Archives of the General Land Office of Texas*. Austin: Lone Star Press, 1955.

Thorp, N. Howard. "Rio Arriba County. The County Up the River (1937)." Rio Arriba County, WPA Files, County Histories, Folder 220. Joseph Halpin Records Center and Archives, Santa Fe, N.Mex.

Tijerina, Reies Lopez. *Mi Lucha por la Tierra*. Mexico City: Fondo de Cultura Economica, 1978.

Torrez, Robert. "The Tierra Amarilla Land Grant: A Case Study in the Editing of Land Grant Documents." *Southwest Heritage* 13 (fall 1983 and winter 1984): 2–4.

Tuan, Yi-Fu. "New Mexican Gullies: A Critical Review and Some Recent Observations." *Annals of the Association of American Geographers* 56 (December 1966): 573–97.

U.S. Army Corps of Engineers. *General Design Memorandum on Abiquiu Dam and Reservoir, Rio Chama, Rio Grande Basin, New Mexico*. Albuquerque: U.S. Army Corps of Engineers, February 1955.

Utah Land Board, Intermountain Forest and Range Experiment Station, U.S. Forest Service, and the Utah Agricultural Experiment Station. *Report of Utah Flood Survey, 1931, 1932*. Special Collections. Merill Library. Utah State University, Logan, Utah.

Van Ness, John. "Hispanic Land Grants: Ecology and Subsistence in the Uplands of Northern New Mexico and Southern Colorado." In *Land, Water, and Culture*, 141–214.

Varjabedian, Craig, and Michael Wallis. *En Divina Luz: The Penitente Moradas of New Mexico*. Albuquerque: University of New Mexico Press, 1994.

Warren, Louis. *The Hunter's Game: Poachers and Conservationists in Twentieth-Century America*. New Haven: Yale University Press, 1997.

Westphall, Victor. *Mercedes Reales: Hispanic Land Grants of the Upper Rio Grande Region*. Albuquerque: University of New Mexico Press, 1983.

———. *The Public Domain in New Mexico*. Albuquerque: University of New Mexico Press, 1965.

Wozniak, Frank, Meade Kemrer, and Charles Carrillo. *History and Ethnohistory Along the Rio Chama*. Albuquerque: U.S. Army Corps of Engineers, 1992.

Chapter 7

The character of the Trickster Coyote in this chapter is of course based on the figure who appears so widely in Native American folktales across the continent. The tale of Coyote and Wolf here came out of my head—but it could have happened this way!

Audubon, John James. "Missouri River Journal," vol. I, *Audubon and His Journals*, 2d ed., edited by Maria Audubon and Elliott Coues. New York: Dover Press, 1986.

Bednarz, James. *The Mexican Gray Wolf: Biology, History, and Prospects for Reestablishment in New Mexico*. Albuquerque: U.S. Fish and Wildlife, Endangered Species Report 18, 1988.

Botkin, Daniel. *Discordant Harmonies: A New Ecology for the 21st Century*. New York: Oxford University Press, 1990.

Bowden, Charles. "Lonesome Lobo." *Wildlife Conservation* (January/February 1992): 45–53, 73.

Boyd, Diane. "International Movements of Recolonizing Wolf Populations in the Rocky Mountains." Paper presented at the Second North American Symposium on Wolves, Edmonton, Alberta, August 1992.

Braudel, Fernand. *The Structures of Everyday Life*. Translated by Stan Reynolds. New York: Harper & Row, 1981.

Brown, David, ed. *The Wolf in the Southwest: The Making of an Endangered Species*. Tucson: University of Arizona Press, 1983.

Brown, Reagan. *Proceedings of the Predator Control Summit*. Austin: Texas Department of Agriculture, 1980.

Brunner, Jim. "The Mexican Gray Wolf Plan." *Rangelands* 16 (August 1994): 140–42.

Caughley, Graeme. "Eruption of Ungulate Populations, with Emphasis on Himalayan Tar in New Zealand." *Ecology* 51 (Winter 1970): 53–72.

Collinson, Frank. "Silver Gray, Arctic, Buffalo, or 'Lofer'—He Was a Big Bad Wolf." *Amarillo Sunday News and Globe*, 5 February 1939.

Dawidoff, Nicholas. "One for the Wolves." *Audubon* (July–August 1992): 38–45.

Eberhardt, L. L., and K. W. Pitcher. "A Further Analysis of the Nelchina Caribou and Wolf Data." *Wildlife Society Bulletin* 20 (1992): 385–95.

"Expert Figures Skull Is from Wolf-Dog." *Missoulian* (Missoula, Mont.), 26 November 1992.

Fischer, Hank. "The Wolf Settles in at Yellowstone." *Defenders* 73 (summer 1998): 21–28.

——. *Wolf Wars: The Remarkable Inside Story of the Restoration of Wolves to Yellowstone*. Helena, Mont.: Falcon Press, 1995.

Fish and Wildlife Service, U.S. Department of the Interior. *Reintroduction of the Mexican Wolf Within Its Historic Range in the Southwestern United States: Final Environmental Impact Statement*. Albuquerque: U.S. Fish and Wildlife Service, 1996.

Fogelman, Valerie. "A Case of Mistaken Identity: The Eastern Timber Wolf in the United States." Lubbock, Tex., 1985.

Frémont, John Charles. *The Expeditions of John Charles Frémont*, vol. I, edited by Donald Jackson and Mary Lee Spence. Urbana: University of Illinois Press, 1970–84.

Fritts, Steven, et al. "The Relationship of Wolf Recovery to Habitat Conservation and Biodiversity in the Northwestern United States." *Landscape and Urban Planning* 28 (1994): 23–32.

Gasaway, William, et al. "The Role of Predation in Limiting Moose at Low Densities in Alaska and Yukon and Implications for Conservation." *Wildlife Monographs* 120 (1992): 1–59.

Gunson, John. "Historical and Present Management of Wolves in Alberta." *Wildlife Society Bulletin* 20 (1992): 330–39.

"Family CANIDAE—Wolves, Coyote, Dogs, and Foxes." In *The Mammals of North America*, vol. II, edited by E. Raymond Hall and Keith Kelson. New York: The Ronald Press, 1959, 842–64. See especially map 444 (p. 849), a North American subspecies map for *Canis lupus*.

Harrell Family Papers. "The Last Wolf Killed in the Panhandle." Oral History Tape, Panhandle-Plains Historical Museum Archives, Canyon, Tex.

Hesse, Hermann. *Steppenwolf*. 1929. New York: Holt, Rinehart & Winston, 1963.

Keith, Lloyd. *Wildlife's Ten-Year Cycle*. Madison: University of Wisconsin Press, 1963.

Mech, L. David. *The Way of the Wolf*. New York: Voyageur Press, 1992.

——, and Patrick Karns. *Role of the Wolf in a Deer Decline in the Superior National Forest*. St. Paul: USDA Forest Service Research Paper NC-148, 1977.

Moody, Joan. "El Lobo's Homecoming." *Defenders* 73 (spring 1998): 6–9.

Moulton, Gary, ed. *The Journals of the Lewis and Clark Expedition*. Vol. IV. Lincoln: University of Nebraska Press, 1984–.

Nowak, R. M. "Another Look at Wolf Taxonomy," in *Ecology and Conservation of Wolves in a Changing World*, edited by L. N. Carbyn et al. Edmunton: Circumpolar Press Institute, 1995.

Paradiso, John, and Ronald Nowak. "Wolves: *Canis lupus* and Allies." In *Wild Mammals of North America: Biology, Management, Economics*, edited by Joseph Chapman and George Feldhamer. Baltimore: Johns Hopkins Press, 1982, 460–74.

Robbins, Jim. "Wolves Across the Border." *Natural History* (May 1986): 6–15.

Schwarz, Joel. "Crying Wolf." *American Way* 19 (March 4, 1986): 68–72.

Schwennesen, Don. "Matriarch Wolf Killed in Canada." *Missoulian* (Missoula, Mont.), 12 February 1993.

"Snarls Dominate Lightly Attended Wolf Hearings." *High Country News*, 20 September 1993.

"Wolves Thinning Yellowstone Coyotes." *Missoulian* (Missoula, Mont.), 28 September 1997.

"Yellowstone Critter Looks Like a Wolf." *Missoulian* (Missoula, Mont.), 7 October 1992.

Young, Stanley, and E. A. Goldman. *The Wolves of North America*. 2 vols. New York: Dover Press, 1944.

Index